Gender, Conflict and Migration

Other volumes in the series

Women and Migration in Asia, Volume 3

SERIES EDITOR: MEENAKSHI THAPAN

Gender, Conflict and Migration

Editor
Navnita Chadha Behera

SAGE Publications
New Delhi/Thousand Oaks/London

First published in 2006 by

Sage Publications India Pvt Ltd
B-42, Panchsheel Enclave
New Delhi 110 017
www.indiasage.com

Sage Publications Inc      **Sage Publications Ltd**
2455 Teller Road   1 Oliver's Yard, 55 City Road
Thousand Oaks, California 91320   London EC1Y 1SP

Published by Tejeshwar Singh for Sage Publications India Pvt Ltd, phototypeset in 10/12 pt Aldine 401 BT by Star Compugraphics Private Limited, Delhi and printed at Chaman Enterprises, New Delhi.

Library of Congress Cataloging-in-Publication Data

Gender, conflict, and migration/editor, Navnita Chadha Behera.
    p.cm.—(Women and migration in Asia; 3)
  Includes bibliographical references and index.
1. Women refugees—South Asia. 2. Refugees—South Asia.
3. Forced migration—South Asia. 4. Conflict management—South Asia. I. Behera, Navnita Chadha. II. Series.

HV640.4.S67G62   305.9'06914—dc22   2006   2005036059

ISBN: 0–7619–3454–5 (HB)   81–7829–604–7 (India-HB)
      0–7619–3455–3 (PB)   81–7829–605–5 (India-PB)

Sage Production Team: Ankush Saikia, Shinjini Chatterjee, Mathew P.J. and Santosh Rawat

Contents

Series Introduction

Migration and the movement it entails has always accompanied civilisation in every stage of its development. Historically, people have moved from one place to another either by force in terms of slavery, or for reasons of colonisation. Towards the late 19th and early 20th centuries, international migrations began to be prompted by industrialisation and urbanisation. A shift in base and settlement, prompted by varied reasons and sponsored by different agents, is thus not a new concept. Unlike the early migrations, which were largely directed towards the north and the west, migration today cannot be understood in linear terms but rather in terms of fluid movements, within structural constraints and continuities, the movements being marked by turbulence and change, and undertaken in multiple directions. In the contemporary context of globalisation, as has often been noted, the world is in a constant state of flux. People are presented with multiple worlds, images, things, persons, knowledge and information at the same time and at an ever-increasing pace. Moreover, the life cycle of each of these has been drastically shortened, such that the world we encounter is perceived and consumed largely in temporary terms. Change, then, is the only constant and the changes that characterise this external world we inhabit are internalised by us and have a significant impact on our lives and our perceptions about time and space. Individuals are forced in one way or another to respond to the larger forces operating on them since no one remains completely removed from the turmoil that surrounds them; the world having come closer, globalisation has facilitated the process of migration considering the forces of demand and supply, needs and gratifications, and the increased and easier possibility of movement and communication.

In this process of movement, one undoubtedly leaves behind a familiar world to explore one's chances in an alien land. The process of migration may thus have a constraining effect on us not only in structural terms, of the choices made available, or cultural terms, but also in the sense in which it may include abuse, exploitation, and emotional and psychological distress. However, migration is largely undertaken with the positive hope of a better life in an unseen world. There is therefore a need to investigate the nuances and complexities entailed in this process and the way in which it impacts the lives and identities of the individual migrants in a world which is in constant flux and movement.

Migration has earlier been explained in dual terms of the push and pull factors, i.e., the voluntarist perspective. It has also been understood from a structuralist perspective, whereby migration is mapped in dichotomous terms of centre-periphery, industrialised-peasant based, west and north-east and south. However, both perspectives have limitations since the former has understood it in simplistic terms of an individual's rationally calculated decision while the latter ended in economic determinism. In order to understand the phenomenon in all its complexity, a more holistic approach is required. Any theory of migration must account for it in terms of race, religion, nationality, sense of belonging and nostalgia. More significantly, much of the early literature on migration has been silent on the issue of 'gender' and there is thus a need to analyse the migration process and the differential experience of women and men in the context of a gendered world. Migration no doubt constitutes a complex subject of study, and an understanding based on the gender dimension serves to further enhance the complexity when we consider the multiple and heterogeneous backgrounds and experience of migrant women and the very complex category of 'woman' herself.

Within this framework, the initiative to publish the five volumes on aspects of 'Women and Migration in Asia' emerged from the ongoing programme on Gender Perspectives on Asia located at the Developing Countries Research Centre, University of Delhi. The first activity of this programme was the international conference on Women and Migration in Asia in December 2003. The conference was attended by participants from all over the world, including representatives from Canada, Australia, Pakistan, Nepal, China, Singapore, France, Italy, Bangladesh, the UK, Israel, the Netherlands, Philippines, Japan, Korea, Taiwan and Trinidad, as well as from within India.

The five volumes are based on themes that emerged from the conference. It was proposed that the publication of these volumes would disseminate the deliberations, and their publication is a collective enterprise aimed at understanding the gender implications of the migration processes, for women, within and across Asian societies and globally.

Women and Migration in Asia

Essentially, the endeavour to publish these five volumes is a critical response to migration theories that have failed to take into consideration the gender aspect, thereby failing to account for the complex experience of migrant women. Migration is often perceived as being mainly a male movement, with women either being left behind or following their men folk as dependents. However, figures suggest that women have migrated in almost the same numbers as men; for example in the year 2000, there were 85 million female migrants as compared to the 90 million male migrants (Zlotnik, quoted in Jolly et al. 2003: 6). Women account for 46 per cent of the overall international migration from developing countries (ibid.).

In addition, as compared to other continental regions, Asia has the maximum number of international migrants. There exist, however, disparities within the region in the sense that countries in South-East Asia allow women greater mobility owing to relatively more liberal attitudes, than other South Asian and Arab countries. While men still form the majority of international migrants in Asia, there is an ever increasing number of women migrating in the region, as shown in Table 1:

Table 1: Proportion of Female Migrants as a Percentage of Total International Migrants by the Region

	1990	2000
South Asia	44.4	44.4
East and South East Asia	48.5	50.1
West Asia	47.9	48.3

Source: Zlotnik, in Jolly, Bell and Narayanswamy. 2003.

Despite the rising number of female migrants, women are not given equal importance as compared to men in matters of migration, since they are still not perceived as equal actors worthy of being accounted for. According to official records, the majority of women migrate legally merely as a part of family reunions. Those who migrate for employment purposes find themselves doing so illegally, considering the rigid cultural and state ideologies and limiting visa policies and work permits regarding the movement of women, especially in countries like Bangladesh and Pakistan. Thus, while viewing women migrants as dependents, we may often ignore their individual economic contributions, and an analysis based solely on official figures would give an inadequate account of the actual migration flows pertaining to women.

Women may migrate alone or along with their families or community. Their migration may be associational (for example through marriage) or women may be independent migrants. Women may be compelled to migrate owing to their economic condition, in search of better work opportunities, or they may opt to migrate as an escape from an oppressive marriage and the traditional patriarchal norms. They may be driven by individual needs and aspirations which most often coincide with those of the family, or migration may be structured and facilitated by the state. Whichever the case may be, migration has undeniably become a prominent reality in the modern world, and the feminisation of migration is an even more significant, although less explored, aspect of this reality.

Poverty and a search for employment have been the predominant propellants of the migration of people, which affords them the opportunity to explore their life chances. The decisions of women to migrate are informed by the twin forces of opportunities and constraints and are taken primarily by the family and, when taken independently, familial and cultural considerations have a great influence. Apart from the cultural and societal restrictions, structural factors like the demand for female labour and the trends in industry and agriculture also affect their decision to migrate. In migration, women, owing to their structural position in society, have limited access to information and resources which determines the differential experience of men and women, on transit and entry. Women are more vulnerable to physical and sexual abuse, lower wages and other forms of exploitation. Migration is thus undertaken with the aim of betterment, in terms of employment and economic gains, and as an escape from cultural and societal constraints in terms of achieving greater autonomy and independence. However, while it may afford them material gains, whether migration enables women to completely break free of the binding patriarchal and traditional norms remains questionable.

Migration: Themes and the Volumes

The volumes in the present series bring out the extent to which a gender perspective makes a contribution to migration theory and the manner in which it aids a comprehensive understanding of women's experience of migration, and how in the process, migration simultaneously emphasises certain gender related aspects pertaining to the specific contexts addressed by each volume. It is the migration flow of women in South Asia around which most of the papers in the five volumes are centred. At the same time, the comparative dimension is present in all the volumes, which are essentially concerned with the Asian region but provide cross-cultural and regional diversity in their understanding of the issues under consideration. The five volumes are clearly also the result of an attempt to address the issues in an interdisciplinary perspective while being rooted in their particular disciplinary domains. This has in fact resulted in the volumes using very eclectic theoretical approaches as well as a focus on particular issues in their complexity and variety. It is also the case that the subject of study is rather complex and cannot be wholly dealt with in terms of a single volume. In order to understand and encompass the multiple realities and identities of migrant women, analyses from different perspectives and vantage points become important and necessary. All the volumes are held together by a set of common themes and each volume must be viewed as providing a significant insight into the larger picture, while the series should be seen as a coherent whole.

While migration viewed along the axis of gender is the overall focus of this series, the aim is to address the issue in terms of particular contexts like conflict, family and marriage, trans-nationalism, work and poverty, and to do justice to each. Thus, while all the volumes are interconnected owing to the common issues they address, within the larger framework, however, each volume makes a valuable contribution in terms of their particular vantage point and the specific context they aim to address and emphasise.

Situated in the larger context of globalisation and the ever increasing rate of cross-border movements thereof, the volumes serve to analyse the varied motivations that propel a woman to migrate, discovering the gap between the migrant woman's aspirations and expectations and the resulting reality. Most of the papers in the volumes point to the fact that the migrant woman's experience cannot be understood merely in terms of the material benefits that may accrue as a result of migration. The social structures and relations that inform the migrant's experience to a great extent also need to be considered for a holistic understanding of the complex experience of such women.

The volumes find common ground in examining the difference between forced and voluntary migration in general (common to men and women), and serve to highlight the voluntary and independent aspect of women's migration, exploring the element of 'choice' and the extent of agency they have in framing their own experience. Woman's agency in different contexts is in fact a critical component of the analyses across the volumes. The notion of 'agency' is thus problematised and examined in terms of personal experience and in relation to the state and legal systems.

The focus is on women on the move. Through their papers, the volumes question the assumption that women essentially migrate as dependents, their migration being seen as largely associational. Women even in the most empathetic discourse are thus at best represented as victims. The indifference towards or denial of the independent aspect of migration of women, in the dominant discourses, as has been argued across the five volumes, serves to ignore the dialectics between these women and the larger social structures and gender relations both in the home and host countries in terms of the reciprocal impact that each has on the other. It is this dominant official discourse which has predominated in various disciplinary approaches to migration within which women are inadequately represented and assumed to form one homogeneous category characterised, in traditional terms, as being submissive, dependent and largely confined to the household sphere. The volumes in this series provide an insight into the gap between the dominant narratives and those of the women themselves, attempting to reach reality as closely as possible.

The collection of papers on 'Transnational Migration and the Politics of Identity' highlights the fact that migration today does not imply a complete break from the past; rather, the migrant must be understood as inhabiting two worlds simultaneously. It explores the ways in which a migrant woman constructs her identity in an alien land, the problems she confronts and the strategies she deploys in making life in the host country more liveable. There is not only fluidity in the experience and construction of identity but also in the manifold ways in which there is a 'back-linking' with the past and the country of origin, whether this is in terms of rituals, practices and values, relationships and family ties, or even in the 'idea' of the country that is carried to the new lands. At the same time, however, the migrant woman is constrained by the structures of the host country, its regulatory regimes and practices, and the limits imposed on her. The volume thus brings out the significance of the fluid nature of a migrant's identity without however ignoring the fact that this fluidity itself and her identity is regulated and structured to a certain extent by the state and other social institutions. Moreover, it examines the manner in which she negotiates with the larger structures and institutions such as the state, patriarchy, family, welfare institutions, etc. which impinge on her everyday personal experience and how this struggle helps in defining and reconstructing her identity in different ways.

In the context of internal migration, and even more in terms of transnational migration, the impact of state policies on the experience of the migrant becomes crucial and has been examined in most of the volumes in terms of the motives of the state in facilitating or curtailing migration out-flow and in-flow respectively, and the extent to which the state/s carries out its/their responsibilities. The volume on 'Poverty, Gender and Migration' focuses on the relationship between state policies and poverty, and the manner in which shifts in state policies bring about corresponding changes in patterns of migration. It explores how transnational migration has unfolded as a continuing process of exclusion and deprivation, whereby state policies have promoted migration, but on the other hand withdrawn from assuring protective support. Internal migrations too, in the light of the shifts and continuities, show a similar link between state policies, poverty and migration. The volume further argues that the experiences of poor women in migration are informed not only by poverty but also by the ideological dimensions of work which is visible in their concentration in jobs in the informal sector that are characterised by a sexual division of labour. The volume thus highlights the common theme that the larger structures affect the personal experience of migrants, and that there is a strong social, cultural and political context to migration by women. In the transnational context, not only does the social and structural categories of the recipient country affect the migrant's experience, the culture, tradition and customs of the home societies and the dominant familial discourse grounded in patriarchy also continue to inform the construction of the migrant woman's identity and experience.

The volume on 'Gender, Conflict and Migration' attempts to break through the homogeneous 'victimhood' image, presented in the dominant discourse, of women migrants affected by war and conflict and seeks to explore the space for women's agency in these situations. It simultaneously highlights the suffering that women are subjected to in a conflict situation as well as the survival strategies adopted by them. The volume thus attempts to break the homogeneity of state discourses by bringing in women's experiences, which make it more complex. It raises a methodological issue in questioning the extent to which recording women's testimonies empowers them, or whether it is a traumatising experience since it rips open the memories of their 'traumatic pasts'. Further, the volume also examines the ethical dilemma of the researcher's subjective involvement in the 'manipulation of their memories' to serve their own ends and its impact on the researchers themselves. The volume seeks to contribute to the literature on migration in terms of the 'cyclical' character of most 'conflict' and 'peace' situations, the phenomenon of 'internally displaced persons' and, to some extent, forced migrants as well.

Migration may thus be either voluntary or forced, may involve individuals or families and even whole communities. One therefore needs to consider the life choices and circumstances of all categories of migrant women while simultaneously addressing the range of gender-specific types of work and their impact on women. Feminisation of the labour force gained momentum after the Second World War when immigration became a state sponsored project, undertaken in response to the labour shortage in the developing and industrialising countries which was to be filled by the Third World countries supplying labour. Women thus migrated to work in export processing zones in the Asian region, as domestic labour, and in the entertainment and sex industries. This highlights the ways in which women in different circumstances and owing to different reasons cross the boundaries of home and community to engage in work in completely different surroundings.

The volume on 'Migrant Women and Work', by focusing upon women who migrate for work, provides indicators to the patterns that are discernible in the migration of women. The volume highlights the specific conditions under which they migrate, the preponderance of women in certain sectors of the labour market, specifically the reproductive and the care sector, the social, economic and political discrimination that particular groups of women are confronted with and the strategies they adopt to cope with such circumstances. It also makes an important contribution to the literature on migration in terms of studying gender and migration in the significant context of women who migrate alone or are the primary migrants, citing case studies of women who are 'solo' migrants. The volume also puts forth the idea that the structural ramifications of women's migration extend beyond the lives of migrant women themselves, insofar as the labour of such women is an important factor in shaping the gender relations found in the societies of both the migrants and their hosts, thereby suggesting new ways of looking at issues such as gender equality, household division of labour and the state policies regarding welfare provisions.

The collection of papers on 'Marriage and Migration' focuses on several aspects of marriage and migration in intra- and transnational contexts. It poses questions as to how the institution of marriage in and of itself may often effectively imply women's migration through the operation of 'kinship' rules of marriage and (post-marital) residence; how marriage can become a strategy to enable individuals and their families to migrate; the dynamics of match-making and marriage negotiations in the context of migration, including the transfer of resources through marriage payments; and, more broadly, how intra- and international migration affects the institution of marriage and wider relations within the family in the Asian context.

The papers in this volume contend that marriage in new contexts of migration may unravel euphemised and gendered practices and relationships. Migration may also impinge on the institution of marriage and transform familial relationships in a variety of ways. It may introduce new considerations into the process of match-making, reinforce or amplify traditional patterns of family and marriage and, in many cases, put the conjugal relationship and relationships between the generations under particularly severe strain, resulting in domestic violence and international custodial disputes. This raises the important question of policy orientations and commitments, in an international dimension, towards women migrants.

Policy Implications

Migration and the focus on women demands that the policies of the sending and receiving countries regarding migration be reviewed and restructured keeping in mind the migrant's interest. While there do exist laws aimed at safeguarding the interest of migrant women and their protection, they are either inadequate or lack effective implementation. In this light, the conference proposed that the distinction between voluntary and forced migration be emphasised such that the policies for each are based on the specific considerations of their particular context. Further, in order to effectively protect the rights and ensure the well-being of specific groups, their particular motivations for migration must be assessed.

The complexity of the process, the multiple and heterogeneous backgrounds of the migrants, and the differential experiences of women and men make policy analysis difficult in this area. Moreover, the countries involved may have different policy goals, the concerns of one may not concern the other. While one country may encourage migration for the positive economic benefits in terms of remittances, the other may do so for acquiring cheap labour. In this sense, both the sending and receiving countries have their regulatory mechanisms to protect and enhance worker welfare. Women like men contribute through their labour and remittances; however, the restrictions on migration imposed by the two countries limit the benefits that may accrue through migration both to the migrant as well as to the involved countries.

Migration has been institutionalised to an extent in terms of the employment brokers managing the entire process for the migrants; however, by curtailing movement, these governments, in a sense, serve to strengthen and perpetuate the exploitation and abuse of women. These women in turn migrate illegally, in search of work, and are thus left to the whims and fancies of these middlemen in transit and employers on arrival. In order to make migration beneficial for the two countries as well as the migrant woman, there is a need to rid the existing laws of their restrictive features and to incorporate in the policies protective measures that would ensure women their rights and welfare. Further, to reduce the power of the mediating agencies, the governments of these countries must devise policies to regulate and standardise the recruitment procedure so that these agencies can not harass potential migrants (Labour Watch in Jolly, Bell and Narayanswamy 2003).

Considering the increased movement in the region, the sending and receiving states may be called upon to build networks between them and share the relevant information with each other and with the women, so as to ensure that migrants move in a well planned environment whereby their experience is not left to fate and chance and they are aware of the migration channels in the receiving country. The governments of the host regions must endeavour to assist migrants in adjusting to the new world, by creating conditions approximate to those in their home

nations. In order to help them cope with the social/psychological consequences of migration, the sense of dislocation, alienation and loss of a
sense of belonging, the governments in both regions must have policies
regarding certain provisions of skill training, for instance, in the language
of the destination country, that would equip these women to find their
way about in the new situation.

The heterogeneous aspect of the migrant population and their backgrounds highlights the need for a group specific and country specific
approach, as that would view the migrant woman's problems more real-
istically, accounting for her particularities. A holistic approach towards
migration is called for that would include apart from the lower classes
the situation of the middle class migrant as well. The analysis must be
based on a complete consideration of the specific context within which
the migrant is located, in order to effectively formulate policies. Moreover, there is a need to focus attention on the manner in which women
migrants are represented in the official discourse, their movement having
been rendered invisible by law. These women in reality engage in negotiations with the larger institutions and the state; however, the latter by
silencing them makes their agency negligible. While formulating policy,
there is a need to therefore ensure a just and visible representation of
women.

Meenakshi Thapan
Series Editor
Women and Migration in Asia

Reference

Jolly, Susie, Emma Bell and Lata Narayanswamy. 2003. *Gender and Migration in Asia:
Overview and Annotated Bibliography*. No. 13. Bridge, Institute of Development Studies,
Sussex, UK.

Acknowledgements

This volume has been a collective venture that has depended on the contributions of several individuals and institutions. First and foremost, I would like to thank Neera Chandoke for inviting me to participate in the Developing Countries Research Centre's (DCRC) programme on 'Gender Perspectives on Asia' during the winter of 2001–02 while I was still at the Brookings Institution, Washington D.C. I am indebted to Meenakshi Thapan for her constant support for this volume and for leading the whole group while shouldering extra responsibilities by being the series editor. Thanks are due to Manoranjan Mohanty, Director of DCRC and other members of the editorial team, which include Anuja Agrawal, Sadhna Arya, Patricia Uberoi, Rajni Palriwala and Anupma Roy, for their valuable inputs in several brainstorming sessions organised over the past three years.

The DCRC organised a mega-international conference on 'Women and Migration in Asia' at New Delhi in December 2003, an event attended by more than a hundred scholars from all over the world. This volume has emerged from the panel on 'Conflict, War and Violence' organised at this conference. I would like to take this opportunity to thank all the panellists, discussants and participants who enriched its deliberations. The DCRC team did a wonderful job in handling the organisational matters. I also wish to acknowledge the generous funding and support extended to this conference by the Department of International Development (British High Commission), the Japan Foundation, the University of Delhi, the Friedrich Ebert Stiftung, the Indian Council of Social Science Research, the Planning Commission (Government of India) and the India International Centre.

I am deeply indebted to the authors for their patience and hard work, and for cooperating so generously in this venture. Without their time and efforts this book would not have materialised. A special word for my research team is in order. Anisha Kinra and Poonam Kumari were of enormous help in planning, coordinating and executing the entire effort of organising this panel for the conference. Sonali Huria painstakingly prepared the bibliography and extended tremendous support throughout the preparation of the manuscript. To all of them, I owe a deep sense of gratitude.

I wish to thank Wendy Harcourt, editor, *Development*, at Sage Publications for granting permission to reprint Saba Gul Khattak's paper on 'Floating Upwards from History: Afghan Women's Experience of Displacement', *Development*, 45 (1), March 2002: 105–10, *www.sidint.org/development*. I also wish to acknowledge *Economic and Political Weekly* for granting permission for reprinting Rita Manchanda's paper, 'Gender, Conflict and Displacement: Contesting "Infantalisation" of Forced Migrant Women', XXXLX (37), September 2004: 4179–186, in this volume.

As ever, I wish to thank my husband Ajay for his unfailing support, and my daughter Miska, for her little albeit precious generosities in allowing my 'absence' at all those times we should have been together.

List of Abbreviations

ABSDF	All Burma Students Democratic Front
BJP	Bharatiya Janata Party
BNP	Bangladesh National Party
BWU	Burmese Women's Union
CEDAW	Convention on Elimination of All Forms of Discrimination Against Women
CFA	Ceasefire Agreement
ECHR	European Convention on Human Rights
EPG	Eminent Persons Group
EXCOM	Executive Committee
GoSL	Government of Sri Lanka
ICRC	International Committee of the Red Cross
IDPs	Internally Displaced Persons
IPKF	Indian Peace Keeping Force
INGOs	International Non-Governmental Organisations
JVP	Janatha Vimukthi Peramuna
JVT	Joint Verification Team
LTTE	Liberation Tigers of Tamil Eelam
SAFHR	South Asian Forum for Human Rights
SDPI	Sustainable Development Policy Institute
TULF	Tamil United Liberation Front
UNHCHR	United Nations High Commission for Human Rights
UNHCR	United Nations High Commissioner for Refugees
UNICEF	United Nations International Children's Emergency Fund
WCAR	World Conference Against Racism
WE	Women's Exchange
WLB	Women's League of Burma

1

INTRODUCTION

Navnita Chadha Behera

Feminist scholarship in migration studies is still evolving both in the conceptual and empirical domains. Conceptually, being alert to the power relations of gender enables us to see features of migration that are otherwise overlooked. Empirically, it has led to new topics of concerns: transnational identity, health and human rights of migrant women, and forced migration as a result of conflicts and political violence, apart from new research on traditional concerns such as migrant labour systems.

This volume begins by conceptually unpacking the three key variables—gender, conflict and migration. A review of the existing literature shows that research on this subject is broadly organised along the twin axis of gender and conflict/war, and, gender and migration. The issue of conflict-driven migration and understanding its gendered character, however, tends to fall between the two stools—a gap this volume seeks to fulfil. The remainder of the introduction focuses on three sets of critical points for intervention—conceptual, methodological and policy-related—as identified by our contributors.

Gender

The concept of gender, as understood in this volume, has been defined with reference to three debates: 'sex and gender', the 'woman' and gender, and the plurality of feminisms. The 'sex and gender' debate relates to the ontological basis of the differences between men and women: are these differences determined biologically or socially?

(Assister 1996; Butler 1990; Hondagneu-Sotelo 1994; Scott 1986). Sex refers to what is biological while gender is a social construction. 'We *are* a certain sex but we *learn* or *perform* certain gender roles which are not predetermined or tied rigidly to biological sex' (Goldstein 2001: 2). Rather than being a fixed trait 'given' by nature that does not change over time, gender is constructed through social and cultural ideals, practices and symbols, producing subjective identities through which we 'know' the world. Gender explicitly rejects biological explanations for sexual divisions of labour, power and dispositions as well as hierarchies of inequality that privilege men and disadvantage women. A gender analysis then alerts us to socially inculcated and purposive rather than natural differentiation between the sexes.

Gender is often mistakenly used to signify 'women only'. The debate on the 'women and gender' question represents an attempt to introduce an analysis of how power relationships between men and women impact their lives (Ferree and Hess 1987: 17; Gerson and Peiss 1985; Margolis 1985; Stanley and Wise 1983). In the early feminist analyses, all gender references concerned women; men had no gender. Such analysis about the basis and the boundaries of the categories 'woman' and 'man' were problematised in post-structuralist and post-modernist frameworks of analysis. Gender, it is argued, is not about women or men as separate and independent categories, but is a relational concept. 'It focuses on understanding how the terms of man-woman and masculine-feminine are mutually constituted and interdependent, that is, they presuppose each other' (Peterson 1992: 9). To quote her:

> The appropriate metaphor is not 'A and B' or 'A1 and A2' but 'A and not A'. 'Man', 'masculinity' and 'male worlds' are literally defined by their exclusion of (and disdain for) that which constitutes 'woman', 'femininity' and 'female worlds'. This has systematic implications for evaluating andocentric knowledge claims since the 'zero sum' construction of A-not A, man-woman, and masculine-feminine suggests that 'A' (man) cannot be fully understood without knowledge and understanding of 'not A' (woman) and *vice-versa*.

Studying gender is, therefore, important not only for its insights about women alone, but chiefly due to its transformative implications for any claims to knowledge.

The third debate pertains to the plurality of feminist analyses. There has been a growing awareness of the diversity within the categories of 'men' and 'women'. That is, there is no universal 'man' or 'woman' or 'woman's experience'. Different feminisms have highlighted the ways in which gender is cross-cut by class, nationalism, ethnicity, sexuality, age and other social variables. The masculine and feminine are always categories within every class, race and culture in the sense that women's and men's experiences, desires and interests differ within every class, race and culture. At the same time, class, race, ethnic group and culture are always categories within gender, since women's and men's experiences, desires and interests differ according to class, race, ethnic group and culture (Harding 1987: 7). This research demonstrates the impossibility of generalising 'male' and 'female' experiences as such and underlines the need to talk about feminisms only in the plural since there is no single set of feminist principles or understandings. So, from a theoretical standpoint, the post-modern feminist school of thought[1] that sees gender itself as 'fairly fluid, contextual and arbitrary' (Goldstein 2001: 49) best captures the arguments presented in this volume. Post-modernism generally rejects the idea of a single objective reality. They share a general scepticism about established categories and methods of knowledge, and emphasise the role of culture in shaping experience. And, post-modern feminism delves into the connections among gender, race, ethnicity, nation, class and other aspects of identity. It embodies a tension, however, between the post-modern emphasis on the diversity of women's experience and the feminist assumption that women constitute a meaningful category (Butler and Scott 1992; Darby 1997; Harrington 1992; Pettman 1996; Walker 1988).

It is also important to avoid essentialising the experiences of Third World women through the Western eye. That is because the character of post-colonial states as well as the relationship there between state and civil society are of a qualitatively different nature (Kandiyoti 1988, 1991; Mohanty, Russo and Torres 1991; Parker et al. 1992; Rai 1996; Waylen 1996). Women in Third World countries are more removed from the state in all its manifestations than are Western women. The lack of education, economic vulnerability, weak infrastructural social support and unavailability of information leave women in these states more dependent upon their own resources, which in themselves are meagre. Rai argues that 'because of the deep "embeddedness" of most Third World states in the civil society . . . both [are] complex terrains: fractured, oppressive, threatening and also providing spaces for struggle and negotiation' (Rai 1996: 32, 35). For women, 'the reinforcing of bureaucratic capacity by social norms in the garb of national, religious and ethnic identities as fashioned male-directed movements of various kinds can be a terrifying combination threatening any attempt to change their lived reality' (ibid.: 35). In the legal domain, Oishik Sircar in this volume for instance stresses upon the need for advancing an alternative asylum jurisprudence in South Asia to challenge and counter the existing constructs of the Eastern-native-disempowered-woman applying for asylum in the developed countries, which at best victimises and at worst infantilises them. Finally, the term feminism as such has different connotations for women caught up in nationalist struggles and ethnic conflicts in the Third World. Mary O'Kane provides an excellent illustration of this point. In communities from Burma, she points out, the English word 'feminist' and it's Burmese and ethnic language equivalents are strongly associated with notions of Western cultural imperialism, sexual orientation and negative social disruption. While most women activists from Burma agree with many feminist principles such as gender equality and empowerment, to publicly call themselves 'feminist' is to invite widespread criticism and further political marginalisation, amongst other complex responses. It is therefore important to recognise the particularities of women's experiences in what are diverse historical and cultural situations.

Conflict

The term conflict is understood within a broad framework that includes the entire spectrum of inter-state wars, internal conflicts, ethnically-driven insurgencies and secessionist movements. Political violence unleashed by communal riots, caste conflicts and terrorist attacks, however, remain outside the purview of this volume. Although our main focus remains on the consequences of these conflicts in terms of internally displacing people or rendering them as refugees, it is important to briefly address the changing character of warfare to understand its implications for causing forced migration.

There is a clear and distinct shift in the emerging discourse on conflict analysis from the traditional warfare-military contests between nation-states to defend their territorial integrity and independence to the 'new wars' or intra-state conflicts where the state is only one among many other players in a conflict that includes guerrilla groups, ethnically mobilised armies and mercenaries. In the period 1989–98, 92 out of 108 wars were domestic wars, with the highest number in Asia, followed by Africa and Europe (Kaldor 1999; Schmeidl 2001; Wallensteen and Sollenberg 1999). Second, the changing nature of warfare, especially in internal wars, means that it happens in the middle of human communities rather than battlefields distant from civilian life. The dividing lines between the 'battle front' and the 'home front' or rear have increasingly blurred, if not disappeared. The 'new wars,' as Darini Rajasingham-Senanayake highlights in this volume, tend to be increasingly waged in multicultural urban spaces and neighbourhoods and pit those who once were neighbours of different ethno-religious or linguistic communities against one another. An estimated 90 per cent of the victims of contemporary civil war and internal conflicts are civilians (Independent Commission on International Humanitarian Issues 1986: 25). 'From 1990 to 1995, 70 states were involved in 93 wars which killed five and a half million people' (Smith 1997: 13). As a result, individuals, families, and at times whole communities have been forced to migrate because of some generalised fear or due to destruction of livelihoods, identities and life worlds. A look at the correlation between wars and refugee migration shows that in the 1990s, all but three (Bhutan, Uzbekistan, Zaire) of the sixty refugee flows coincided with an intra-state conflict during some point in time. In two more cases, intra-state conflicts resulted in internal displacement (Lebanon, the Philippines). Third, there is no abrupt cut-off between war and post-war periods. Armed conflicts are often converted not into constructive political process but into non-specific or sporadic acts of revenge. As conflicts acquire a cyclical character, the post-war period is sometimes better called 'inter-bellum', or a pause before the fighting begins again.

Finally, the earlier literature on armed conflicts and wars was mostly gender-blind, with women's participation simply not identified. Waging wars as well as political violence within the state were seen as male domains, executed by men, whether as armed forces, guerrilla groups, paramilitaries or peace-keeping forces (Enloe 1993). Feminist analysis seeking to locate the 'missing women' made attempts to correct the male bias in data collection and analysis. However, this 'add and stir' approach was very limiting. Later analysis also tended to portray a simplistic division of roles and gender dichotomies: men were the perpetrators (in defence of the nation and their wives and children), while women were victims, particularly of sexual abuse and abduction (Kelly 2000; Yuval-Davis 1997). Similar to this was the notion that 'men make wars' and 'women make peace'. These, however, played into unfortunate stereotypes that characterised men as active and women as passive; men as agents, women as victims; men as rational, women as emotional (Tickner 1999: 4). Even when men were victims on the battlefield, they were portrayed as omnipotent, masculine heroes (Burguieres 1990). This under-representation or misrepresentation of the gendered causes, costs and consequences of violence has resulted in insufficient recognition of women's involvement and participation, both unavoidable and deliberate, in violent conflicts (Jacobs et al. 2000; Lentin 1997). There is a growing recognition that claiming inherent differences between women and men contradict the real-life actions of men and women. History has demonstrated that many men resist war through a refusal to participate, draft evasion and outright protest, and on the other hand, many women express their citizenship or even nationalism by proudly sending their men to wars or directly joining the ranks of militants in insurgency situations. Likewise, feminists have rejected idealistic associations of women with peace, which have long served to 'disempower women and keep them in their place, which is out of the "real world" of international politics' (Tickner 1999: 8).

Overall, the literature on 'women and war' and 'women and peace' has focused on issues such as women's human rights abuses during conflict (Bunch and Carrillo 1992; Byrnes et al. 1997; Schuler 1995), women's testimonies of their experiences of conflict (Bennett et al. 1995; Turshen and Twagiramariya 1998; Women's Initiative 1994), the linkages between militarisation and patriarchy (Chenoy 2002; Enloe 1983, 1993) and women's role in the peace negotiations or their exclusion from the peace processes (Brock-Utne 1989; Butalia 2002; Manchanda 2001; Roach-Pierson 1987; Ruddick 1989). The concerns of internally displaced or refugee women tend to be subsumed within the frameworks of understanding the gendered nature of conflict and are not addressed in their own right. Women and men's experiences of being violently uprooted and forced into migration entail different dynamics which are not taken into account in such analyses. On the larger plane, feminist perspectives on conflict studies have proliferated in the past 20 years, yet they remain marginal to the predominantly male mainstream of political science or international relations.[2]

Migration

The story of feminist perspectives in migration studies follows a similar trajectory. Although the concept of migration has been studied in many disciplines (Brettel and Hollifield 2000), for much of its history it has tended to be blind to the gender dimension (Willis and Yeoh 2000). In the early migration studies dominated by economic theory, the neo-classical approach explained migration as a rational response by individuals to imbalances in the means of production, with the purpose of maximising returns for their labour, while the structuralist approach illustrated it as a phenomenon to be explained in terms of structural features of capitalist development. In both cases, migrants were either assumed to be non-gendered beings, or it was assumed that both men and women were subject to the same motivations to migrate. Research in sociology and anthropology focused almost exclusively on issues of ethnicity and class.

In international relations, neo-realist analyses failed to address the refugee question because of their state-centric analysis and excessive focus on power-politics, while the neo-liberal approach only addressed the managerial and governability dimensions of refugee problems (Basu 2001: 403). The literature on refugees was predominantly descriptive with scholars concentrating on the refugee situations and policies of individual nations (Ferris 1987; Loescher 1992; Loescher and Scanlan 1986; Zucker and Zucker 1987), and on the causes of refugee flows (Rystad 1990; Weiner 1996; Zolberg et al. 1989). Legal scholars focused their analyses primarily on the United Nations High Commission for Refugees (UNHCR) statute and the legal provisions of national and international refugee instruments pertaining to refugee definition, asylum and protection (Chimni 2000; Goodwin-Gill 1983; Hathaway 1991). Historians undertook detailed studies of refugee movements and the role of international organisations during and after the two World Wars (Holborn 1975; Miserez 1988; Proudfoot 1957; Stoessinger 1956; Vernant 1953), as well as during the Cold War period (Saloman 1991). Quantitative studies sought to identify the structural causes of refugee flows (Schmeidl 2001). An important similarity in these diverse accounts of migration lay in their failure to recognise or account for gender.

Gender and migration research gained salience in the early 1980s and was initially concerned with 'adding women' to existing migration research. For example, in some models of the neo-classical approach, the availability of marriage partners became an extra factor influencing female migrants (Chant and Radcliffe 1992: 20). Many of the anthropological studies, which disengaged with the neo-classical approach and started building structuralist models, were disaggregated by gender, but 'explicit or implicit gender role typing was endemic' whereby men were cast in urban settings and women in rural areas (Wright 2000: 8). The problem with such a gendered division of labour was that it was deemed to be natural, and so 'its origins were not questioned', and 'exceptions to it tended to be dismissed as deviant and/or irrelevant' (ibid.). The growing recognition of the importance of gender led to new research interests in micro-scale studies, often concerned with gender norms in source communities and gender relations within sending households. Scholars also grappled with the questions of why and how gender division of labour right at the heart of the migrant labour system came into being, so developing an analysis of gender at distinct levels: the micro-level of individual behaviour/agency; the macro-level of political economy; and the meso-level of the household (ibid.: 12). As compared to anthropology and sociology, however, international relations remain far behind in integrating gender-aware analyses within its disciplinary foundations. The theoretical constructions of feminist literature are only beginning to make their presence felt. The discipline appears more like one where 'women are allowed the space to engage with feminist critiques at the first level, whilst the men tend to get on with what they regard as the "serious work"' (Pankhurst and Pearce 1998: 158).

An important distinction between theoretical models explaining migration in all these disciplines pertains to the extent of determination accorded to human agency in relation to social structure. The structuration model of migration, in this context, broke new ground in recognising that 'structure is not as much external to human action, and is not identified solely with constraint' (Giddens 1987: 61). This model allowed analytical space for understanding an individual's role in constituting the migrant labour system, without overlooking the fact that the system in turn conditions and mediates their agency. Early accounts of migration seeking to reconcile agency and structure, however, tended to perpetuate the neglect of gender. They recognised that not all migrants were equal in terms of their potential to influence social events, but it was on class distinctions between migrants, and racial distinctions between migrants and settlers, that attention had been focused, while differences based on gender were overlooked or subjected to biological determinism.

It is important to deploy the feminist approach because gender is relational rather than essential. Recognising gender as simultaneously being structural and a component of individual identity prompts attention to the macro and micro 'structures' without privileging one at the expense of the other. In other words, feminist scholarship attends to the subjective and everyday while relating these to the historical and structural relations within which specific data or studies are situated (Peterson 1992: 10). Most of the gender and migration research, however, focuses on issues of labour, households, reproduction and the impact of transnationalism on the migrants' identity—themes explored in the other volumes of this series.

While problematising the notion of choice and coercion, this volume focuses on the 'forced' rather than 'voluntary' elements of migrant experiences. This is important both for migration studies as well as for feminist literature. The world refugee map tallies almost perfectly with the world conflicts map, driving home the importance of understanding the dynamics of conflict-induced migration. Quantitative studies have also shown that refugee flows are affected by state implosions and/or the formation of new states, genocidal violence, and internal struggles, particularly those fuelled by foreign military interventions (Schmeidl 2001: 84–85). Although women outnumber men in the refugee populations experiencing forced displacement (Keely 1992; Martin 1991), there is little recognition of the gendered nature of refugees and internal displacement. The term 'internally displaced' refers to those persons who have fled their homes but remain within the borders of their countries, whereas refugees leave their countries of origin.

Gender is an integral part of the refugee experience in that it permeates women's experience of being dislocated, displaced or becoming refugees during their flight, processes of seeking asylum and resettlement as well as availing humanitarian assistance in refugee camps (Boyd 2001: 105–06). More importantly, conflict-generated migration represents a crisis point and presents possibilities of transformations in social relations of men and women. The contributors to this volume seek to understand how status, identities and power relations among men and women change from conflict situations at home to the migrant camps, and when they return home.

In studying conflict-induced migration, it is important to keep in mind certain characteristics of borders in post-colonial states, especially in the context of South Asia. Baud and van Schendel provide a most lucid exposition on the typology of borders. Using Oscar Martinez's classification, Baud and van Schendel say that:

> ... borderlands—i.e., that space that lies on both sides of the border—can be classified as *alienated*, in which routine cross-border exchange is practically non-existent, largely due to mutual hostility; *co-existent*, in which minimum cross-border exchange is allowed; *interdependent*, in which societies on both sides are linked symbiotically, making for considerable flow of human and economic resources; and finally, *integrated* borderlands, when all barriers to trade and human movement are removed (Baud and van Schendel, cited in Menon 1999: 160).

Except for the last one, the South Asian region provides us with examples of all: India and Pakistan of the first type; India and Bangladesh of the second; and India and Nepal of the third. Another distinguishing feature of the region is that, barring India and Nepal, all its borders were consequent upon Partition and remain contested or porous to this day. The protracted conflict over Kashmir between India and Pakistan; 'the rebelliousness' (Baud and van Schendel's characterisation) along the Bangladesh–Tripura–Mizoram border and the Chakma insurgency in Bangladesh; simmering discontent in Punjab and Assam in India; and Sind and Baluchistan (now violent) in Pakistan, 'dates back in some measure to Partition and old migrations' (ibid.). Although states are at pains to protect and safeguard their borders from being redrawn or erased, in reality all borderlands are actually quite porous and people engage in all manner of cross-border interactions and exchange. On India's eastern border, migration continues to this day as a steady stream or trickle depending upon the exigencies of the situation. Overlapping ethnic and/or familial linkages cutting across borders within the South Asian region makes this constant migration not only possible, but also facilitates it.

Finally, keeping in mind the cyclical nature of conflicts outlined earlier, conflict-driven migration too happens in cycles. Saba Gul Khattak explains in this volume the three phases of the Afghan conflict: the first phase of Afghan resistance against Soviet rule lasted from 1979 to 1992; the second phase of inter-mujahideen warfare from 1992 to 1996; and, the third phase that began with the coming of the Taliban in 1996. These phases not only produced different kinds of refugees, but there were also many who repatriated and then returned to Pakistan when the violence and war did not subside. Within Sri Lanka, internally displaced Tamils have returned to Liberation Tigers of Tamil Eelam (LTTE) controlled Tamil areas, but when fighting between Sri Lankan forces and the LTTE intensifies, they are pushed out yet again. Likewise, the minority community of Hindus who had stayed behind in Pakistan at the time of Partition come under pressure every time bilateral relations between India and Pakistan deteriorate, and are forced to become refugees across the border in Rajasthan.

The remainder of this introduction lays out the central themes that run through the volume, and discusses certain key conceptual, methodological and policy-related issues.

Conceptual Issues

This section explores new thematic and theoretical connections. This volume, as pointed out earlier, is situated between the large literatures in gender and conflict and gender and migration. Although both literatures have been burgeoning in the past decade, they have often followed divergent pathways. Contributors to this volume have sought to make these pathways intersect, especially in the context of migrant women's experiences in Asia.

Problematising Migration through a Gender Lens

Deploying a gender lens brings to focus the thin dividing lines between choice and coercion in the case of conflict-driven migration. Urvashi Butalia explains it with reference to the partition of India in 1947—the largest exodus in human history—that took place amidst terrible violence and fear. In theory, everyone had a choice to migrate or to stay, but in practice, staying on was virtually impossible. Khan's paper documenting the Pakistani experiences, too, records that most people wanted to just save themselves—a point well captured in an interviewee's remark: 'nassan wali ghal karo' (there is no other option but to run away). While such choices were mostly imposed on the people, this process played out differently for men and women. It was men who decided whether women should migrate—often forcibly sending them away—stay, or be killed by their own (male) family members if their safety during flight could not be ensured. Sealdah station in Calcutta was flooded with women who had been forcibly sent away by their men from East Pakistan where they had their ancestral homes, because the men felt that East Pakistan was no longer secure (Chakravarty 2004). In Punjab, on the other hand, many Sikhs and Muslims proudly recounted stories of having killed their wives and daughters in order to protect their honour and save them from the *kafirs* (infidels). In both situations, the 'choice' of whether to move or to stay or indeed to sacrifice their own lives were constantly choices that were being made for women. The underlying assumption was of course that they were incapable of making these choices themselves. In the case of abducted women who crossed the border between the two countries twice—at the time of abduction, and then their 'recovery' by the respective state authorities—neither move was of their own free will. Women's experiences such as these problematise the understanding of conflict-induced migration and makes it difficult to label them into neat categories of being 'migrants', 'refugees' or simply 'dislocated' women.

Rita Manchanda also questions the utility of determining voluntary and coercive reasons for explaining the complex web of factors that underlie migration. She points to the blurred lines of distinction between life-threatening and livelihood-threatening situations, in view of the structural violence many people, especially women, in many parts of South Asia are routinely subjected to. For example, the Rohingya Muslims from Myanmar's eastern state of Arakan have fled discrimination and persecution from the majoritarian Burman (Buddhist) state and co-ethnic Rakhine (Buddhist) community. However, in Bangladesh—their 'first site of refuge'—they are deemed 'illegal aliens'. Starvation rations, intimidation by the police and fears of being pushed back makes them—adolescent girls and young widows in particular—'voluntarily opt' to being trafficked as illegal migrants to Karachi. The story of Tamil women refugees from Sri Lanka seeking refuge in the Indian state of Tamil Nadu follows a similar trajectory. In order to escape the oppressive conditions in the refugee camps exacerbated by the willful indifference of the host state's government towards their security, many 'choose' to be re-cruited as 'maids' for the Gulf countries by agents scouring the camps.

The scenario is not much different for the women of Nepali origin fleeing from Bhutan to Nepal due to persecution, or Afghan women fleeing to Pakistan. The testimonies of these women expose the nominal notion of choice or the idea of voluntarism as understood in the rational choice theory.

Manchanda also criticises the characterisation of internal displacement of an estimated 150,000–200,000 people by the Maoist insurgency in Nepal as 'a spurt in seasonal migration'. Officially, the government recognises only 7,343 persons/families, the criteria being 'a person who has been displaced due to murder of a family member by the terrorists'. Since one out of three persons in Nepal depends upon seasonal migration for family survival, she stresses the need to interrogate the usefulness of definitions of 'voluntary migration' in a situation of structural violence unleashed by the conflict between the Maoists and the Nepalese Army. Generalised violence, forced recruitment, the use of food as an instrument of war, and the disruption of agricultural production, food for work programmes, education and health services has not permitted thousands of people to return from seasonal migration. Against this backdrop, the strategy of the International Committee of the Red Cross to view displacement as a mere increase in normal migration rates, she points out, raises questions for humanitarian politics as well as definitional parameters of conflict-driven migration.

Analyses of conflict-induced migration usually focus on internally displaced persons and refugees. By using a gender perspective, Manchanda introduces a third category of those who are 'internally struck' and are often the most vulnerable. Those who cannot flee conflict situations are women, children, the elderly and the disabled. They are left behind to face increasing deprivation and the wrath of soldiers, many of whom use rape as a weapon of war. During the liberation struggle for Bangladesh in 1971, men had either joined the guerrillas (the Mukti Bahini) or fled across the border to get arms training and women were left behind to protect their homes and children. Likewise, the ongoing Maoist insurgency in Nepal has left many villages with few able-bodied men. They have melted into the jungles, joined the rebels or migrated to cities across the border in India. Women have to take on new roles of using the plough, dealing with the local government and often trading sexual favours for male labour to thatch their houses, and are also at the receiving end of violence perpetrated by the Nepalese Army. With regard to resettlement, too, a gendered pattern can be discerned in the case of Sri Lankan and Afghan refugees where women were reportedly sent back first to test whether it was safe to return.

Migration studies have focused on the effects of migration on the poor, oppressed and women, while the experiences of middle class 'refugees' are conspicuously absent. Nayanika Mookerjee, in this volume, critiques the construction of the poor and the raped migrant woman—a romantic underclass that needs to be represented either as a victim or with agentive subjectivity—as the subalterns during times of armed conflict and resulting displacement. She argues that the exclusion of the experiences of middle class refugees and an emphasis on poor, women refuges as victims or agents disallows an exploration of the class and gendered identities and gendered social relations during wars. *Muktir Gaan* (Songs of Freedom) is the lens through which her paper highlights the heterogeneity of migrant experiences as a result of war. By focusing on middle class men and women migrants of varied religious backgrounds assigned with the agency of raising morale during war and juxtaposing them with poor migrants and raped women, *Muktir Gaan* is able to interrupt the binaries of agent-victim, male-female and class.

Mookerjee further argues that migration studies have been unable to address how migration during war while being threatening may also be imbued with adventure and excitement precisely by virtue of one's class position. During wars there are varied migrant experiences which do not fit the subaltern imagery and hence are not included within academic and policy understandings of refugee experiences. The younger middle class generation in their responses to *Muktir Gaan* emphasised precisely the aesthetics of the liberationary and sensual feeling of the film. Viewing it primarily as a road movie, the adventure and its concurrent excitement and eroticism are further heightened by the context of the ravages, fears and pain of war tinged with the prospect of freedom. Quite a few young men and women in contemporary Bangladesh expressed that they wished they were young when the war was on as it was so exciting and sensual; there was so much freedom for men and women to travel without family and one could have a sense of responsibility in the midst of armed conflict. Thus while migration is seen to result in the breakdown of processes of economic development, Mookerjee highlights how romanticism linked to the idea of the adventure of war reveals the political economy of migration, namely, who can migrate and under what conditions.

Re-examining Feminist Assumptions through Migrant Women's Experience

The public-private binary forms the core of feminist theories. Although it has been criticised as being an inadequate tool for analysing constructions of civil societies in post-colonial nations (Chatterjee 1990), the boundary between the public and the private especially blurs in situations of violent conflict. They open up for women the public sphere predominantly controlled by men. As armed groups and security forces wage wars amidst multicultural civilian spaces, civil society is suppressed and the public sphere of men collapses. Patriarchs can no longer play the role of the protector as women are literally and metaphorically forced to come out on the streets.

Several authors in this volume argue that violent conflict blurs the divide between the private sphere of women and the public sphere of men, and in doing so, questions the validity of the divide. For example, growing up in traditional Hindu patriarchal families as young girls, all the three protagonists of Raychaudhury's paper—Amiyaprova Debi, Surama Debi and Sarajubala Debi—had rarely stepped out of the *andarmahal*s of their respective houses. But when the country was partitioned and riots broke out in Bengal, men and women alike were on the streets. The traditional values imposed by the patriarchal society became irrelevant due to the violence unleashed by Partition. Therefore, when these women began to reconstruct their lives in an unknown territory on the other side of the border, the boundaries between public and private space had already become blurred for them.

Mary O'Kane makes the same point that in the foundationless, fluid and morphing transversal spaces of the Burma–Thailand borderlands, distinctions between public/private, politics/survival, mother/activist, freedom fighter/illegal alien collapse and become inseparable experiences. The collapse and significant restructuring of how these binary categories of relations are lived in the borderlands has caused tensions between many women and members of their communities resulting in shifts and transformations in women's identities. Likewise, Rajasingham-Senanayake points out that in the north and east of Sri Lanka, the reality of war for women has been the loss of their men folk, physical safety, psychological insecurity and a struggle for survival and sustaining the family. As a result women have crossed the private/public barriers to contend with the military, to compete in the market and to survive economically. In doing so, many women have been forced to take on the responsibility of traditionally male roles such as becoming the head of a household or the principal income generator in their families.

Drawing upon the public-private binary, feminists also view home—a private space guarded by patriarchal traditions that remains outside the purview of the state due to the social contract—with suspicion. Migrant women, however, tend to remember 'home' in a positive spirit. Khattak points out that the word for country and home is used interchangeably: *watan*. When Afghan refugee women talk of going home, they talk about going back to their *watan*. Raychaudhury, too, uses the term 'refugee' to refer to a person who has been uprooted from her *desh*—a term translated as 'foundational homeland' by Dipesh Chakraborty. Home is thus intricately woven into the idea of belonging—belonging to a place and a community. In this sense, a person derives her/his sense of self from home. Refugees and migrants are never quite at home in the countries and places that they live in since the sense of belonging and home is missing. This is because home also represents a way of life, a way of being, a culture and a way of thinking. Khattak thus interprets home as a positive locus of identity for women rather than uncritically adhering to the feminist position of considering home to be primarily the first site of oppression for women.

Home, she argues, becomes a symbol of violence when it comes to a woman's relationship with a man and patriarchal authority. However, her own relationship with the house/home is different in that it represents a sanctuary—even if it is a patriarchal sanctuary. Home is the source of primary identity for women not only because both are associated predominantly with the private sphere, but also because home is the locus of self, culture and belonging. This is true for men as well as women; however, due to the historical role that women play in the making of home, they identify much more with it. Women's understanding and representations of home involve multiple themes that relate to both the physical as well as imagined and intangible aspects. Aside from being a reflection of self, and social and economic status, home represents the space where women can be happy and secure, where they can be creative and enjoy familial support.

Perhaps that is why one of Raychaudhury's protagonists, Amiyaprova Das, an elderly woman of about 75, can vividly remember her *janmobhite* (ancestral house), *desher bari* (original home), *khelar math* (playground) where she used to play her favourite game *dariabanda* (a traditional sport of East Bengal, particularly popular among young girls) with her elder brother, sisters and younger cousins. She especially remembers the days of the Durga puja when she used to receive new clothes and had fun with her cousins. Sarajubala Debi, despite her apparently incoherent utterances, can also remember clearly their *pujor ghor* (room for worshipping) where they celebrated Kali puja, Monosha puja and Shitola puja. In the loneliness of the refugee camps, both looked back with nostalgia to their *desh* where they had everything.

Butalia on the other hand underlines the shifting notion of 'home' for migrant Hindus who seek naturalisation and citizenship of the 'host country', that is India. In other words, they are seeking a home, a sense of belonging and a nation (symbolised also in the desire to have an identity as established by a state document, the Indian passport) to call their own. But for many of them, these notions keep shifting. Is 'home' where they now are, or where they have spent much of their lives? Is the nation where they have now set up camp or is it the country whose passports they continue to hold? For many migrants, while they may be located in a new state, home remains elsewhere, the land they left behind.

Mookerjee's paper seeks to destabilise the relationship between militarisation and patriarchy (Enloe 2000). The role of both men and women as peace activists, using peaceful tools like songs to provide support to the Bengali liberation fighters to fight wars jars the feminist interpretation of gendered relations during wars (Elshtain 1987; Goldstein 2001; Lorentzen and Turpin 1998; Reardon 1985; Vickers 1993). This is also reflected in the gendered social relations and activities within the cultural troupe depicted in *Muktir Gaan* where the women are engaged in the masculine idiom of reading newspapers while the men are engaged in feminised practices of practicing songs. The relationship between militarisation and patriarchy, Mookerjee argues, is further complicated by exploring the idioms of feminisation through visuals of the landscape and songs within *Muktir Gaan*. In identifying the role of women and identity politics rather than women per se, feminisation—applicable to both men and women—is a positive attribute. Feminisation is able to evoke empathy and emotive nostalgia while also constructing the role of men and particularly women during the war as agentive. If migrant women's experiences add new nuances to the fundamental assumptions of feminism, they also provide new sites for raising their gender consciousness.

Migration as New Sites for Raising Gender Consciousness

O'Kane discusses in detail how women began to challenge established norms of gender relations in response to new and different situations faced in the Burma–Thailand borderlands and what transformations it wrought on women activists' understanding of gender in relation to their being displaced to refugee camps, joining political dissident communities or staying on as undocumented migrants.

Through performing welfare duties in line with their traditional gender roles under the intensely pressured conditions of displacement and refugee camps, some women, she points out, came to question, then challenge, aspects of traditional gender norms through pursuing non-traditional roles in the community and education. The driving need to find solutions to immediate and long-term crises led women to self-advocacy, including demands for meaningful political participation in relevant decision-making processes. Their growing contacts with international organisations not only provided new resources, but also an awareness about the gendered nature of abuse suffered by exploited women from their communities. The need to take coordinated action on behalf of women migrants and their families led to the establishment of women's organisations such as the Shan Woman's Action Network in 1998 and the Pa-O Women's Union in 2000.

Likewise, many female students, particularly those who had taken leading roles in organising demonstrations during the 1988 uprising inside (erstwhile) Burma, felt marginalised and discriminated against on the basis of gender. The 'student' component of their identities was suddenly given lesser respect as they were forced to perform traditional female roles in the organisation of the student resistance. Feeling unjustly constrained by conventional gender roles imposed on them, women began questioning previously assumed meanings of politics and gender in ways that caused a shift in gender consciousness. It led to the formation of the first women's organisation by a group of seven women in a remote jungle army camp on the Burmese side of the border in 1995. Without access to funding, communication technologies, information or education of formal bodies of feminist knowledge, they organised the Burmese Women's Union and quickly established a branch on the China–Burma border. To quote O'Kane:

Women activists understood that to increase their capacities in the face of structural gender discrimination within the broader male-dominated Burmese opposition movement, they needed to unify on the basis of gender.... Uneven social, political and economic status, as well as different experiences of conflict and displacement character-ised the relations between women as they embarked on this challenge for unification. Initial encounters between women activists revealed much to themselves about the extent to which militarised society inside Burma had generated a 'divide and rule' culture amongst politico-ethnic communities, and how the social structures of dis-placement in the borderlands operated to perpetuate these divisions in the absence of a collective women's rights consciousness.... [So,] they needed to form alliances across ethnic boundaries to put forward a unified voice, not only on 'women's issues', but political processes in general. Intricately related to this, women's vision for political transition in Burma demands the participation of women at all levels of political dialogue which also demands reconciliation across ethnic boundaries.

This demonstrates the transformative implications of deploying a gender perspective, which not only throws new light on understanding the experiences of migrant women but goes much beyond in raising fundamental questions about the conflict, migration and politics as such.

State, Citizenship and Migrant Women

Feminists believe that the state is the main organiser of power relations of gender. Studying migration from their standpoint, therefore, helps in uncovering the patriarchal character of the state in appropriating the civil and political rights of migrant women. Menon and Bhasin, and Butalia's work on thousands of women who were abducted and then 'recovered' by the respective state authorities during the post-Partition era illuminates the paternalism of the Indian state (Butalia 1998; Menon and Bhasin 1998). It took on the role of protector and provider and insisted on determining where women and their children belonged. For women who were dislocated, destitute, widowed and col-lectively described in policy terms as 'unattached', the state stepped in as the surrogate paterfamilias, and once again inherited the mantle of protector.

Most post-colonial states saw themselves as agents of social and economic transformation and through their constitutions, laws and legislation sought to change and develop societies. This was particularly true for north India, especially Punjab, where 'the government has always been characterized as *ma-baap* (mother-father). As [such] it is duty bound to provide a rich, warm, nurturant relationship (the *ma* part) as well as paternal protection from the dangers of life (the *baap* part)' (Stephen Keller 1975: 47). In both cases, however, 'the state was acting as custodian and guardian on behalf of missing or wronged men—in the case of widows, the men were permanently absent or missing; in abduction, it was the women who were "missing"—and the patriarchal bias of its intervention and ideology were evident in both' (Menon and Bhasin 2001: 78).

The Abducted Persons Act was remarkable for the impunity with which it violated every principle of citizenship—fundamental rights and access to justice. That is because the terms and context in which this bill defined 'abducted persons' saw them solely as missing members of naturalised communities of families or religious groups on whose behalf choices had to be made, never as citizens of the new state who would otherwise exercise their civil and political rights. The extended debate on forcible recovery as violating the constitutional and fundamental rights of abducted women, as *citizens*, is evidence of this conflict; the resistance by abducted women themselves further demonstrates their attempt to realise citizenship by acting independently and autonomously—of community, state *and* family (ibid.: 77). The attempt was thwarted through a consensus reached by all three on the desirability and necessity of women preserving community and national honour by subordinating their rights as individuals and citizens to the rights of the community and the will of the state.

The patriarchal basis of state intervention was also evident in deciding the fate of these abducted women's children. The government had passed an ordinance that those women whose babies were born in Pakistan would have to leave them behind, and those children that were born in India would have to stay in India, implicitly acknowledging that *the child belonged with the father, Hindu or Muslim* (Menon 1998: 26). In implementing the government policy, the authorities actively discouraged women from taking their children with them and pressured those who were pregnant to have abortions before they returned to their families.[3] Ironically, such women and children were often spurned by their extended families and communities because they were now considered 'impure'.

More than two decades later, the story was repeated during another partition when East Pakistan seceded to become Bangladesh in 1972. Nearly 200,000 to 300,000 Bengali women were raped by Pakistani soldiers during the liberation struggle for Bangladesh. The state valorised them in the post-war period by declaring that all raped women of 1971 were *birangonas* (war heroines). Ostensibly, this was an attempt to reduce social ostracism towards these women and enable their smooth social re-absorption, but the hard reality was that they were diseased, malnourished and traumatised, and many were killed by their husbands because they had been dishonoured. The *birangonas* were also never given the right as a *citizen* of the newly-created state to decide the fate of their children. The state assumed the role of a patriarch when Mujib-ur-Rehman, the 'father of the nation', publicly denounced the children born of the raped Bangladeshi women-citizens as aliens. As the first President of Bangladesh, he decided to give up the more than 30,000 'war babies' for adoption, in many cases against their mother's wishes.

Feminist analyses show that citizenship is, historically as well as conceptually, not a gender-neutral phenomenon (Gardezi 1997; Parker et al. 1992; Pateman 1988; Shaheed 1997; Yuval-Davis 1997). The relationship of women with the state is still mediated by the family and the concept of direct citizen-state is absent for the female population. However, in the modern state system, individual's rights or the right to have rights flow from being recognised as a citizen of a sovereign nation-state. O'Kane explains that in fleeing to Burma's borderlands, women activists' relationship as citizens with the state of Burma has been severed. Their displacement from Burma and lack of acceptance into any other state means they are not recognised as belonging to any political community. Their exclusion from membership of a state forcibly situates them in a liminal space outside the paradigm of the nation-state. What complicates this issue further is the women activists' deliberate *choice* to remain on the Burma–Thailand border rather than seek resettlement through the United Nations High Commission for Refugees (UNHCR) in third countries. They believe that the borderlands provide the most suitable environment to continue their political resistance. In exercising their choice to stay, women highlight the contradictory and ambiguous character of borders as important sites of dis/connection with inside Burma.

The repudiation of their own country's political borders by citizens can be most subversive. An Indian film *Mammo*, by Shyam Benegal, beautifully depicts this phenomenon. Mammo, the protagonist of the film, defies the boundaries created by Partition by returning to her sister's home in Bombay in India and refusing to go back to Pakistan upon expiry of her visa. In an extreme act of resistance, she fakes her own death certificate, thus confounding the laws of entry and citizenship of both countries, and in a triumphant rejection of borderlines imposed by both states, she asserts her 'right to be in India by inserting her very body into the place she calls "home"' (Menon 1999: 162).

Understanding conflict-induced migration from a legal perspective, albeit infused with a gender spirit, brings to fore the question of state responsibility. Oishik Sircar, in this volume, discusses the vexed problem of the state's role in the persecution suffered under the asylum law. Traditionally in refugee law, persecution was understood as an act of the state or those acting in their capacity as state agents. A central concern of feminists is, therefore, that forms of persecution suffered by women in more private settings are less likely to be recognised as grounds for persecution. And, the indirect roles of the state in generating and/or sustaining harmful acts are not likely to be acknowledged. In some situations, the state may be the agent denying basic human rights, or it may fail to offer protection even though such protection is within its capacity. At other times, women experience acts of harm either because of their association with others and/or because the state does not protect them. Also, the emphasis on the violation of civil and political rights both deflects attention away from the affirmative duty of the state to ensure rights, and ignores the existence of societal-wide discrimination against women (Connors 1997). The state has an affirmative obligation to protect and prevent violence. Sircar argues that the state's inability to do so is not only in breach of its obligations under international law, which requires it to punish those individuals—government agents or private actors—who commit human rights violations, but also amounts to persecution from nonfeasance, that is, liability is conferred on the state for commission of those persecutory acts.

Meta-narrative of the State and the Disruptive Stories of Women

A state's meta-narrative is almost always a history of the elites, focusing more on their heroic deeds which are supposed to have been singularly responsible for determining the roadmap for the creation, governance and future of a nation-state. Furrukh Khan argues in this volume that in such histories, voices which challenge this meta-narrative are sidelined at best and totally silenced at worst, so that alternative histories and perspectives that might break the selective linearity of the state's version are institutionally marginalised. This indeed is the case of women's stories, which are completely absent from the state's version of history. Women's stories of Partition are denied any mode of 'official' transmission beyond their 'private' space, and issues of violence, especially sexual brutalisation, are rarely allowed to be passed on to the next generation. Implied in their coerced silence is the usurpation of their right to speak by the patriarchally inspired state's meta-narrative, which perceives the oral stories by women as a disturbing influence on the grand narrativisation.

Khan describes the meta-narratives of the state as linear, unbending and unrelenting, vertical in structure yielding no space for the debate as they are also shaped by patriarchical influences. Women's narratives are, on the other hand, non-linear, almost anarchic and radically horizontal, cuting across boundaries imposed by the state. Khan, Butalia and Raychaudhury's contributions to this volume attempt to break the homogeneity of state discourses by bringing in women's experiences, which make it more complex. Butalia, for instance, points out that the dominant narrative of Partition is one of mass migration with iconic pictures of large columns of people moving in both directions. And it is this narrative that lends itself to the accompanying narrative of the making of the nation-state: here were millions of 'the nation's' people making their way out of a violent situation into a new home, a new country. The newly formed nation-state responded as a parent does to their suffering, with care, offering rehabilitation, relocation, jobs and compensation. But within this narrative lie the stories of those who do not quite fit in—the abducted and forcibly recovered women. Their narratives question, resist and sometimes disrupt the meta-narrative and help us to unpack the seemingly unproblematic category of migrants. In their refusal to return to their families, some abducted women further complicate the meta-narrative by refusing to accept, *and own*, the borders that now separate the two nations.

Beyond Victimhood: Migrant Women's Agency

The agent-victim binary tends to be exacerbated in the case of migration due to conflict. There are two schools of thought. The first focuses on the double victimisation of female migrants and the disempowering albeit differential impact of conflict-driven migration upon women. To quote Manchanda: 'The woman refugee represents the epitome of the marginalisation and the disenfranchisement of the dislocated. Her identity and her individuality are collapsed into the homogenous category of "victim" and of her community. She is constructed as devoid of agency, unable and incapable of representing herself, powerless and superfluous'. Refugee and displaced women, it is argued, are in double jeopardy owing to their gender, which heightens their vulnerability to the most pervasive and egregious forms of human rights abuses (Saigol 2000; Wali 1993).

The forms of abuse common to refugee and displaced women and girls include rape, forced prostitution, trafficking, domestic violence, sexually-related torture and murder, abduction and the demand for sexual favours in exchange for basic relief items such as food, water, fuel, documentation and transportation to relief centres. They also often serve as their children's sole caretakers as many of them are widows or separated from their spouses and other extended family. So, refugee women must seek food and safety not only for themselves but also for their children who also need health care, housing and an education. They play a central economic role though lacking in decision-making power in their societies.

Two sets of explanations are offered to elucidate the 'double jeopardy' thesis. The first argues that patriarchy is recomposed in intensified forms after a period of disintegration due to displacement and dislocation (Wali 1993). In the case of Afghan women, for instance, the norm is towards greater control of women rather than creating new spaces for their agency. Their mobility in refugee camps was severely restricted and there was a resurgence in camps of the Islamic practice of veiling and seclusion of women. Through campaigns of public violence, women had even been restricted from participating in the so-called service delivery programmes. Fatwas or religious decrees during Friday prayer sessions were used to provoke public violence against Afghan women who disobeyed socio-religious mores. The incidence of domestic violence has been observed to increase in refugee situations as a result of male frustration with the inability to perform 'the male role'. This is especially because living off women's earning is anathema to Afghan, particularly Pashtun patriarchy. Angry and 'conflict-impotent' husbands, thus, tend to vent their frustrations upon women for becoming breadwinners and going out to earn (Saigol 2000).

Rajasingham-Senanayake makes the same point with reference to the Tamil conflict, i.e., men who refuse to fight or who are forced to live off humanitarian aid in refugee camps suffer from feeling de-masculinated because they often cannot support their families and play the socially prescribed role of protector and breadwinner of the family. The result is low self-esteem and a sense of failure that might lead to suicidal tendencies among men and boys. Reports from those living in refugee camps indicate that alcoholism is high, as is increased domestic violence. She further argues that the tendency to view women as 'victims' in the armed conflict has been fuelled by a number of popular and human rights discourses. Anthropological, sociological and literary ethnography has also tended to represent Tamil women as living within a highly patriarchal caste-ridden Hindu cultural ethos, particularly in comparison to Sinhala women whose lives are seen to be less circumscribed by caste ideologies and purity/pollution concepts and practices.

Feminist ethnography on the other hand, Rajasingham-Senanayake points out, has emphasised the subordinate status of Tamil women in the Hindu caste structure, while frequently noting the split between the ideology of *Shakti* or female power as the primary generative force of the universe (also associated with the pantheon of powerful Hindu goddesses) and the reality of women's apparent powerlessness in every-day life (Thiruchandran 1997). By and large, however, women have rarely been centred in debates on caste, and when they have been, they are more often than not constructed as victims rather than agents of culture. Popular romanticisations of home as well as constructions of internally displaced people as victims (the Sinhala term '*anathagatha kattiya*' literally means the abandoned people, while the Tamil term *veedu attavargal* means people without a home), like the victim discourse concerning women in conflict in the human rights field, often obscure the realities of living at home during conflict.

While there is little doubt that women in a war's interregnum carry a double burden, viewing women as merely victims of their culture, war and patriarchy elides women's agency in violence. Positioning women as victims might also mean that they are subject to secondary victimisation since victimhood also often entails carrying the burden of a social stigma. Women who are widowed and/or raped, as were the abducted women during India's partition in 1947 and Bengali women during the Bangladesh liberation struggle in 1971, are particularly vulnerable to the double complex of stigmatised victimhood.

The second school of thought questions stereotypical essentialising of women as 'victims' that denies their agency and assumes universal, simplified definitions of such phenomenon (Moser and Clark 2001):

> The notion of agency attributes to the individual actor the capacity to process social experience and to devise ways of coping with life even under the most extreme forms of coercion. Within the limits of information, uncertainty and other constraints that exist, social actors are 'knowledgeable' and 'capable'.... For women as much as men, the experience of violent conflict and migration, as with social life, is not built upon a single discourse. As social actors, they face alternative ways of formulating their objectives, however restricted their resources (2001: 5).

Rajasingham-Senanayake argues that the social disruption caused by conflicts has tended to open up new forms of migration and spaces of agency, even as different communities tend to react in different ways to violence. She explores the changing shape of women's agency in the midst of displacement by exploring the new roles that women increasingly perform in their everyday activities where the armed conflict has transformed social structures. Women have taken on many new and unaccustomed roles such as becoming the head of households and principal income generators. They have also begun to play new public roles of dealing with authorities from the government agencies to the military and the humanitarian aid agencies. They file documents, plead their cases and implement decisions in public and private in the presence or absence of their men folk who are increasingly disempowered or disappeared. Displacement has also provided a liberating displacement of caste and gender hierarchies. The erosion of caste ideology and practice, particularly among the younger generation in the camps, had contributed to women's mobility and sense of empowerment. Unlike in Jaffna, where village settlement was caste and region based, in the camps it was difficult to maintain social and spatial segregation, caste hierarchies, and purity pollution taboos for a number of reasons.

A generation of young Tamil war widows who have been displaced to and in the border areas for many years are, for instance, increasingly challenging conventional Hindu constructions of widowhood as a negative and polluting condition which bars their participation from many aspects of community life. Rajasingham-Senanayake cites the examples of several young widows working in Vavunia town, but resident in the camp and in Batticaloa, who displayed their sense of independence by wearing the red *pottu*, the auspicious mark reserved for married Hindu women, despite being widows or women whose husbands had abandoned them. They refuse to be socially and culturally marginalised and ostracised because they lack husbands and children. Displacement along with the fragmentation and reconstitution of families around women in a conflict appears to have provided a space to redefine traditional Hindu Tamil perceptions of widows and single women as inauspicious beings. There is, thus, growing evidence to suggest that despite the psychosocial traumas that displacement entails, long-term displacement has provided windows of opportunity for greater personal and group autonomy, and experiments with identity and leadership for displaced people, particularly women.

O'Kane makes an equally powerful argument as to how women activists, displaced from Burma and marginalised at multiple intersecting levels—gender, ethnicity and effective statelessness—have transformed dimensions of this extreme marginalisation into relative advantage. As occupants of transit zones, they make the uninhabitable habitable and remake spaces according to their needs. Her narrative of women activists from refugee camps, and migrant and political dissident communities reflect how, through travel and relocation, women moved back and forth through their memories to assess and reassess their past in relation to the present and visions for the future. In the process, they formulated new understandings, developed new ideas and meanings and asked new questions concerning gender roles. Transformations in these women's gender consciousness, in turn, led to either a transformation of the frameworks in which established women's organisations worked, or to the formation of new women's organisations.

Methodological Concerns

Feminist methodology rejects the positivist division between theory and practice, between the researcher and the 'object of research'. The positivist science does not take into account elements that are present in scientific knowing but devalued because they denote feminine values—intuition, empathy, emotion, passion—and eventually distort the actual process of undertaking scientific inquiry (Ferree and Hess 1987: 13). Feminist social scientists 'reclaiming the value of the female, legitimate these very elements that have been denied and repressed in science itself' (ibid.). They advocate closer interaction as research is considered to be an interactive process, a communal exercise where the people, the subject of the research, are equally involved with the research process from the conception of research. The whole process of research, it is felt, should eventually create a non-hierarchical base for intervention and sharing (Thiruchandran 1999: 12). The best feminist analysis, to quote Harding:

> ... insists that the inquirer her/himself be placed in the same critical plane as the overt subject matter, thereby recovering the entire research process for scrutiny in the results of research.... We are often explicitly told by the researcher what her/his gender, race, class, culture is, and sometimes how she/he suspects that this has shaped the research project.... Thus, the researcher appears to us not as an invisible, anonymous voice of authority, but as a real, historical individual with concrete, specific desires and interests.... The beliefs and behaviours of the researcher are part of the empirical evidence for (or against) the claims advanced in the results of research. *This* evidence too must be open to critical scrutiny no less than what is traditionally defined as relevant evidence.... Introducing this 'subjective' element into the analysis in fact increases the objectivity of the research and decreases the 'objectivism' which hides this kind of evidence from the public (1987: 9–10).

Contributors to this volume have employed a variety of feminist research methods including ethnographic research, in-depth interviews, dialogue, oral history, textual analyses, consciousness-raising techniques, i.e., role-playing, and establishment of networks and communication.

Raychaudhury's contribution is based on the life history of three elderly dispossessed women, Amiyaprova Debi, Surama Debi and Sarajubala Debi. Khan's research involved interviewing over 50 women from various economic and social backgrounds, with a particular focus on the lower and lower-middle (economic) classes. These were conducted in several cities including Rawalpindi, Islamabad, Sialkot and Lahore, as well as in smaller towns like Narowal and Shakargarh. He took help of the local people and female research assistants for making initial contact, which facilitated the task of gaining access and allowed the interviewees to feel more comfortable.

Khattak's paper is based on a collection of more than 50 qualitative in-depth interviews with Afghan refugee women that were conducted during 2000–01, with an objective to understand the gendered effects of conflict upon women. The interviews were conducted in the local languages of Pushto and Dari and these were later transcribed and translated. Rajasingham-Senanayake's contribution draws from ethnographic field research conducted during several fieldwork stints over a number of years (1996–2000) to study the two decades long armed conflict and patterns of forced migration that began in 1983, as well as the most recent phase of the peace process that started in 2001 between the Government of Sri Lanka (GoSL) and the LTTE in the north-east of Sri Lanka. These were conducted among communities in the border areas, both 'cleared'— held by the military—and uncleared—land controlled by the LTTE— areas. Her observations on displaced women are drawn from interviews conducted with women living in three different settings of displacement: welfare centres or refugee camps where people are housed in sheds, schools or structures constructed by UNHCR and other relief agencies working with the government; residents of border villages who have been displaced many times by the fighting, shelling and bombing, but chose to return to their villages; and new settlements in the border areas of Vanni where the GoSL settles landless displaced families from the same province on new plots of land.

Butalia draws upon her earlier ethnographic research and oral testimonies of the abducted during India's Partition in 1947 and more recent interactions with Hindu Singh Sodha, a leader of the Hindu migrant communities from Pakistan that are now living in the Thar region of Rajasthan. O'Kane conducted 27 qualitative interviews in 2000–01 with 24 politically active women from Burma based on the Burma–Thailand borderlands for her paper. Belonging to diverse ethnic nationalities from Burma—Karen, Karenni, Shan, Mon, Pa-O, Padaung, Burman, Kachin and Tavoy—these activists, aged between 20 and 55 years, had lived on the borders for varying lengths of time. Some women had been on the border for most of their lives while others arrived in the aftermath of the 1988 pro-democracy civil uprising. Most of the interviews were conducted in English. O'Kane acknowledges that cross-cultural, cross-linguistic exchanges of this kind are laden with biases inherent in unequal power relations of researcher/subject, Western/Asian, race, class, native language/non-native language, and so on. She is very much cognisant of the absence of shared native languages and cultural and historical experiences between herself and the women she interviewed. As a 'cultural, linguistic and racial outsider,' she draws 'consciously and unconsciously from her experiences of living and working directly with them as a volunteer' for short durations in 1999 and 2001, and the friendships developed during that period, which, over time, had blurred her 'outsider' status.

Why is feminist ethnography important? What are its different techniques? What kind of problems do scholars face in using feminist methodologies? And, what are the 'special' problems involved in researching the experiences of political violence as such in conflict situations? In such situations, researchers are dealing with the most painful and traumatic of human experiences. An interview can easily bring to surface painful memories that people may actually be attempting to forget (Butalia 1998; Menon and Bhasin 1998; Mohsin 2002; Perera 1999). Therefore a number of methodological and ethical issues have to be faced and engaged within such situations. The following section debates some of these issues.

Oral Testimonies

Oral history has enriched the process of remembering and recording events of the past due to its ability to include voices which Robert Perks describes as those 'hidden from history' (cited in Khan's paper in this volume). Disregarding the violence against women would be disregarding and silencing an entire spectrum of experiences related to that violence. As White and Reynolds put it: '...these women's experience is invaluable to our collective knowledge of ourselves as a society in conflict; that this experience has in the past been denied the authority it warrants; that if no concerted effort to record it is made it may be irretrievably lost to our future' (cited in Perera 1999: 1). Orality has resulted in a comparatively more democratic portrayal of social and political events. Nationalist historiography has generally seen the partition of India as an unfortunate outcome of sectarian and separatist politics. Much of the literature—historical, socio-political, philosophical, and religious—treats Partition as if sexual and gender differences did not make a difference.

Khan's paper addresses the question of inclusion, that is, the extent to which women's experiences are represented in historical accounts. Interviewing these women, he argues, would evince the multiplicity of their narratives not just for themselves, but to add, even a discordant voice to the parochial, patriarchal and elitist meta-narrative of the experience of Partition. Their deliberate assertions fill the gaping holes not just in the social but the political construction of the recent past of Pakistan. There were numerous occasions in which interviewees had been witness to the savagery inflicted on women from one group by men from another, including amputation of breasts, mass rape, parading them naked through public and religious places, cutting open the wombs of pregnant women, and tattooing their bodies with nationalistic and religious slogans. Most of such graphic details are never part of any written history, be it by the state or the individual. Oral literature, on the other hand, is how most of the population of Pakistan, remembers its collective ordeal. This form of articulation of memory of Partition has been marginalised for long enough, and suffered because of the postcolonial nations' obsession with the colonial version of collecting and articulating a national history which has always been in a written form. Orality demonstrates the complexities of remembering that cannot be captured in written literature and hence adds a dimension missing from the otherwise linear narrative. These collective voices, he stresses, need to be tapped into in order to create new and hybridised forms of national autobiography.

Interestingly, Mookerjee adopts a different approach. Rather than citing pure testimonies and narratives, she seeks to address how one relates to these testimonies and narratives. In fact, an exploration of the oral history and testimony within *Muktir Gaan* allows an understanding of 'documentation of both the witness as he makes testimony and the understanding and meaning of events generated in the activity of testimony itself' (Young cited in Mookerjee in this volume). The film is deemed to be a narrative and musical story of a unique movement in history when a nation is born. In the film, the Bangladesh Freedom Struggle Cultural Squad—a group of young middle class men and women refugees—travelling on a truck are juxtaposed with stereotypical scenes of poor, impoverished women refugees who are fleeing to India. Naila Marium's 'stroll' through the camp, for instance, is juxtaposed with the narrations of the experiences of terror and pain of various refugees. In fact for the audiences of *Muktir Gaan*, juxtaposition of the heterogeneity of refugees and the confrontation of refugees allow different kinds of identification with gendered migration images. This is particularly significant for independent Bangladesh, where *Muktir Gaan* evoked a very emotive response two decades after it was filmed.

Mookerjee argues that there is a significant parallel between the middle class refugees documenting and being a witness to the plight of other refugees and that of the researchers working on migration who are also engaged in making testimony in the process of being a witness. Through this the varied identifications that one has as a middle class refugee or as a researcher with varied migrant identities is identified. The paper raises questions as to what kinds of discomfort are caused by the study of middle class refugees and what kinds of binaries are hence disrupted. These are significant questions, which precisely address the reflexive and discursive understandings of migration study researchers and their identification with varied refugee identities.

'Her' Story in 'Her' Words

The nexus of language, culture and personal experience, O'Kane points out, plays a crucial role informing both the expression and interpretation of experience, ideas and opinion. She cites Hallah Ghorashi's study of Iranian political activists in exile in the Netherlands to illustrate the impact of language in interpreting and analysing interviews. Ghorashi's psychological responses to the language and terminology interviewees used to discuss their identity revealed insights unavailable to people outside their particular political experiences (Ghorashi as cited in O'Kane in this volume). It is indeed important to let the women speak their own idiom, their own phrases and proverbs, in their own language and dialect. In recounting multiple notions of home evoking different themes regarding violence, peace, displacement, loss, death and hope, Khattak notes her conscious effort to let the women's voices speak and derive her analysis from their words, rather than any preconceived ideas. Raychaudhury, too, attempts to share the feelings, experiences and trauma of the contemporary displaced women and to look at their life and times through their own eyes. However, if the researcher does not share the language of his/her interviewee, he/she may adopt different methods. O'Kane, for instance, points out that without Burmese or other ethnic language skills, she relied heavily on observation, and her own culturally informed notions, of non-verbal forms of communication including body language, emotional and psychological 'fallout' reactions and consequences. As the women also responded to her reactions of what was going on at any particular time, she notes, both were constantly challenged to clarify and articulate their meanings and intentions in a way that reflexively adjusted their understandings of events and relationships. Nonetheless, O'Kane acknowledges the significant methodological and epistemological limitations of her paper because there are always some aspects of these women's lives and work that remains hidden from her and beyond her appreciation, such as political meanings communicated through culturally and linguistically specific humour or the complications of bridging traditional and modern forms of relations.

Role Conflicts in Research Settings

Feminist methodological approaches have for the most part tended to emphasise closeness rather than distance with the 'subject' of their research. Some feminist scholars have, however, recently begun to address the difficulties that closeness with the subjects may impose on the research process (Behar 1995; Davidman 2002). Janet Jacobs in her research on evolving a feminist ethnography of holocaust victims encountered the problem of 'double vision', wherein the researcher is at once both a witness to crimes against humanity and an ethnographic observer in search for qualitative data (2004: 227). As a witness to crimes against humanity, the researcher enters into a deeply personal relationship with her or his subjects that, according to Dori Laub (1992), often obscures the boundaries between the researcher and the researched, a blurring of subjectivity that is intensified by bonds of gender and ethnic kinship. Historical scholars of the Holocaust have approached this troubling aspect from the standpoint of psychoanalytic thought and termed it as a 'phenomenon of transference', which is described by Saul Friedlander as follows:

> The major difficulties of historians of the *Shoah*, when confronted with echoes of the traumatic past, is to keep some measure of balance between the emotion recurrently breaking through the 'protective shield' and numbness that protects this very shield. In fact, the numbing or distancing effect of intellectual work on the *Shoah* is unavoidable and necessary; the re-occurrence of strong emotional impact is often unforeseeable and necessary (1993: 130).

Davidman endorses this viewpoint saying that the success of her own research study—a feminist ethnography of newly orthodox women in the context of the Holocaust—relies on her ability to separate her intrusive memories and emotions from the research perspectives that she brought to the fieldwork settings (2002: 24–25). Jacobs in her research, however, feared that in creating and sustaining emotional distance from women, she would be at the risk of exploiting their pain and degradation (2004: 229).

Ethical Dilemmas

Interviewing female migrants who have been violently uprooted from their homes and abducted or raped can be traumatising for them. The unethical character of talking about personal matters does indeed cause a moral dilemma. Researchers are compelled to ask: What is our right and why should these women be duty bound to talk to us with terrible pain in mind? So, Khan constantly grapples with a moral dilemma: 'At what point does recording the borne and witnessed traumatic experiences of human suffering cross from documentation of the critical memory to the manipulation of the survivor for cold academic dramatic effect?'. That is because, he notes, the strain of the interviews conducted was always the tension between the horror of atrocity and the controlled suppression, which had very rarely been allowed to surface. It was apparent how this sustained pressure had accentuated the chasm that ironically separated a number of women from their own experiences. They repeatedly raise questions about the legitimacy of their own witnessing and suffering.

That is also because approaching such issues from the perspective of gender representation requires the observer to focus his or her attention primarily on women-centered imagery and atrocities, a subjective point of view in which the women become larger, more obvious in their degradation, suffering and humiliation, while the children and men recede into the ethnographic background. In taking photographs of Holocaust victims for the purpose of evolving a feminist ethnography, Janet Jacobs 'experienced a "crisis" of observation' in which she 'questioned not only [her] ... betrayal of Jewish men and children but [her] ... responsibility for a research project that by its very nature could contribute to the dissemination of images of women's subjugation and degradation that were already so pervasive in Holocaust memorial culture' (2004: 232). She was often particularly troubled by the fact that 'through a process of ethnographic selectivity, she therefore, has to choose which memory to privilege and which to trivialise, a choice that in the face of genocidal histories, raises serious ethical questions' (ibid.: 231).

On the other hand scholars, especially psychologists, argue that interviewing victims of violence can have a therapeutic value. In recording the oral testimonies of Tamil women who were heads of households in Sri Lanka, Selvy Thiruchandran noted some such responses including, 'I am happy I talked to you. I talked about my worries, shared them with you and found an outlet It hurts and is painful to keep within us. I am relived now of the distress' (Thiruchandran 1999: 118). Stacey suggests that while the methods of ethnography preclude the possibility of a totally feminist research process, a 'partial' feminist ethnography, in which the moral consequences of representing the other is stressed, is both a worthwhile and necessary scholarly endeavour (Stacey 1988). Jacobs cautiously agrees in admitting that while all ethical dilemmas are not in fact resolvable, stress must be laid on the 'value of a self-reflexive methodological approach that insists on the need for moral self-examination within feminist research', because the 'intellectual honesty that such reflexivity brings to the field of social science can contribute greatly to a more thoughtful and sensitive analysis of gendered memory' (2004: 236).

Voyeurism of Violence

The very act of researching as well as the representation of terror and experiences of political violence in academic and human rights discourse could in themselves be problematic. Stirrat, as cited in Perera, argues that what begins for many as an intellectual interest in specific problems of violence later becomes something akin to a voyeuristic fascination with 'a pornography of violence' (Perera 1999). This problematic situation, he insists, has mostly arisen among academics from countries in the 'North'. According to Stirrat:

> What I have suggested as a voyeuristic and pornographic interest in violence can best be sustained when the analyst is at a safe distance from the events described, or where the academic through colour

and nationality, and of course a return airline ticket, can observe the violence of others. This indeed is a form of contemporary orientalism in which violence has to be added to the list of characteristics of the 'other' and if not associated with 'race' is all too often conflated with 'culture' or a close synonym (ibid.: 8).

This also refers to the problem of space between those who study violence and those who experience violence. Perera argues that the problem of personal experience and social distance generally applies to both foreign and local professionals. In both an academic/professional sense as well as in a socio-cultural and class sense, local professionals are also as distant from the sites and survivors of violence as their foreign counterparts (ibid.: 9). Moreover, one should be careful in not taking these experiences out of their specific context. A crucial issue, according to Veena Das, is whether the form evolved in writing about the experiences of victims of violence is simply used to titillate. Does it tear the facts of violence out of context? Does the author stand in relationship of a voyeur to the narratives of suffering? She argues that 'to be the scribe of human experience of suffering creates a special responsibility towards those who suffer. While there cannot be a single answer to the nature of this responsibility, one cannot simply hide behind the axiological neutrality of Max Weber. We shall have to ask: did we take this responsibility seriously?' (Das 1990: 33).

Non-Narratability of Pain

Perera argues that the problem of understanding and writing about human suffering is made even more difficult by the non-narratability and non-communicability of the language of pain and suffering. This is particularly true when we are dealing with excessive pain as well as pain that is culturally perceived as abnormal or immoral and relatively restricted as an experiential category such as torture (Perera 1996: 12). Scarry contends that 'whatever pain achieves, it achieves in part through its resistance to language' (Scarry 1985: 4). Perera explains this with the example of a young Sri Lankan man in his late 20s who was tortured by a group of people whom he considered to be JVP (Janatha Vimukthi Peramuna) activists. While attempting to express his experiences, he often lapsed into long spells of silence. Often he emerged from these spells of silence by stating that 'I do not have the words to describe the pain and all that happened'. In this case, the inability to share pain was expressed in terms of existing linguistic expression, which nevertheless did refer to pain's resistance to language (Perera 1996: 12). The language has merely been successful in describing the fact that people are in pain, not what it is like.

Policy Implications

Women refugees outnumber men refugees. Yet the over-representation of women in refugee flows reverses to under-representation in claims and/or settlement in industrial countries such as Australia, Canada, the Netherlands, France, Sweden, Switzerland and the United States (Boyd 1995; Hovy 1997; UNHCR 1997; UN Secretariat 1995). These 'sex-selective outcomes in settlement reflect that gender is deeply embedded in the processes generating refugee flows and providing humanitarian assistance' (Boyd 2001: 104). In other words, gender influences both the processes of determining who is a refugee and who gets humanitarian assistance meant for refugees. Just as using a gendered lens makes a difference to what one sees of conflict and migration, applying gender analysis in decision-making could make a difference to what one does about it. And this is not only, of course, to see, but it could potentially act as an instrument for transformative change.

Gendered Character of the Refugee Determination Process

International refugee instruments are gender-biased because they do not make a distinction between male and female refugees. No single women representative was present or consulted in the drafting of the seminal international instrument conceptualised in Geneva in 1951—the 1951 UN Convention Relating to the Status of Refugees. Furthermore, the UNHCR's *Handbook on Procedures and Criteria for the Determination of Refugee Status* makes no reference to the female gender. The Convention was of course meant to apply to women and men equally, but it has increasingly been argued that its omission of sex from the list of Convention reasons, coupled with the Convention's use of masculine pronouns throughout, led to distinctively female experiences being marginalised (Crawley 2001: 5). The key criteria for being a refugee are drawn from the public realm dominated by men. With regard to women's activities in the private sphere there is primarily silence, which assigns the critical quality 'political' to mostly public activities. Thus, state oppression of a political minority is likely to be considered political unlike gender oppression at home. Moreover, in rejecting gender as a legitimate ground for persecution, state authorities may easily dismiss people, especially women whose economic, cultural and social rights have been violated, as 'economic migrants' (Raj 2001: 170). Persecution, too, takes different forms according to the gender of the person, and it is experienced differently by men and women. So, 'what constitutes persecution and what criteria are necessary to determine eligibility for settlement evokes images of behaviours and characteristics that drew selectively from gender identities, gender roles, gender power relations and systems of gender stratification' (Boyd 2001: 104).

Anthony Good in this volume however contests feminist critics for assuming that women are discriminated against in asylum decision-making and argues that the reality seems more complex. It does not seem to be the case that women as a whole are less successful than men in their asylum claims; if anything, rather the reverse, but that the asylum cases of men and women are always different. In other words, the refugee identities of *both men and women* are gendered social constructs. What is more, the parties involved in processing their claims—the immigration officers or case workers who interview them on behalf of the state, their own legal representatives who record their statements, the administrative officials who make initial decisions on their claims, and the judges who determine their appeals—tend to construct these identities using such received gender stereotypes as masculine rationality, activity, and autonomy, or feminine emotionality, passivity, and dependence (Spijkerboer cited in Good in this volume). So, women are less likely to meet the eligibility criteria for refugee status not only because of non-recognition of gender-based persecution, but also because of the social and political context in which their claims are adjudicated.

Another consequence of the Convention's 'gender-neutrality' is that it is generally unclear which 'Convention reason' is the most appropriate peg upon which to hang a claim of gender-based persecution. Because the Convention itself provides no guidance, female asylum applicants face particular difficulties in demonstrating that their experiences, however horrific, can be brought within the scope of the Convention. For example, courts may fail to recognise gender-related differences in how political opinions are expressed in conflictual situations. Good examines these issues with special reference to asylum applicants from Sri Lanka, Pakistan and India in the British courts and looks at the implications of key cases in the international jurisprudence. In Sri Lankan appeals, for example, the Secretary of State almost always argues that sexual assaults were individual actions not condoned by the state, and hence did not amount to persecution—even when rape has been perpetrated against detainees by those very agents of the state who were holding them in custody. Many decisions are grounded on the erroneous view that rape, even in the context of generalised conflict, is primarily an act of sexual gratification rather than of violence (Crawley 2001: 35), Good illustrates the point with reference to several cases of Tamil women who were raped. For example, the rape of 'Anne', a Tamil woman from Jaffna, was precipitated by her refusal to provide rice for the men who raped her, yet the Dutch authorities did not even consider the possibility of interpreting this as a political act of opposition to the LTTE (Spijkerboer 2000: 47, 51). In another case, a Tamil woman referred to as 'D' had been detained twice by the authorities, and her entire family was suspected of association with the LTTE. As for 'TM', another Tamil woman aged 50, her brother had joined the LTTE, her father had been shot dead by the security forces, and she herself had been questioned and later required to report regularly to the authorities under suspicion of having provided medical care to wounded LTTE cadres. Yet the British courts downplayed these political contexts and assumed that sexual desire was the primary motive. Good also points to evidence that such presumptions are ethnically determined. Thus, while the rape of Tamil women are usually considered by the British courts to be sexually-driven offences committed by delinquent individuals, rapes of Bosnian women tend to be seen as examples of politically motivated ethnic cleansing (Spijkerboer 2000: 101).

Sircar analyses the dilemmas of female migrants in the context of the South Asian region, where none of the states are signatories to the 1951 Convention or the 1967 Protocol. And, the UNHCR's protection mandate is subject to bilateral agreements. Thus refugee determination, protection and care become ad hoc and vulnerable to competing strategic and economic compulsions, particularly national security concerns. There is very little legal input available in a gendered sense for the protection of women fleeing violence, and governments have been insensitive in failing to recognise the special needs and requirements of women refugees (Hans 2003: 356). As a result, there are a growing number of internally displaced women who are at greater risk because the government that should have protected them often commits the abuses they seek to escape. Moreover, because they have not crossed any international border to seek refuge or asylum, displaced persons can claim only minimal protection from international law (Human Rights Watch 1995: 101). Sircar argues that South Asian women forced to migrate due to gender-based persecution can be best protected through the establishment of regional and national 'gender asylum law' regimes.

Gendered Character of Humanitarian Aid in Refugee Camps and Other Sites of Migration

The institutional gender bias of the refugee regime has direct consequences for women refugees in refugee camps and other border areas. Refugee determination procedures frequently reproduce existing gender hierarchies where men are considered heads of households and women are viewed as dependents. When women flee in the company of male relatives (spouses, fathers, brothers), often, the men are treated as the 'primary' asylum seeker, even if it is the women's experiences that might more clearly fit the requirements granting an asylum. They may not be asked about their own experiences except to corroborate those of the male family members (Hinshelwood 1997; Martin 1991; Newland 2003). The practice of linking women to men also exists when issuing documents. In countries of asylum, documents such as identification cards, or even papers granting the right to remain, may be issued to men, but not women family members.

Manchanda, for example, refers to the UNHCR and the Government of Nepal's practice of using a registration and ration distribution system based on household cards listed under the name of the male household head. The Government of Nepal would issue a separate ration card to a woman only if she obtains a legal divorce. But under Nepalese law divorce endangers a woman's custody of her children and has implications for their claims to property rights on their eventual return to Bhutan. It also prevents them from participating in the verification and categorisation process that would allow them to be repatriated to Bhutan. Refugee men can register children born of non-refugee women, but women cannot transfer citizenship to their children. This discriminatory policy denies unregistered children access to rations of food, clothes, education and health, and makes them ineligible for repatriation to Bhutan. Moreover, the verification process places women at a disadvantage to have their claims fairly considered. The Joint Verification Team (JVT) conducting interviews at Khudanabari camp in 2003, for instance, had no women members in the team. Women were unable to have independent interviews even if they were separated from their husbands. Furthermore, women and children who had found safety by living separately from abusive heads of households remain linked to and dependent on them for purposes of verification and repatriation.

Gender stratification in refugee camps often results in refugee men occupying important mediating positions, who, in turn, control all the important aspects of camp administration and allocation of resources. It is not surprising, therefore, that woman's needs are often overlooked or misunderstood and aid is misdirected. Frequently bearing additional social responsibilities as heads of households, women face discrimination in food distribution, access to health, welfare and education services—doubly disadvantaged as refugees and as women. In fact, 'the refugee, by definition, becomes "he" and projects intended to provide training, employment and incomes are geared primarily to "him"' (Hall 2000: 508). Women are generally relegated to the status of a 'special' minority group within these programmes, and are often included in projects for the old and handicapped undertaking traditional, marginal and unproductive welfare activities.

While Manchanda, O'Kane and Rajasingham-Senanayake's contributions echo this viewpoint to underline the gendered character of refugee camps as well as humanitarian aid administered to female migrants, they also highlight women's abilities to transform such marginalised spaced into an enabling environment. O'Kane, for instance, notes that women's gender identities in camp-based organisations are mostly reinforced in line with traditional ethnic roles for women. However, their work to locate funds and resources to provide even the most basic survival needs for newly arrived refugees and individuals in immediate crises made women aware of the male control of political and military decision-making and weaponry, women's susceptibility to rape and other forms of sexual abuse, increased domestic violence and increased vulnerability to maternal and infant mortality and morbidity. The driving need to find solutions to such crises led women to self-advocacy, including demands for meaningful political participation in relevant decision-making processes. The vast majority of undocumented migrant women face a different set of challenges because of the lack of access to humanitarian aid, geographical dispersal and black market employment. Significantly, O'Kane notes that it was predominantly loose coalitions of migrant women rather than the male-dominated political organisations in the opposition movement that first began to respond to the needs of undocumented migrant communities.

Structural Social Transformations and Altering the Gender Status Quo

Long-drawn out conflicts have not only opened up new spaces for women's agency, as argued earlier, but also entailed deeper social and economic transformations, which have changed family and community structures. A generation of feminist studies of women in conflict has suggested that a return to peace is often signified as a return to the pre-war gender status quo (Enloe 1983; Jayawardena 1986). That analysis, argues Rajasingham-Senanayake, was based on the study of an older generation of conventional inter-state wars between militaries in Europe, as well as de-colonisation struggles and revolutions in Asia (Vietnam, China). She suggests that the 'new war' in Sri Lanka that has been sustained and subsidised by a network of local-global actors—developmental, humanitarian, criminal and diaspora—and thrust women into new roles, has also enabled women to subtly and creatively craft their identities and destinies, often manipulating the 'victim' identity that is thrust upon them in the humanitarian and post-conflict policy discourse as they are displaced or widowed.

While there is growing recognition among those involved in humanitarian relief and rehabilitation work about the need for gender sensitive relief and rehabilitation work, few programmes have systematically explored how relief might aid recovery from individual trauma and social suffering, and facilitate women's empowerment in and through conflict. Manchanda refers to the cultural specificity approach of 'going through the men', for example in the Afghan refugee camps, something which tends to reinforce oppressive local patriarchies. Casting all women in the 'victimhood' mould props up local patriarchies and justifies the claimed necessity of male protection for women (Saigol 2000). Humanitarian protection and aid discourses, especially service delivery strategies, underline the need to be sensitive to the culture and tradition of the Afghan tribes. However, their notion of 'culture' tends to be very static. Saigol rightly argues that international advisors do not problematise 'culture and tradition' that are constantly being reformed, especially in the social upheaval conditions of conflict. Violently uprooted and dislocated from their homes, the loss of the male identity as breadwinner and the exigencies of the mixing of tribal ethnicities in a refugee situation produces and reforms 'tradition' and 'culture' as evinced in the re-construction of the majority Pashtoonwali identity. In a refugee situation, the group's need to preserve community and culture intensifies. The jihad comes to be aggressively centred on women's bodies by making them invisible. A fatwa issued by the United Ulema of Afghanistan detailing restrictions on women reveals the hysterical paranoia of a conflict-destabilised society. The more insecure the men the stricter the seclusion of women, the more extra domestic activities are denounced and the more aggressiveness and domestic violence mark the male identity. Saigol argues, that 'when women are helped in ways that reinforce an oppressive status quo the only people helped are the powerful males of the group' (ibid.). Rajasingham-Senanayake as well as Manchanda stresses the need to validate the possibility of conflict producing spaces for ambivalent empowerment that is crucial for reshaping humanitarian policy responses, peace-building and post-conflict resettlement policy frameworks and shoring up women's rights. It involves the recovery of women's experience of conflict-induced displacement as a resource, and value and policy frameworks that recognise women are not just passive victims structured in the humanitarian discourse as 'dependent' on aid hand-outs.

Rajasingham-Senanayake also points out that many internally displaced women who have given up the dream of return are in the paradoxical position of being materially and psychologically displaced by humanitarian interventions and human rights discourses and practices that define them as victims who need to be returned to their original homelands for their protection and for the restoration of national and international order and peace. For the 'assumption of return' is a fundamental premise of state, international and NGO policies vis-à-vis internally displaced people. The victim ideology that pervades relief and rehabilitation as well as social health and trauma interventions for female migrants needs to be problematised because these policies might be contributing to prolong the conflict and be a cause of trauma, for especially for those women who wish to settle in the place were they have found refuge. But instead of being assisted to build new lives and livelihoods they are kept dependent on relief handouts. Thus, ironically, relief might be prolonging the trauma of the very people it is supposed to assist. Moreover, it arouses anxieties lest a 'return to peace' and 'return home' would mean a return to the pre-war caste and gender status quo. Rajasingham-Senanayake however argues that the changes wrought by 17 years of armed conflict, displacement and humanitarian-relief-development interventions in terms of altering the structure of family, caste, land rights and the gender status quo among communities in the border areas affected by the conflict in Sri Lanka are too deep, too complex, structural and fundamental. Unlike in the past, when women who took on various non-traditional gender roles in situations of social stress, conflict, war and revolution were 'pushed back into the kitchen after the revolution' as part of a return to everyday life, this time, she argues, that the great threat and the greater challenge to the gender status quo come less from the women in fatigues who might be asked to do desk jobs after the conflict, and more from the women who refuse to erase the red *pottu*, the unsung civilian women who daily struggle to sustain their families and themselves.

She urges social scientists, development workers and activists to address the issue of how social structural transformations wrought by long-term armed conflicts might have also brought desirable changes to entrenched social hierarchies and inequalities such as caste and gender, among people exposed to it. That is because for many women who have lost family members, peace can never be a simple return to the past. Rather, peace necessarily constitutes a creative remaking of cultural meanings and agency—a third space between a familiar, often romanticised past and the traumatic present. Finally, she seeks to evolve a new culturally appropriate idiom to articulate, legitimate and support women's transformed roles and empowerment in the midst of conflict, social disruption and displacement. That is because for social transformation to be sustained there needs to be cultural transformation—the acceptance of the legitimacy of women performing their new roles.

Conclusion

This volume highlights the importance of 'taking gender seriously' in migration research to improve both migration theory and conflict research. It seeks to open up alternative spaces for engaging in new intellectual inquiries that address the multifaceted conceptual, methodological and policy-related issues in the context of conflict-driven migration as also to develop cross-connections between them. This is important not only for rectifying the wrong—neglecting gender—done in the past, but equally significant for its emancipatory possibilities in the future.

Notes

1 Gender traditionalism makes gender visible but leaves it unquestioned. A modernist, liberal position stressing upon the similarity of men and women and on the equality between them is also flawed as it obscures the fact that, in the world as it is, gender differentiation and male power live on. Gender liberalism can combine in unfortunate ways with gender traditionalism to prevent gender from being seen as significant or explanatory (Cockburn 2001: 14).
2 Goldstein notes that the omission of gender is measurable by counting the number of headings and sub-headings in a book's index on topics relating to gender. The typical political science and history books about war—the 'big' books about the origins of wars and their history—score zero. Most political science studies of gender roles in war come from a feminist perspective, and are written by women. The authors and editors of 25 international relations books that address war and peace from explicitly feminist perspectives consist of 21 women and one man (Goldstein 2001: 34–37).
3 Of the children born to mothers in Pakistan and recovered by India, only 102 had come to India as of 21 July 1952; the total number of women recovered was 8,206.

References

Assister, Alison. 1996. *Enlightened Women: Modernist Feminism in a Postmodern Age*. London: Routledge.
Basu, Gautam Kumar. 2001. 'Refugee Studies and International Relations Theory', in Sanjay K. Roy (ed.), *Refugees and Human Rights: Social and Political Dynamics of Refugee Problem in Eastern and North-Eastern India*, pp. 391–407. New Delhi: Rawat.
Behar, Ruth. 1995. 'Writing in My Father's Name: A Diary of "Translated Woman's" First Year', in R. Behar and D.A. Gordon (eds), *Women Writing Culture*, pp. 65–101. Berkeley: University of California Press.
Bennett, O., J. Bexeley and K. Warnock (eds). 1995. *Arms to Fight, Arms to Protect: Women Speak out about Conflict*. London: Panos.

Boyd, Monica. 1995. 'Migration Regulations and Sex Selective Outcomes in Developed Countries', in *International Migration Policies and the Status of Female Migrants*, pp. 83–98. New York: United Nations (United Nations Department for Economic and Social Information and Policy Analysis, Population Division).

———. 2001. 'Gender, Refugee Status, and Permanent Settlement', in Simon, Rita James (ed.), *Immigrant Women*, pp. 103–23. New Brunswick: Transaction Publishers.

Brettel, Caroline B. and James F. Hollifield. 2000. 'Introduction', in Caroline B. Brettel and James F. Hollifield (eds), *Migration Theory: Talking Across Disciplines*, pp. 1–26. New York: Routledge.

Brock-Utne, Birgit. 1989. *Feminist Perspectives on Peace and Peace Education*. New York: Pergamon.

Bunch, C. and R. Carrillo. 1992. *Gender Violence: A Development and Human Rights Issue*. Dublin: Attic Press.

Burguieres, Mary K. 1990. 'Feminist Approaches to Peace: Another Step for Peace Studies', *Millennium: Journal of International Studies*, 19(1): 1–18.

Butalia, Urvashi. 1998. *The Other Side of Silence: Voices from the Partition of India*. New Delhi: Viking Penguin.

——— (ed.). 2002. *Speaking Peace: Women's Voices from Kashmir*. New Delhi: Kali for Women.

Butler, Judith. 1990. *Gender Trouble: Feminism and the Subversion of Identity*. New York: Routledge.

Butler, J. and J. Scott (eds). 1992. *Feminists Theorise the Political*. London: Routledge.

Byrnes, Andrew, Jane Connors and Lum Bik (eds). 1997. *Advancing the Human Rights of Women: Using International Human Rights Standards in Domestic Litigation*. London: Commonwealth Secretariat.

Chakravarty, Gargi. 2004. *Coming Out of Partition: Refugee Women of Bengal*. New Delhi: Shristi.

Chant, S. and S. Radcliffe. 1992. 'Migration and Development: The Importance of Gender', in S. Chant (ed.), *Gender and Migration in Developing Countries*, pp. 1–29. London: Belhaven Press.

Chatterjee, Partha. 1990. 'The Nationalist Resolution of the Women's Question', in Kumkum Sangari and Sudesh Vaid (eds), *Recasting Women: Essays in Colonial History*, pp. 233–53. New Delhi: Kali for Women.

Chenoy, Anuradha M. 2002. *Militarism and Women in South Asia*. New Delhi: Kali for Women.

Chimni, B.S. (ed.). 2000. *International Refugee Law: A Reader*. New Delhi: Sage Publications.

Cockburn, Cynthia. 2001. 'The Gendered Dynamics of Armed Conflict and Political Violence', in Caroline O.N. Moser and Fiona C. Clark (eds), *Victims, Perpetrators or Actors? Gender, Armed Conflict and Political Violence*, pp. 13–29. New York: Zed Books.

Connors, Jane. 1997. 'Legal Aspects of Women as a Particular Social Group', *International Journal of Refugees*, Autumn Special Issue Supplement, 9: 114–28.

Crawley, Heaven. 2001. *Refugees and Gender: Law and Process*. Bristol: Jordans.

Darby, Phillip (ed.). 1997. *At the Edge of International Relations: Postcolonialism, Gender and Dependency*. New York: Pinter.

Das, Veena. 1990. 'Introduction', in Veena Das (ed.), *Mirrors of Violence: Communities, Riots and Survivors in South Asia*, pp. 1–33. Delhi: Oxford University Press.

Davidman, Lynn. 2002. 'Truth, Subjectivity and Ethnographic Research', in J. Spikard and S. Landres (eds), *Personal Knowledge and Beyond*, pp. 17–26. New York: New York University Press.

Elshtain, Jean Bethke. 1987. *Women and War*. New York: Basic,

Enloe, Cynthia H. 1983. *Does Khaki Become You? The Militarisation of Women's Lives*. London: South End Press.

———. 1993. *The Morning After: Sexual Politics at the End of the Cold War*. Berkeley: University of California Press.

———. 2000. 'The Prostitute, the Colonel and the Nationalist', in Cynthia H. Enloe, *Manoeuvres; The International Politics of Militarising Women's Lives*, pp. 49–107. Berkeley: University of California Press.

Ferree, Myra Marx and Beth B. Hess. 1987. 'Introduction', in Myra Marx Ferree and Beth B. Hess (eds), *Analysing Gender: A Handbook of Social Science Research*, pp. 9–30. Newbury Park, Beverly Hills, London: Sage Publications.

Ferris, Elizabeth G. 1987. *Central American Refugees and the Politics of Protection*. New York: Praeger.

Friedlander, Saul. 1993. *Memory, History and the Extermination of the Jews in Europe*. Bloomington: University of Indiana Press.

Gardezi, Fauzia. 1997. 'Nationalism and State Formation: Women's Struggles and Islamisation in Pakistan', in Neelam Hussain, Samiya Mumtaz and Rubina Saigol (eds), *Engendering the Nation-State*, vol. 1, pp. 79–110. Lahore: Simorgh Publications.

Gerson, J. and K. Peiss. 1985. 'Boundaries, Negotiation, Consciousness: Reconceptualising Gender Relations', *Social Problems*, 32(4): 317–31.

Giddens, A. 1987. *Social Theory and Modern Sociology*. Cambridge: Polity Press.

Goldstein, Joshua S. 2001. *War and Gender: How Gender Shapes the War System and Vice Versa*. Cambridge: Cambridge University Press.

Goodwin-Gill, Guy. 1983. *The Refugee in International Law*. Oxford: Clarendon Press.

Hall, Eve. 2000. 'Vocational Training for Women Refugees in Africa', in Katie Wills and Brenda Yeoh (eds), *Gender and Migration*, pp. 91–107. Massachusetts: Edward Elgar.

Hans, Asha. 2003. 'Refugee Women and Children: Need for Protection and Care', in Ranabir Samaddar (ed.), *Refugees and the State: Practices of Asylum and Care in India, 1947–2000*, pp. 355–95. New Delhi: Sage Publications.

Harding, Sandra. 1987. 'Introduction: Is there a Feminist Method?', in Sandra Harding (ed.), *Feminism and Methodology. Social Science Issues*, pp. 1–14. Bloomington: Indiana University Press.

Harrington, Mona. 1992. 'What Exactly is Wrong with the Liberal State as an Agent of Change?', in V. Spike Peterson (ed.), *Gendered States: Feminist (Re)Visions of International Relations Theory*, pp. 65–82. Boulder: Lynne Rienner.

Hathaway, James. 1991. *The Law of Refugee Status*. London: Butterworth.

Hinshelwood, Gill. 1997. 'Interviewing Female Asylum Seekers', *International Journal of Refugees*, 9 (Autumn Special Issue Supplement): 159–64.

Holborn, L.W. 1975. *Refugees: A Problem of Our Time. The Work of the UNHCR, 1951–72*, vol. 1&2. Methuen: Scarecrow Press.

Hondagneu-Sotelo, Pierrette. 1994. *Gendered Transitions*. Berkeley: University of California Press.

Hovy, Bela. 1997. 'The Sex and Age Distribution of Refugees and Others of Concern to UNHCR: Statistical Evidence', paper presented at the annual meeting of the Population Association of America, Washington, D.C., March.

Human Rights Watch. 1995. *The Human Rights Watch Global Report on Women's Human Rights*. New Delhi: Oxford University Press.

Independent Commission on International Humanitarian Issues. 1986. *Refugees: The Dynamics of Displacement*. London: Zed Books.

Jacobs, Janet Liebman. 2004. 'Women, Genocide, and Memory: The Ethics of Feminist Ethnography in Holocaust Research', *Gender and Society*, April 18(2): 223–38.

Jacobs, S., R. Jacobson and J. Marchbank. 2000. *States of Conflict: Gender, Violence and Resistance*. London: Zed Books.

Jayawardena, Kumari. 1986. *Feminism and Nationalism in the Third World*. London: Zed Books.

Kaldor, Mary. 1999. *New and Old Wars: Organised Violence in a Global Era*. Stanford: Stanford University Press.

Kandiyoti, Deniz. 1988. 'Bargaining with Patriarchy', *Gender and Society*, 2(3): 274–90.

———. 1991. 'Identity and Its Discontents: Women and the Nation', *Millennium: Journal of International Studies*, 20(3): 429–43.

Keely, Charles. 1992. 'The Resettlement of Women and Children Refugees', *Migration World*, 20(4): 14–18.

Keller, Stephen. 1975. *Uprooting and Social Change*. Delhi: Manohar.

Kelly, Raymond C. 2000. *Warless Societies and the Origins of War*. Ann Arbor: University of Michigan Press.

Laub, Dori. 1992. 'Bearing Witness, or the Vicissitudes of Listening', in S. Felman and D. Laub (eds), *Testimony: Crises of Witnessing in Literature, Psychoanalysis and History*, pp. 57–74. New York: Routledge.

Lentin, R. (ed.) 1997. *Gender and Catastrophe*. London: Zed Books.

Loescher, Gil. 1992. *Refugee Movements and International Security*. Adelphi Papers 268. London: International Institute for Strategic Studies.

Loescher, Gil and John Scanlan. 1986. *Calculated Kindness: Refugees and America's Half-Open Door*. New York: Free Press.

Lorentzen, Lois Ann and Jennifer Turpin (eds). 1998. *The Women and War Reader*. New York: New York University Press.

Manchanda, Rita (ed.). 2001. *Women, War and Peace in South Asia: Beyond Victimhood to Agency*. New Delhi: Sage Publications.

Margolis, D. 1985. 'Redifining the Situation: Negotiations on the Meaning of "Women"', *Social Problems*, 32(4): 332–47.

Martin, Susan Forbes. 1991. *Refugee Women*. London: Zed Books.

Menon, Ritu. 1998. 'Reproducing the Legitimate Community: Secularity, Sexuality, and the State in Postpartition India', in Patricia Jeffery and Amrita Basu (eds), *Appropriating Gender: Women's Activism and Politicised Religion in South Asia*, pp. 15–32. New Delhi: Kali for Women.

———. 1999. 'Cartographies of Nations and Identities: A Post-Partition Predicament', *Interventions*, 1(2): 157–66.

Menon, Ritu and Kamala Bhasin. 1998. *Borders and Boundaries: Women in India's Partition*. New Delhi: Kali for Women.

———. 2001. 'Her Body and Her Being: Of Widows and Abducted Women in Post-Partition India', in Margaret Jolly and Kalpana Ram (eds), *Borders of Being: Citizenship, Fertility, and Sexuality in Asia and the Pacific*, pp. 58–81. Ann Arbor: The University of Michigan Press.

Miserez, Diane (ed.). 1988. *Refugees: The Trauma of Exile: The Humanitarian Role of Red Cross and Red Crescent*. Dordrecht: Martinus Nijho Publishers.

Mohanty, C., A. Russo and L. Torres. 1991. *Third World Women and the Politics of Feminism.* Bloomington, Indiana: Indiana University Press.

Mohsin, Amena. 2002. 'Gender, Nationalism and Security', in Navnita Chadha Behera (ed.), *State, People and Security: The South Asian Context*, pp. 202–19. New Delhi: Har-Anand Publications,

Moser, Caroline O.N. and Fiona C. Clark (eds). 2001. *Victims, Perpetrators or Actors? Gender, Armed Conflict and Political Violence.* London: Zed Books.

Newland, K. 2003. 'Seeking Protection: Women in Asylum and Refugee Resettlement Processes', Issue Paper for the United Nations Division for the Advancement of Women, Expert Consultation on Migration and Mobility and How this Movement Affects Women. Malmo: Sweden.

Pankhurst, Donna and Jenny Pearce. 1998. 'Engendering the Analysis of Conflict: A Southern Perspective', in Haleh Afshar (ed.), *Women and Empowerment: Illustrations from the Third World*, pp. 155–63. London: Macmillan Press.

Parker, Andrew, M. Russo, D. Sommer, and P. Yaeger (eds). 1992. *Nationalisms and Sexualities.* London: Routledge.

Pateman, C. 1988. *The Sexual Contract.* Cambridge: Polity Press.

Perera, Sasanka. 1996. 'Against the Making of a Violence Industry: A Personal Reflection on Methodological and Ethical Problems in Studying Human Suffering'. Unpublished paper, Colombo.

———. 1999. *Stories of Survivors. Socio-Political Contexts of Female Headed Households in Post-Terror Southern Sri Lanka*, Volume I. New Delhi: Vikas Publishing House.

Peterson, V. Spike. 1992. 'Introduction', in V. Spike Peterson (ed.), *Gendered States. Feminist (Re)Visions of International Relations Theory*, pp. 1–29. Boulder: Lynne Rienner.

Pettman, Jan Jindy. 1996. *Worlding Women: A Feminist International Politics.* New York: Routledge.

Pierson, Ruth Roach (ed.). 1987. *Women and Peace: Theoretical, Historical and Practical Perspectives.* New York: Croom Helm.

Proudfoot, Malcolm J. 1957. *European Refugees, 1930–1952: A Study in Forced Population Movement.* London: Faber and Faber.

Rai, Shirin. 1996. 'Women and the State in the Third World', in Haleh Afshar (ed.), *Women and Politics in the Third World*, pp. 25–39. London: Routledge.

Raj, S. 2001. 'The Gender Element in International Refugee Law: Its Impact on Agency Programming and the North-South Debate', *Indian Society of International Law Yearbook on Humanitarian and Refugee Law*, 1: 164–82.

Reardon, Betty A. 1985. *Sexism and the War System.* New York: Teachers College Press.

Ruddick, S. 1989. *Maternal Thinking: Towards a Politics of Peace.* London: The Women's Press.

Rystad, G. (ed.). 1990. *The Uprooted: Forced Migration as an International Problem in the Post-War Era.* Lund: Lund University Press.

Saigol, Rubina. 2000. 'At Home or in the Grave: Afghan Women and the Reproduction of Patriarchy', paper presented at a WISCOMP Conference on 'Women and Security', New Delhi.

Salomon, K. 1991. *Refugees in the Cold War: Toward a New International Refugee Regime in the Early Postwar Era.* Lund: Lund University Press.

Scarry, E. 1985. *The Body in Pain: The Making and Unmaking of the World.* Oxford: Oxford University Press.

Schmeidl, Susanne. 2001. 'Conflict and Forced Migration: A Quantitative Review, 1964–1995', in Aristide R. Zolberg and Peter M. Benda (eds), *Global Migrants, Global Refugees: Problems and Solutions*, pp. 62–94. New York: Berghahn Books.

Schuler, Margaret (ed.). 1995. *From Basic Needs to Basic Rights: Women's Claim to Human Rights*. Washington D.C.: Women, Law and Development International.

Scott, Jean. 1986. *Girls with Grit: Memories of the Australian Women's Land Army*. Boston: Allen and Unwin.

Shaheed, Farida. 1997. 'Women, State and Power: The Dynamics of Variation and Convergence Across East and West', in Neelam Hussain, Samiya Mumtaz and Rubina Saigol (eds), *Engendering the Nation-State*, vol. 1, pp. 53–78. Lahore: Simorgh Publication.

Smith, Dan. 1997. *The State of War and Peace Atlas*. New York: Penguin.

Spijkerboer, Thomas. 2000. *Gender and Refugee Status*. Aldershot: Ashgate.

Stacey, Judith. 1988. 'Can there be a Feminist Ethnography?', *Women's Studies International Forum*, 11: 21–27.

Stanley, L. and S. Wise. 1983. *Breaking Out: Feminist Consciousness and Feminist Research*. London: Routledge.

Stoessinger, J. 1956. *The Refugee in the World Community*. Minneapolis: University of Minnesota Press.

Thiruchandran, Selvy. 1997. *Ideology, Caste, Class and Gender*. Delhi: Vikas Publishing House.

———. 1999. *The Other Victims of War: Emergence of Female Headed Households in Eastern Sri Lanka*, vol. II. New Delhi: Vikas Publishing House.

Tickner, J. Ann. 1999. 'Why Women Can't Run the World: International Politics According to Francis Fukuyama', *International Studies Review*, Fall, 1(3): 3–11.

Turshen, M. and C. Twagiramariya (eds). 1998. *What Women Do in War Time: Gender and Conflict in Africa*. London: Zed Books.

United Nations Secretariat. 1995. 'Measuring the Extent of Female International Migration', in *International Migration Policies and the Status of Female Migrants*, pp. 56–79. New York: United Nations (UN Department for Economic and Social Information and Policy Analysis, Population Division).

UNHCR. 1997. *The State of the World's Refugees 1997–98: A Humanitarian Agenda*. Oxford: Oxford University Press.

Vernant, Jacques. 1953. *The Refugee in the Post-War World*. New Haven: Yale University Press.

Vickers, Jeanne. 1993. *Women and War*. London: Zed Books.

Wali, S. 1993. *Uprooted People: Third Annual Report on the State of World Hunger*. Washington, D.C.: Bread for the World Institute on Hunger and Development.

Walker, R.B.J. 1988. *One World, Many Worlds: Struggles for a Just World Peace*. Boulder: Lynne Rienner.

Wallensteen, Peter and Margareta Sollenberg. 1999. 'Armed Conflict 1989–1999', *Journal of Peace Research*, 36(5): 533–606.

Waylen, G. 1996. *Gender in Third World Politics*. Buckingham: Open University Press.

Weiner, Myron. 1996. 'Bad Neighbours, Bad Neighbourhoods: An Inquiry into the Causes of Refugee Flows', *International Security*, 21(1): 5–42.

Willis, Katie and Brenda Yeoh (eds). 2000. *Gender and Migration*. Massachusetts: Edward Elgar.

Women's Initiative. 1994. *Women's Testimonies from Kashmir: 'The Green of the Valley is Khaki'*. Bombay: Women's Initiative.

Wright, Caroline. 2000. 'Gender Awareness in Migration Theory: Synthesising Actor and Structure in Southern Africa', in Katie Willis and Brenda Yeoh (eds), *Gender and Migration*, pp. 3–23. Massachusetts: Edward Elgar.

Yuval-Davis, Nira. 1997. *Gender and Nation*. London: Sage Publications.

Zolberg, A. et al. 1989. *Escape from Violence: Conflict and Refugee Crisis in the Developing World*. New York: Oxford University Press.

Zucker, Norman L. and Naomi Flink Zucker. 1987. *The Guarded Gate: The Reality of American Refugee Policy*. San Diego, California: Harcourt Brace Jovanovich.

2

MUKTIR GAAN, THE RAPED WOMAN AND MIGRANT IDENTITIES OF THE BANGLADESH WAR

Nayanika Mookherjee

We were always told that women had been victims. This shows
the women did do things during *Muktijuddho* (the Bangladesh war
of liberation in 1971). My legs are shaking. I am absolutely over-
whelmed—*Muktir Katha* (Words of Freedom, 1999). (A young
woman responding to *Muktir Gaan* [Songs of Freedom, 1996] in its
sequel *Muktir Katha*).[1]

In 1996, *Muktir Gaan* (Songs of Freedom), a documentary film, was
released in Bangladesh. This film shot in 1971 by the American photo-
grapher Lear Levin follows a cultural troupe of young Bengali middle
and upper middle-class men and women from Dhaka who had fled to
Calcutta in India during the nine-month-long duration of the Bangladesh
war. Tareque and Catherine Masud, two documentary filmmakers, re-
trieved these reels from Lear Levin's cellar in New York and released it
as *Muktir Gaan* in Bangladesh. The film documents the activities of the
Bangladesh Freedom Struggle Cultural Squad, a group of young middle
class men and women who in 1971 toured various refugee camps, training centres of liberation fighters and liberated zones and sang songs to
provide moral support and inspiration to the refugees and liberation
fighters. The popularity of *Muktir Gaan* in Bangladesh in the mid-to-
late 1990s as evidenced in the aforementioned response elevated the
young men and women in the documentary to the position of celebrities
24 years after their activities were documented and aroused an emotive
nostalgia of a Bengali identity.

In 1947, the independence of India from British colonial rule had resulted in the creation of a new homeland for the Muslims of India by the carving out of the eastern and north-western corners of the country, which came to be known as East and West Pakistan respectively. Thus in the formation of Pakistan, Islam was the sole principle of nationhood unifying two widely disparate units, separated not only geographically but also by sharp cultural and linguistic differences (Bhuiyan 1982; Sisson and Rose 1990). Over the years, various West Pakistani administrative, military, linguistic, civil, and economic controls led to a liberation war in 1971. Though India joined the conventional war on Bangladesh's side only in December 1971 (for the final 10 days),[2] it was providing guerrilla training to the *Mukti Bahini* (Bengali liberation fighters) led by General Osmany during the nine-month struggle (Alama 1992; Rahamana 1982–85). This culminated in the establishment of a People's Republic of Bangladesh on 16 December 1971.[3]

During the nine months of the war, the Pakistani Army with the assistance of local collaborators (Razakars, Al Badr, Al Shams, Shanti Bahini),[4] killed some three million Bengali men and women from all walks of life and social classes—intellectuals, journalists, students, workers and villagers. Amidst this carnage 200,000 to 300,000 women were raped.[5] As the war was being waged and nearly one crore 'refugees'[6] poured from across the border into India, East Pakistan was suddenly catapulted from relative obscurity into the headlines of the international press. The atrocities committed by the Pakistani Army and their Bengali collaborators were widely viewed as human rights abuses by the international community. This was highlighted with the 'Help Bangladesh' concert held by George Harrison and Joan Baez in Madison Square Garden, New York in August 1971. After the war various aid agencies, charities, doctors and medical personnel from several western countries came to Bangladesh in order to pool their resources and services to help the newly-created nation. In the documentary *Dateline Bangladesh* (1972) the Prime Minister of India Mrs Indira Gandhi justified the Indian military support to the Bangladeshi struggle by commenting, 'Shall we sit and watch their women get raped?' Hence Bangladesh from its conception had been the focus of being a nation born out of human rights abuses[7] and in need of help.

Muktir Gaan is the lens through which this paper seeks to highlight the heterogeneity of migrant experiences as a result of war, particularly that of the middle class refugees. This allows juxtaposition and encounters between various refugees and thereby examines the identifications with varied refugee subjectivities in contemporary Bangladesh. The paper attempts to outline this through a discursive exploration of various visual images of a migrant's figure as a raped woman, a poor woman and that of the middle class refugee. Rather than citing pure testimonies and narratives, it seeks to address how one relates to these testimonies and narratives. In fact, an exploration of the oral history and testimony within *Muktir Gaan* allows an understanding of 'documentation of both the witness as he makes testimony and the understanding and meaning of events generated in the activity of testimony itself' (Young 1988: 157–71).

This would enable an interrogation of the victim-agent, class and gendered binaries through which migrant experiences are predominantly studied. This is because migration studies have focused on the effects of migration on the poor, oppressed and women who I have argued in a subsequent section in this paper constitute the 'subalterns' (Guha 1983)[8] for migration studies. It is conspicuous with the absence of the experiences of middle class 'refugees'. The paper should not be misunderstood as making a reactionary case for including the experiences of middle class refugees as a category within migration studies, nor is it a search for the experience of the subaltern. Instead, the paper critiques the construction of various subalterns through the emphasis on the poor refugees as subalterns, Bangladesh as a subaltern with its poverty-struck and disaster prone image, and the poor and the raped as the subalterns during times of armed conflict.

All these subalterns are fused together in the context of the 1971 Bangladesh war, which the paper seeks to discursively explore. The paper argues that the exclusion of the experiences of middle class refugees and an emphasis on poor, women refugees as victims or agents disallows an exploration of the class and gendered identities and gendered social relations during wars. Instead the paper explores the aesthetics/sensibilities[9] and symbolic capital (Bourdieu 1995)[10] of the middle class refugees, which allows the middle class refugees to represent the migrant experiences of the raped women and the poor during the 1971 war and in an independent Bangladesh in the 1990s.

This also allows an exploration of the way *Muktir Gaan* destabilises the role of women as peace activists and the relationship between militarisation and patriarchy.[11] More significantly the paper seeks to highlight the different connotations of war, particularly how war maybe experienced as erotic, as an excitement and an adventure, a 'libidinal economy' (Goodwin 1997).[12] The paper argues that the aesthetics of middle class identifications as depicted in *Muktir Gaan* precisely makes it a success in evoking in the 1990s the varied experiences and emotions of the war.

The paper attempts to do this by identifying why the refugee has not been part of the war story. Further it critiques the construction of the subaltern within the triad of refugee studies: the study of wars, migration and Bangladesh. It elaborates this in the analysis of the image of the raped refugee woman in various films in Bangladesh, and the juxtaposition of middle class refugees with the raped and impoverished. In the first section it explores the literature on women and war. Next it explores the search for the subaltern within the triad of studies on wars, migration and Bangladesh. The next section addresses the images of the refugee as poor and raped and juxtaposes this with the refugee accounts in *Muktir Gaan*. It explores the encounter of different refugees in refugee camps, the ontological identification as refugees and maps the daily lives of the middle class refugees. In the final section it seeks to highlight the distinctiveness that *Muktir Gaan* brings to various assumptions existing within refugee studies, and as a result allows a discursive and reflexive interrogation of researchers engaged in refugee studies.

Women and the War Story

Wars have primarily been studied as a militaristic and gender-neutral phenomenon. Throughout the 1980s and 1990s, feminist scholars revisited wars in history to study their causes and outcomes as well as the ways in which they were fought and to establish the link between patriarchy and militarisation (Bennett et al. 1995; Butalia 1998; Cooke and Rustomji-Kerns 1994; Das 1995; Elshtain 1995; Enloe 1989, 1993, 2000; Menon and Bhasin 1998; Meyer and Prügl 1999; Peterson and Runyan 1993; Tickner 1992; Lorentzen and Turpin 1998; Waller and Rycenga 2000). Their findings revealed that although war has been neatly classified as genderless, it is in fact one of the most gendered of human activities. This new scholarship shows how the deliberate omission of women—except as nurses, long suffering wives, mothers, sisters and camp followers—from the story of war has allowed the fiction of an ungendered domain to persist. War has been considered the purview of those few who have experienced combat. Since women have predominantly not been part of the combat, clearly they had no authority to speak of the dead and dying.

There are different dimensions of the women and war story that appear in the existing literature. The women, who have evolved their own way of coping with conflict situations, demand that the meanings attached to war be reviewed and revised so that accounts of war also reflect gendered experiences. On the one hand, countless women spoke of discovering new skills, capabilities and confidence in wartime, and new opportunities (Bop 2001) and new responsibilities—most notably economic provisions—for their families, but also new forms of management, decision-making, and administrative tasks, such as dealing with officials and governments.

On the other hand wars may also destroy chances of marriage and motherhood for women because of rape and subsequent social rejection, or women may be seen as being too old by the end of hostilities. In fact women's prominence as guerrilla fighters, as military targets of bombs and rapes, and as subjects of debate about the gendering of the military and of combat has complicated the telling of the war story. The women and war story however does not only entail the events during the war but also what happens after the war, which is sometimes equally violent and conflictual. Feminists have hence insisted that women's struggle must become part of the nation's struggle and that this integration must be theorised so that both the nationalist and the feminist narratives are understood to be mutually necessary (Yuval-Davis 1989; 1997; 1999). This position is however not without its specific historical and political problems, as nationalist projects might often co-opt feminist issues for a broader struggle. However in post-liberation phases feminist issues are often sidelined from the national agenda. Hence any research needs to focus on oral narratives of both during and after the war. It is this most damaging aspect of war—the way the economic and social costs can last for generations—which comes across so powerfully through personal testimony, with its human detail and variety. Women documenting their memories of war are a crucial element of the waging of peace and the creation of a woman's mythology of war and peace. Remembering is a crucial strategy for survival. Women's contestatory narratives can create alternative spaces and in these new spaces conflicts may be resolved without automatic resort to organised and lethal violence (Cooke 1996; Cooke and Rustomji-Kerns 1994).

However it is important to qualify the term 'women' by pointing out that the effects of war are not the same among all women, as women is not a homogeneous term and experiences vary according to class, age, status and the various social contexts in which women are located and which also helps/restricts women to deal with the events after the war. Not only their experiences differ but also their connections to the conflict, and these experiences and connections determine their position in the aftermath (Bop 2001: 20). So initial studies of armed conflict do not take into account women's and refugees' experiences as they are seen to be non-combative and civilian and hence without any agency worthy of accounts of valour and war. This has been redressed by recent focus on refugee and gendered experiences of war by feminists, which the paper suggests is hinged on the construction of the refugee as a victim, poor and female. By not focusing on the experiences of middle class refugees and their encounters with the victim, poor and female refugees, migration studies have not able to highlight the gendered and classed relationships between refugees which are integral to the understanding of gendered social relationships during times of conflict. This paper attempts to redress this by precisely focusing on these differential migrant experiences and the identifications with the varied refugee subjectivities in independent Bangladesh.

The Quest for the 'Subaltern'

The interrogation of two interlinked stereotypes, namely the study of Bangladesh and the study of migrants, and the dialectical relationship between them, are central to the arguments of this paper. Bangladesh is stereotypically seen as a country ravaged by floods, cyclones and poverty and within South Asian studies is a central laboratory for the developmentalist genre. As a result constructions of the country have become synonymous with the notions of disaster and impoverishment juxtaposed with a saviour paradigm—the need to save and civilise Bangladesh through the international aid economy, which operates as a parallel government in the country. This infantilising model of Bangladesh is omnipresent in NGOs, international policies and national governments (as evidenced in Mrs Gandhi's articulation). Bangladesh is truly the 'subaltern' (Guha 1983) within South Asian studies.

The study of migration also has its own subalterns. Predominantly migration studies have focused on the effects of migration on the poor, oppressed and women, and rightfully so. The reasons behind trans-national migration are multifarious. People are either escaping eco-nomic, political and violent oppressions or seeking newer economic lives beyond their familiar shores. People may migrate in search of better economic opportunities, impelled by war, violence, natural disasters, political chaos, unemployment and poverty. However migration studies have not only focused on female migrants as victims; there has also been a recent focus on the agency and survival strategies of poor, migrant women. However this focus hinges on the assumption of the migrant woman as poor and has to be hence shown to be agentive. The com-plicated relationship between well-off migrant women who are seen to have agency by virtue of their symbolic and social capital, remain unexplored.

The agent-victim binary in the case of poor migrant women becomes exacerbated in the case of migration due to conflict in the predominant literature on effects of armed conflict on women. Women are most likely to be uprooted by war (Manchanda 2001; Thangarajah 2003). More than four-fifths of war refugees are women and young girls who also experience additional and often sexualised violence during their flight. By the end of 1992 more than 46 million people had lost their homes; about 36 million of these were women and girls (Lorentzen and Turpin 1998: 4). The Tokyo Declaration formulated in 1997 by women from over 20 countries states that violence occurring during war and armed conflict situations represent the extension of the violence which women face on a everyday basis in male dominated societies (Agrawal 2003: 15). Violence may present itself as a reason for migration—such as war, threat of rape or internal conflict—or as a fall out of migration. Women bear the brunt of the trauma of conflict. They are attacked, harassed, humiliated and separated from their families. I have argued elsewhere about the varied effects of sexual violence during wars on women, their families and their communities (Mookherjee 2002, 2003, 2004, forth-coming). Refugee women also often serve as their children's sole care-takers as many of them are widows or separated from their spouses and other extended family. They must seek food and safety not only for themselves, but also for their children who require healthcare, housing and an education. Refugee women in exile are often the supporters of an extended family network, playing a central economic role yet still lacking decision-making power in their societies (Collett 1998: 323–28).

The saviour paradigm inherent within identifying the agency or victimhood of poor female migrants when combined with the study of female migrants of the Bangladesh war of 1971 assumes a greater intensity in the context of the horrors of the war. However migration studies are conspicuous with the absence of the experiences of middle class migrants. The focus on *Muktir Gaan* attempts to redress that lack and highlight the heterogeneity of migrant experiences as a result of the war of 1971. It not only focuses on the experiences of middle class migrants but also significantly juxtaposes them with poor migrants and the raped woman as the migrant. This allows an exploration of the various subjectivities these various migrant figures embody. This is significant as it allows an exploration of various kinds of victim-agent subjectivity and identifications towards these migrant images, which are in operation in contemporary Bangladesh.

The very fact that the cultural troupe supported the resistance movement for the liberation of Bangladesh through the deployment of predominantly peaceful tools like songs imbued with nationalistic fervour complicates the role of women as peace activists during wars (Lorentzen and Turpin 1998). As a result the relationship between militarisation and patriarchy (Enloe 2000) was also destabilised as the women become part of the military paraphernalia in a civilian capacity and were helping to buttress the military and moral strength of the *Mukti Bahini*. Their activities as a cultural troupe during 1971 evoke the aforementioned emotive response (with which this paper began) to what is perceived as their agentive and combative role during that year. Also, migration studies have been unable to address how migration during war, while being threatening, may also be imbued with adventure and excitement precisely by virtue of one's class position. This allows a rethinking of what war means to different people, as in this case it was also viewed as a 'road story' imbued with adventure, excitement, eroticism, pain and the prospect of freedom. In the following section I juxtapose the migrant as the raped, who is then positioned vis-à-vis the poor and the cultural troupe.

Refugees and Raped Women

After the formation of Bangladesh a large number of films were made which highlighted the impact of the varied horrors of the war. Predominant among them was the plight of the refugees fleeing to India. The horrors of rape and the raped woman as the refugee symbolising the ravaging of a nation also became a predominant issue for documentary and commercial films aimed at raising international awareness. This was legitimised by the post-war government declaration that all raped women of 1971 were war heroines (*birangonas*). This was an attempt to reduce social ostracism towards such women and enable their smooth social re-absorption.

Starting with *Stop Genocide* by Zahir Raihan[13] in 1971, rape was highlighted by showing the quiet, mute face of a 16-year-old girl in a refugee camp. The voiceover narrative explained that six men had raped her while her family was killed, and all along her face spoke volumes about her experience. The close-up of the grim, vacant face of the raped intensifies her silence making it axiomatic that she does not speak. The lingering close-up of her face and body provides its own narrative, making her muteness necessary and her bodily features become the direct recipient of the spectator's looks. In the process, the women in the camp are transformed into illustrations of the raped women and become representative of that invisible 'shamed' group. The 1972 film *Orunodoyer Ognishakhi* (*Witness and Pledge to a New Dawn*), which draws upon the contradictions of the middle class during the war, focuses on the personal trauma of a film actor called Altaf who does not take part in the war and instead seeks safe refuge in Calcutta. On the way to India he encounters various instances whereby women are raped. The image of the *birangona* disrobed of her sari, who is thereby clothed by Altaf's shirt and *lungi*, with her long hair in disarray and a vacant look in her eyes, seems to be testimony of her experience of rape. In the other instances of rape, the women later either commit suicide or become mentally unstable.

The bleak face of the *birangona* comes to stand in as a marker and shame of rape resulting in an inner, muted pain. The women look away from the camera because they might be shameful of their situation, or attempt to assert or retrieve their shame by looking away from the frame so as not to be termed shameless. The captions under the photographs freeze an endless number of possibilities for the image whereby the words give a single certainty. However, while freezing the woman as being raped, the caption enables the spectator to imagine the situation of rape of the woman in the picture. The citation within articles of rape are also an invocation of forensic proof of claims made in the text, as well as those captured in registers of literature and government speeches. In fact the photographs also become proof because of the role of Kishore Parekh and Roshid Talukdar, the photographers who produced most of these images. Overall, the use of faces crystallises the *birangona* as the noble sufferer.

Pictures of the body of a raped woman represented generic pictures of bodies which are mangled and twisted into each other, showing maybe a breast or a leg of a woman with dishevelled hair (*Dateline Bangladesh*, 1972) and hence unidentifiable by the violence inflicted. With the voiceover in the background this becomes the common image of the *birangona*. Along with the facelessness of these pictures, the documentary and evidentiary function is apparent in the picture accompanying the descriptions of rape in Rangpur district with the heading 'Nazi torture pales in comparison to the barbarism of the Invader Army' (*Doinik Bangla*, 14 January 1972). Footage of corpses, vultures and skulls (*Mrittunjoyee*, 1972) emphasises martyrs and the killing of intellectuals. In an Indian government documentary titled *Loot and Lust* (1972), the spatial locations of Rokeya Hall, Dhaka University emphasise the geographical sites of rape. Similarly, generic images of *birangona*s are juxtaposed in *Dateline Bangladesh* with Indira Gandhi's comment, 'Shall we sit and watch their women get raped?' In *The Frost Programme* (1972) Sheikh Mujib agonised over how Muslims could rape Muslim women.

The raped woman thus has various images. She is predominantly a victim who is mute, has a bleak face or can only be identified through her tangled body or by the captions, which freeze her violent encounters. These images of muted victims predominantly help to legitimise the refugee image of the raped. On the other hand as the refugee who is seeking to escape the ravages of war, she can only be identified as mentally unstable and hence has to be protected by a fellow refugee who is also trying to escape the war. As a result there is already a hierarchy of refugee trauma in operation here where the image of raped refugee women exacerbates the pain of other fellow refugees. This pain also allows fellow refugees to acquire an agency vis-à-vis the victim-raped woman by giving her their shirt and *lungi* for protection. The agency of the raped woman is only enabled with the potentiality of her exit through suicide. Hence the varied images of raped women as the name-less or the fleeing victim or the agentive suicidal provide a language of intervention, legitimisation for other fellow refugees and heads of state and make them sole authors of a traumatic, civilising, positive change. This legitimisation is also possible as the raped women in these images are primarily shown as being poor and impoverished.

The 'common' refugees also share this poor and impoverished image of the raped. All the documentary films produced after the war portrayed the squalid conditions under which refugees were leading their lives in the refugee camps. Muted by the trauma of war and its consequent sufferings—namely physical, social, economic, emotional—the endless images of refugees and refugee camps was also a pointer to the high population of Bangladesh and its connotative pathology for the progress of the country. As a result Bangladesh seemed doomed and consigned to impoverishment—an image that persists not only in the West, but also in South Asia. Within this repertoire of existing images, *Muktir Gaan* emerged.

Muktir Gaan and the Heterogeneity of Refugee Experiences

Muktir Gaan is based on the activities of a cultural troupe of young middle class men and women who follow the lives of 'common people' and become a testimony to their suffering during the Bangladesh war of liberation of 1971. This links with the point made by Young (1988: 157–71) earlier, where the act of witnessing the testimony provides a comprehension of the events emerging from the testimonial itself. The impact of *Muktir Gaan* was enormous and widespread, and gave rise to a resurgence of an emotive identity steeped in the nostalgia of being Bengali across all generations. It is important to point out that although there was no specific women's agenda in the nationalist movement during 1971 the mobilisation of middle class women was critical. A small number of women also took up arms and joined the underground resistance in 1971 (though few of them are supposed to have engaged in combat). That these images became so dominant within the national pantheon show that women, apart from being symbols of national culture and tradition, are also symbols of modernisation, liberation and insurrection. The bodily practices[14] of middle class East Pakistani Bengali women became a provocative and visible symbol of resistance. Through their clothing (saris), adornments (flowers in their hair, and wearing *teep*[15]) and actions (singing the songs of Tagore which was banned by the Pakistani government, celebration of Bengali New Years Day and sending their daughters to music and dance school and allowing them to perform on stage) they became the icons of Bengali ethnicity, a vehicle for marking cultural (and territorial) boundaries.[16] Women therefore played an important role in forming middle-class nationalist identities during the *Muktijuddho* (liberation war) as they bore all that was simultaneously culturally oppositional to Pakistan and distinctive of Bangladesh.

Muktir Gaan travelled all across Bangladesh in the 1990s and was shown in villages in various parts of the country.[17] The impact of *Muktir Gaan* is evident in *Muktir Katha*, its sequel, which documents the life histories triggered off among people in response to *Muktir Gaan*. In fact *Muktir Katha* begins with the refugees of 1971, the young middle class men and women singing, 28 years later, the various Tagore songs they had sung during the war, in Dhaka University. These songs are juxtaposed with images of *Muktir Gaan* with these men and women singing under the red banner of the Bangladesh Freedom Struggle Cultural Squad fluttering with revolutionary zeal. The song they sing bring out the pathos of the ravages of the war: 'From land to land we travel singing the sad songs of your cities, fields, forests; it makes my eyes fill with tears.'

The images of the middle class refugees 28 years on is contextualised by the young male voice which points out that for the past 25 years all the ideals of the *Muktijuddho*—namely that of secularism, socialism, nationalism and democracy—that have been lost is being resurrected by a documentary film, *Muktir Gaan*. The film was stuck in the censorship office for five months as it was deemed to be highlighting the role of Sheikh Mujib, the father of Sheikh Hasina, the head of the opposition Awami League in 1995 and the Prime Minister of Bangladesh between 1996–2001. This is because Mujib as the head of the Awami League and the first head of state of independent Bangladesh is deemed by some to be the father of the nation and who led the country through the 1971 war. The censor board also wanted the role of General Zia to be acknowledged in the film. Zia is the assassinated husband of the then (1991–95) Prime Minister Khaleda Zia of the Bangladesh National Party (BNP). On 25 March 1971, when Mujib was arrested by the Pakistani Army, his speech declaring independence of Bangladesh was read out among others by General Zia, something which was deemed to have had a strong inspirational impact on the liberation struggle in Bangladesh. Hence the leadership debate hinges around who actually led the country and provided inspiration to the struggle and hence had to be the deified leader in independent Bangladesh.

In 1995 faced with the lack of a distributor, various young volunteers printed tickets themselves and started having open-air shows of the film in various parts of Dhaka. This elicited various emotional responses, including the one with which this paper begins. Another young woman pointed out that the young generation did not know anything about the war and that someone had to take the blame for keeping them ignorant about the values of the war. It is alleged that during the 15 years of military rule from 1975–90, as well as during the time of the BNP government, history has been 'distorted' and the younger generation fed a manipulated version of history. These distortions include downplaying of the role of Mujib, his speech of 7 March 1971 which is deemed to have triggered off the liberation struggle, the role of the Indian Army in 1971, non-mention of Mujib and allusion to him in terms of the 'degeneracy after 1971', significance given to the role of the military rather than civilians and, more importantly, de-nationalised reference to the army involved as the 'invader army', 'enemy army' or 'friendly army', which has been misinterpreted by the younger generation as the Indian Army being the invaders and Pakistani Army being the friendly army in 1971.

Muktir Gaan begins with an introduction to the Bangladesh Freedom Struggle Cultural Squad, a group of young middle class men and women travelling through refugee camps in India in a truck during the war of 1971. The group of six men and five women of different religion, age and class background consists of a couple, Benu and Shaheen; two sisters Lubna and Naila Marium, the latter a medical student; two other women Sharmeen Murshid and Lata Chowdhury; three Hindu men Bipul Bhattacharya, Debabrata Chowdhury and Dulal Chandra Shil; and two other young men, Swapan Chaudhury and the narrator, a young bespectacled Tariq Ali. The film narrates that the events of the *Muktijuddho* were being followed through the eyes of a troupe of Bengali musicians who travelled in refugee camps and liberated zones amidst the upheaval of the war and had daily interactions with refugees and liberation fighters. Thus through an amalgamation of diverse materials the film is deemed to be a narrative and musical story of a unique movement in history when a nation is born.

In the film the refugees on the truck are juxtaposed with stereotypical scenes of poor, impoverished women refugees who are fleeing to India. The image of a young woman running with her child and looking back at the camera has become the iconic image of the refugee of Bangladesh circa 1971. The images of queues of refugee women and children, caked in mud and seeking help from an unknown god in the sky above, is set to the haunting rendition of Allen Ginsburg's *Jessore Road* sung by Moushumi Bhowmick. This haunting tone also sets the scene for exploring the downcast faces and eyes of some of the refugee women in the queue, and the narrator speculates whether they have been raped, a genre common in the aforementioned documentary films. The lyrics of the song poignantly capture the refugee experience of loss and the horrors of the war: 'that land, body and soul is riddled with bullets', 'people are fleeing from home and soil'. Tariq Ali, the narrator, pauses to look at the 'endless sea of faces of refugees ... who as victims of genocide are coming in millions leaving behind lands, houses, dreams and fields of harvest and joy'. Reflecting on that knowledge of loss he proclaims 'we are also refugees', an ontological state of knowing bringing into existence a reality. But this is a reality precisely tinged with a distinctive refugee identity. The realisation of being a refugee is however distinguished by the fact that as a middle class group they are a different kind of refugee, not just the teeming millions—the stereotypical category for refugee identification. This is because the cultural troupe also has the agency to raise the morale of liberation fighters and other refugees interned in refugee camps.

This existential affirmation of the cultural troupe thereby allows different refugee identities to come face-to-face with each other. Thus the film travels through the various tortuous faces of the refugee camps. Tariq narrates that thousands of people are living in the refugee camps and are living lives no better than animals. This narration is focussed on Naila Marium's beautiful face as she walks through the camp with refugees on either side. Her 'stroll' through the camp is juxtaposed with the narrations of the experiences of terror and pain of various refugees: an old man is seen narrating how his wife was raped and murdered, while an old woman tells of how her whole family was killed in the war. Sharmeen's bangled hands and fringes, Tariq's spectacles and various hands of the other members of the group come into view as everyone tries to console the old woman, hold her hand and dry her tears. This is worse than the Holocaust, Tariq says. Hence the song 'my heart cries out in despair to sing the songs of Bangladesh, the land of Bengal spun from gold is now filled with blood' fills up the space of the refugee camp and brings together the pain, pathos and loss of the various refugees as well as the viewers of the film. The identification with the various refugee identities of those within the film and those watching the film in independent Bangladesh hence comes full circle. Here migrant identity is precisely defined and hinged on a narration of loss, pain and pathos.

The film is also a window to the daily lives of the cultural troupe as they eat, rest and travel together in the midst of the war of 1971. The film brings out the romance of the road movie genre as young unmarried men and women of different religious and class backgrounds travel in the back of a truck huddled together in the December chill. They stop at various villages near the Indo-Bangladesh border and are often offered hospitality and food by different refugee families. With one such refugee family the group eat together as they listen to the family's accounts of death, arson and loss of homes. Tariq comments that he is touched by their hospitality. The group washes their hands in the same bowl of water, thus transcending religious boundaries of purity and pollution. The family also gives a caged parrot to Tariq as he shows interest in the bird. Thereafter the bird is seen to travel with the group in the truck. As Tariq proceeds to teach the bird to say *Joi Bangla* (Victory to Bengal), the clarion call of the war in 1971, he muses that like them the bird is also a refugee. The group is also seen huddled together listening to the broadcast of Independent Bengal Radio in another refugee home. They express happiness when they hear of the assaults on the Pakistani Army. While the women sing together to the songs being broadcast on radio, some of the men start whistling to the songs. The predominant part of the film however focuses on the group singing inspirational songs in refugee camps and among liberation fighters.

The moments of leisure of the group also highlights gendered relations within the group. In a particular clip, Naila, Sharmeen and Lubna are seen reading a newspaper while the men are in the background practicing their songs. Naila is reading aloud an article from the newspaper *The People* to Sharmeen, 'Have you seen this article from the Bangladesh warfront—Pakistani troop carrier blown up. See here, Tangail! This is our district—villages have been burnt to the ground'. Here accounts of victory over the Pakistani military paraphernalia are juxtaposed with an account of personal loss linked to one's regional home in Bangladesh. They also talk about their male relatives who are in the war. Sharmeen asks Naila which sector her father and brother are in and whether she has heard from them at all. She answers in the negative and adds that she is particularly worried about her brother who is a guerrilla. Naila further draws Sharmeen's attention to the article highlighting the demands of the Pakistani Army, 'We are tired— we want wine and women'. 'Have you seen this?' Naila points out poignantly. The voices and haunting melodies of the male troupe members practising their songs in the background add further poignancy to the news of ravage and terror being read out from the newspaper by the women in the warm winter sun.

The daily lives of the cultural troupe as refugees is also hinged on the symbolic connotation of food, which is seen to embody the natural spirit of Bangladesh. Hence the group is filmed while eating rice on banana leaves, both a dominant signifier of the essence of being a Bengali, a Bengaliness which is hinged on the freedom and birth of one's nation. As a result when the group visit the liberated zones they kiss the earth on which they land, put the dust on their forehead and also mould the soil in their hands. However these embodied essences and practices of the nation is juxtaposed with constant narratives of how Pakistani soldiers have been killed and left to the dogs. The smell of freedom and exhilaration of the new nation as signified by the liberated zones is aptly captured with the image of the group walking into the horizon with the fluttering of saris and the red and green flag with the map of the new country in its middle.

Muktir Gaan and the Heterogeneity of Refugee Identifications

While migration studies have predominantly focused on women, the figure of the refugee and migrant has been primarily treated as a non-person. This particularly gets exacerbated with the infantilising model that is used while referring to refugees from Bangladesh fleeing the horrors of the 1971 war. *Muktir Gaan* is able to disrupt this narrative successfully through this group of young middle class men and women from varied religious backgrounds travelling as refugees. This is precisely reflected in the comment of the young woman with which this paper began. By focusing on middle class men and women of varied religious backgrounds assigned with the agency of raising morale during war, it is able to interrupt the binaries of agent-victim, male-female and class, namely of the poor, ravaged, migrant woman who might be assigned her agency, with which migration studies have predominantly been concerned. However, while *Muktir Gaan* is able to break down these stereotypes, that is precisely possible through the locationalities and aesthetics of class, which lends itself to the aesthetics of war as portrayed through the film.

The younger middle class generation in their responses to *Muktir Gaan* emphasised precisely the aesthetics of the liberationary and sensual feeling of the film. Viewing it primarily as a road movie, the adventure and its concurrent excitement and eroticism are further heightened by the context of the ravages, fears and pain of war tinged with the prospect of freedom. This is also highlighted in the film where one could speculate about emotive and erotic attachments among the group, about the 'sexual draw of protest' (Jasper 1997: 217), where 'one's love shapes one's affective map of the world' (ibid.: 114).[18] Quite a few young men and women expressed that they wished they were young when the war was on as it was so exciting and sensual; there was so much freedom for men and women to travel without family and one could have a sense of responsibility in the midst of armed conflict. The relationship between Benu and Shaheen in the film is part of this 'libidinal economy of a movement' (ibid.: 187), where the pursuit of one's love and political goals concur.

Thus while migration is seen to result in the breakdown of the processes of economic development, this paper highlights how romanticism linked to the idea of the adventure of war reveals the political economy of migration; namely, who can migrate and under what conditions. Narratives of experiences during the war as well as after the war bring this out. In the words of Marie from Lebanon (Bennett et al. 1995: 3), 'War is what happens afterwards, the years of suffering hopelessly with a disabled husband and no money, or struggling to rebuild when all your property has been destroyed.'

On the other hand after returning to their house after the war, Sharmeen had commented: 'How come nothing has happened to our house? I thought it would be totally in rubbles. It doesn't feel as if there has been a war'.[19]

Muktir Gaan also shows that rather than forfeiting citizenship rights, this migrant narrative allows a certain conjuring of citizenship rights within the context of violence, war and the nation. One is not sure when Bangladesh would be formed but the dream towards that imaginary citizenship is possible through *Muktir Gaan* because in reality the possibilities of this citizenship is violently disrupted due to the ongoing war.

The narrative between militarisation and patriarchy is also disrupted in *Muktir Gaan*. The role of both the men and women as peace activists and using peaceful tools like songs to provide support to liberation fighters to fight wars jars the feminist interpretation of gendered relations during wars. This is also reflected in the gendered social relations and activities within the group. So the women are engaged in the masculine idiom of reading newspapers while the men are engaged in feminised practices of practicing songs or the masculine idiom of whistling. In fact many of these women also worked in border hospitals as they were deemed a safer place than staying within Bangladesh. The relationship between militarisation and patriarchy is further complicated if we explore the idioms of feminisation through the visuals of the landscape and songs within *Muktir Gaan*. Hence in identifying the role of women and identity politics I would argue that rather than women, here, feminisation, applicable to both men and women, is a positive attribute. Feminisation is able to evoke empathy and emotive nostalgia while also constructing the role of men, and particularly women, during the war as agentive and masculinised. This nostalgia is located next to a dream, an aspiration, adventure, a sense of helplessness, pain, empathy and loss and feelgoodness in contemporary Bangladesh.

In fact for the audiences of the film, the juxtaposition of the heterogeneity of refugees and the encounter of refugees allow different kinds of identification with gendered migration images. On one hand it enables a continuation with the victim-agent binary in terms of identifying with the refugee who is poor and raped. On the other hand the agentive-victim argument gets differently framed to create a more empathetic identification with the middle class agentive refugees, which I would argue is linked to the aesthetics of war.

At this point I would also like to raise a reflexive and political question. There is an important parallel to be drawn between the middle class refugees being a witness to, and documenting, the plight of other refugees, and researchers working on migration who are also engaged in making testimony in the process of being a witness. Through this, the varied identifications that one has as a middle class refugee, or as a researcher with varied migrant identities, is identified. Is the use of established binaries by researchers and middle class refugees, in their search for the subaltern within migration studies, highlighting the various ways in which they identify with the stereotypical refugee figure? How would the study of middle class refugees by middle class researchers disrupt and disturb the neat agentive-victim binary?

Conclusion

Migrant experiences were initially not been made part of the accounts of war as they were seen to represent no real elements of valour. Recent feminist accounts of the war have however made gendered and migrant experiences central to an understanding of the war story. However the construction of the migrant has primarily been that of the poor, migrant woman. This paper is thus primarily a critique of the construction of the subaltern within migration studies—namely the poor, migrant woman—as a romantic underclass who needs to be represented either as a victim or with agentive subjectivity. The paper unpicks the triad of subalterns: the poor, woman in migration studies, Bangladesh within South Asian studies and the poor and the raped within conflict studies. All these three subalterns are fused together in the context of the Bangladesh war of 1971. Yet during wars there are varied migrant experiences which do not fit the subaltern imagery and hence are not included within academic and policy understandings of refugee experiences. Further, in post-war situations refugee experiences are also comprehended and identified through their multiplicities.

Muktir Gaan is the lens through which this paper seeks to highlight the heterogeneity of migrant experiences as a result of war, and the juxtaposition and encounters between various refugees, thereby examining identification with varied refugee subjectivities in contemporary Bangladesh. The film enables an interrogation of the victim-agent, class and gendered binaries through which migrant experiences are predominantly studied. The relationship between militarisation and patriarchy is also dislocated, and that the experience of wars could be sensual and erotic is also highlighted. Thus it shows that accounts of war for different migrant communities also differ.

Through this the paper attempts to examine the kind of migrant experiences that are not addressed within migration studies and analyse discursively and reflexively the need for researchers to study migrant experiences through existing binaries, and the modes of identification that are connotative in such studies. In fact for the audiences of *Muktir Gaan* the juxtaposition of the heterogeneity of refugees and the confrontation of refugees allow different kinds of identification with gendered migration images. Without an account of the multiplicity of migration experiences, what remains obscure is the gendered and classed relationships between refugees, something which is integral to the understanding of gendered social relationships during times of conflict. This is particularly significant for independent Bangladesh where *Muktir Gaan* evoked such an emotive response two decades after it was filmed. This I have argued is because of the varied identifications the audience have with the varied migrant experiences. Particularly, the middle class migrants and their symbolic capital lends to the ravages of war, middle class sensibilities which also allows them to represent and aestheticise the horror experienced by the other poor, raped migrants of the war of 1971.

There is a significant parallel between middle class refugees documenting and being a witness to the plight of other refugees, and researchers working on migration who are also engaged in making testimony in the process of being a witness. Through this the varied identifications that one has as a middle class refugee or as a researcher with varied migrant identities is identified. The paper raises questions as to what sorts of discomfort are caused by the study of middle class refugees and what kinds of binaries are hence disrupted. These are significant questions which precisely address the reflexive and discursive understandings of migration study researchers and their identification with varied refugee identities. Finally this helps to identify the need to do away with the use of binaries when documenting and witnessing migrant experiences.

Notes

1　*Muktir Gaan* (1996) (Songs of Freedom) is a feature length documentary film about a troupe of travelling musicians during the Bangladesh war of liberation of 1971. It was directed by Tareque and Catherine Masud. The sequel to *Muktir Gaan*, *Muktir Katha* (1999) (Words of Freedom) is an oral history documentary about the experience of ordinary villagers during the 1971 war based on their responses to the screening and viewing of *Muktir Gaan* throughout Bangladesh.

2 India's presence in Bangladesh also ensured that it was able to suppress the Naxalite movement (inspired by Maoist principles against oppressive feudalistic land relations) in West Bengal. During fieldwork narratives abounded about the loot and plunder undertaken by the Indian Army after liberation of military hardware, foodgrains, industrial produce and household goods (Salek 1977: 110).

3 For varied accounts of *Muktijuddho* refer to Ahmed 1992; Ayoob et al. 1971; Hayder 1990; Maniruzzaman 1980; Mascarenhas 1971; Muhith 1992; Rahamana 1982–85; Sengupta 1981; Williams 1972.

4 The collaborators are usually considered to be Bihari Muslims who spoke Urdu and came to Bangladesh during the 1947 Partition. Reactionary religious parties like the Jamaat-e-Islami were also considered to be allies of the Pakistani forces (Salek 1977). Today the word 'razakar' is used as verbal abuse for a betrayer similar to Mirjafar (who betrayed the Bengal emperor Sirajudaula to his enemies) or Judas.

5 I am unsure about the historiography of the '3 million dead and 200,000/300,000/400,000 women raped'. After the war, these were the various numbers cited in various government and non-government sources (Rahamana 1982–85). Today the official number of raped women stands at 200,000 and it has become canonised and co-terminus with the *Muktijuddho*.

6 In this paper the migrant experience is predominantly framed within the category of the 'refugee'—namely a welfare and legal term that would help identify their aid receiving and non-legal status.

7 Occurring at the conjuncture of Cold War politics, *Muktijuddho* is still termed as a civil war in the international legal language of human rights (International Commission of Jurists 1972: 27). The killings and rapes of 1971 have not been recognised as genocide, a claim that is made by a majority of intellectuals and social and political activists, and even now *Muktijuddho* is referred to primarily as one of the Indo-Pakistan wars. A search for 'Muktijuddho' on the Internet showed 45 sites while a search for '1971 Indo-Pakistan War' provided links to 3,323 sites. A few examples of such sites which refer to it as an Indo-Pakistan war are: *www.subcontinent.com/1971war*; *www.kids.infoplease.com/ce6/history*; *www.lycos.infoplease.com/ce6/history*; *www.freeindian.org/1971war*; *www.bharat-rakshak.com/IAF/History/1971war*; *www.asia.yahoo.com/arts/humanities/history*; *www.historyguy.com/indo-pakistaniwars.html*.

8 Sarkar (1997) has pointed out a tendency towards essentialising the categories of 'subaltern' and 'autonomy' and non-western 'community consciousness' as a valorised alternative of critiques of western colonial power knowledge, which has enabled the subaltern to be a creation, a reification of historians (Masselos in Ludden 2001). The separation of domination and autonomy disallows immanent critiques of structures that have been the strength of Marxist dialectical approaches.

9 I use middle class aesthetics/sensibilities in multiple ways here. The very notion of aesthetics involves, according to Daniel (1997: 309), the need to bring order out of disorder, to mould form from that in which form is absent. But even though this order may be posited only as a future hope, something to be achieved in the making, this hope is drenched in nostalgia of the imagined glory that once was. This nostalgia in Bangladesh is rooted in its Bengali identity epitomised in the literary tradition, the main readership of which constitute the middle classes. The romanticism that emerges from this also finds its fruition in the 'glamour and sorrow' of the liberation struggle which was rooted in constructions of an essentialised Bengali identity—the constituent elements of the aestheticising sensibilities of Bangladesh's middle class.

10 Symbolic capital exists 'in the form of the prestige and renown attached to a family and a name is readily convertible back into economic capital' (Bourdieu 1995). Here by symbolic capital of the middle class I refer to middle class aesthetics/ sensibilities which have been outlined above.

11 Studies of global politics and armed conflicts have predominantly been seen as the forte of men and the experiences of women have been excluded from this study. Cynthia Enloe (1989, 1993, 2000) and various others have established the relationship between patriarchy and militarisation. Enloe (1989, 1993, 2000) has argued how increased militarisation in terms of global politics is also based on ensuring that women are confined to the domestic sphere, which however also buttresses the military paraphernalia. More recently she (Enloe 2000) has highlighted the everyday militarisation of women's lives, and how the varied responses of women to September 11 has also complicated the relationship between militarisation and patriarchy where women are actively involved in the military paraphernalia as soldiers, mothers and feminists who are in support of the war on terror.

12 As cited in Jasper 1997: 187.

13 While searching for his brother, an intellectual who was picked up from his house in December 1971, in Mirpur, Dhaka in January 1972, Zahir Raihan disappeared. He is alleged to have been killed by pro-Pakistani Biharis in Mirpur.

14 Ardner and Holden (1987) talk about the symbolic use of the body by those lacking an effective political voice. Mahashweta Devi's story 'Draupadi' (Cooke 1996: 136–46) gives a traumatic account of the rape of a low caste woman who refused to be dressed after being gangraped. Similarly, when the women of Greenham smeared their naked bodies with ashes on Nagasaki Day 1984, their actions challenged not only the invisibility of the bodies of victims of 'the nuclear disaster' but also 'men's stereotypes of naked women' (Jones 1987).

15 *Teep* are decorative spots on the forehead worn traditionally by Hindu women to denote marital status. In Bangladesh the wearing of *teep* is very common. It connotes clothing and stylistic practice, and also political practice, emphasising a Bengali identity that exists alongside a Muslim identity.

16 My experience of Bengali New Years Day in Dhaka during my fieldwork surpassed any celebration that I have seen in West Bengal, India, which showed how much this is part of one's identity politics in Bangladesh.

17 Lear Levin's footages became *Muktir Gaan* only in the 1990s.

18 By this Jasper (1997) refers to the erotic and sensual attachments that are associated with various social and revolutionary movements where the pursuit of one's love and one's political goals concur.

19 Interview given to author by Noorjahan Murshid, Sharmeen's mother, who became the Minister for Relief and Rehabilitation under Sheikh Mujib's government, the interview took place in Oxford in October 1998. ·

References

Agrawal, A., S. Arya, N. Chadha Behera, M. Mohanty, L. Murali, R. Palriwala, N. Ranganathan, M. Thapar, P. Uberoi. 2003. *Women and Migration in Asia Handbook*. Delhi: Developing Countries Research Centre, University of Delhi.

Ahmed, S. 1992. *Bangalir Sadhana O Bangladesher Muktijuddho* (The Struggle of Bengalis and Bangladesh's Liberation War). Dhaka: Jatiya Sahitya Prakashan.

Alama, M. 1992. *Gerila Theke Samukha Juddhe*. (From Guerilla to Conventional Warfare). Dhaka: Jatiya Sahitya Prakashan.

Ardener, S. and P. Holden (eds). 1987. *Images of Women in Peace and War: Cross Cultural and Historical Perspectives*. London: Macmillan.

Ayoob, M. et al. 1971. *Bangladesh: A Struggle for Nationhood*. Delhi: Vikas Publications.

Bennett, O., J. Bexeley and K. Warnock (eds). 1995. *Arms to Fight, Arms to Protect: Women Speak out about Conflict*. London: Panos.

Bhuiyan, A.W. 1982. *Emergence of Bangladesh and Role of Awami League*. New Delhi: Vikas Publishing House.

Bop, C. 2001. 'Women in Conflicts, their Gains and their Losses', in S.A. Meintjes, A. Pillay and M. Turshen (eds), *The Aftermath: Women in Post-Conflict Transformation*, pp. 19–34. London: Zed Books.

Bourdieu, P. 1995. *Outline of a Theory of Practice.* Cambridge: Cambridge University Press.

Butalia, Urvashi. 1998. *The Other Side of Silence: Voices from the Partition of India*. New Delhi: Viking Penguin.

Collett, P. 1998. 'Afghan Women in the Peace Process', in L.A. Lorentzen and J. Turpin (eds), *The Women and War Reader*, pp. 323–28. New York: New York University Press.

Cooke, M. 1996. *Women and the War Story*. Los Angeles: University of California Press.

Cooke, M. and Rustomji-Kerns (eds). 1994. *Blood into Ink: South Asian and Middle Eastern Women on War*. Colorado: Westview Press.

Daniel, E.V. 1997. 'Suffering Nation and Alienation', in V. Das, A. Kleinman and M. Lock (eds), *Social Suffering*, pp. 309–58. Berkeley: University of California Press.

Das, Veena. 1995. *Critical Events: An Anthropological Perspective on Contemporary India*. Delhi: Oxford University Press.

Elshtain, J.B. 1995. *Women and War*. London: University of Chicago Press.

Enloe, Cynthia. 1989. 'Gender Makes the World go Around', in Cynthia Enloe (ed.), *Bananas, Beaches and Bases: Making Feminist Sense of International Politics*, pp. 1–18. London: Pandora Press.

———. 1993. *The Morning After: Sexual Politics at the End of the Cold War*. Berkeley: University of California Press.

———. 2000. 'The Prostitute, the Colonel and the Nationalist', in *Manoeuvres: The International Politics of Militarising Women's Lives*, pp. 49–107. Berkeley: University of California Press.

Goodwin, J. 1997. 'The Libidinal Constitution of a High-Risk Social Movement: Affectual Ties and Solidarity in the Huk Rebellion', *American Sociological Review*, 62: 53–69.

Guha, R. 1983. *Elementary Aspects of Peasant Insurgency in Colonial India*. Oxford: Oxford University Press.

Hayder, R. 1990. *1971–Bhoyabhoyo Obhigota* (1971–A Terrifying Experience). Dhaka: Jatiya Sahitya Prokashoni.

International Commission of Jurists. 1972. *The Events of East Pakistan, 1971: A Legal Study*. Geneva: International Commission of Jurists.

Jasper, J. 1997. *The Art of Moral Protest: Culture, Biography and Creativity in Social Movements*. Chicago: University of Chicago Press.

Jones, L. 1987. 'Greenham Common', in S. Ardener and P. Holden (eds), *Images of Women in Peace and War: Cross Cultural and Historical Perspectives*, pp. 179–204. London: Macmillan.

Lorentzen, I. A. and J. Turpin (eds), 1998. *The Women and War Reader*, pp. 323–28. New York: New York University Press.

Ludden, David (ed.). 2001. *Reading Subaltern Studies: Critical History, Contested Meaning and the Globalisation of South Asia*. New Delhi: Permanent Black.

Manchanda, R. (ed.). 2001. *Women, War and Peace in South Asia: Beyond Victimhood to Agency*. New Delhi: Sage Publications.

Maniruzzaman. T. 1980. *The Bangladesh Revolution and its Aftermath*. Dhaka: Bangladesh Books International.

Mascarenhas, A. 1971. *The Rape of Bangladesh*. Calcutta: Vikas Publishing House.

Menon, R. and K. Bhasin. 1998. *Borders and Boundaries: Women in India's Partition*. New Delhi: Kali for Women.

Meyer, M.K. and E. Prügl (eds). 1999. *Gender Politics in Global Governance*. Lanham: Rowman and Littlefield.

Mookherjee, N. 2002. 'A Lot of History: Sexual Violence, Public Memories and the Bangladesh Liberation War of 1971', doctoral thesis, University of London.

————. 2003. 'Gendered Embodiments: Mapping the Body-Politic of the Raped Woman and the Nation in Bangladesh', in Nirmal Puwar and Parvati Raghuram (eds), *Critical Reflections on Gender and the South Asian Diaspora*, pp. 157–77. Oxford: Berg.

————. 2004. 'My *man* (honour) is lost but I still have my *iman* (principle): Sexual Violence and Articulations of Masculinity', in R. Chopra, C. Osella and F. Osella (eds), *South Asian Masculinities*, pp. 131–59. New Delhi: Kali for Women.

————. (forthcoming). 'Remembering to Forget: Public Secrecy and Memory of Sexual Violence in Bangladesh', *Journal of Royal Anthropological Institute*.

Muhith, A.M.A. 1992. *Bangladesh: Emergence of a Nation*. Dhaka: University Press.

Peterson, V.S. and A.S. Runyan. 1993. *Global Gender Issues*. Boulder: Westview Press.

Rahamana, H. (ed.). 1982–85. *Bangladesher Svadhinota Yuddha Dolilpotro* (Documents of the Bangladesh Independence War). 16 volumes. Dhaka: *Gonoprojatantri Bangladesh Sarkar, Tathya Mantralaya* (People's Republic of Bangladesh, Information Ministry).

Salek, S. 1977. *Witness to Surrender*. New Delhi: Oxford University Press.

Sarkar, Sumit. 1997. 'The Decline of the Subaltern in Subaltern Studies', in *Writing Social History*, pp. 82–108. New Delhi: Oxford University Press.

Sengupta, J. 1981. *Bangladesh in Blood and Tears*. Calcutta: Naya Prokash.

Sisson, R. and L. Rose. 1990. *War and Secession: Pakistan, India and the Creation of Bangladesh*. Los Angeles: University of California Press.

Thangarajah, C.Y. 2003. 'Veiled Constructions: Conflict, Migration and Modernity in Eastern Sri Lanka', in K. Gardner and F. Osella (eds), *Contributions to Indian Sociology: Special Issue: Migration, Modernity and Social Transformation in South Asia*, 37(1&2): 141–62.

Tickner, J.A. 1992. *Gender in International Relations: Feminist Perspectives on Achieving Global Security*. New York: Columbia University Press.

Waller, M. and J. Rycenga (eds). 2000. *Frontline Feminisms: Women, War, and Resistance*. New York: Garland.

Williams, R. 1972. *The East Pakistan Tragedy*. London: Tom Stacey.

Young, J.F. 1988. *Writing and Rewriting the Holocaust: Narrative and Consequences of Interpretation*. Bloomington: Indiana University Press.

Yuval-Davis, N. and F.Y. Anthias (eds). 1989. *Woman-Nation-State*. London: Macmillan.
Yuval-Davis, N. 1997. *Gender and Nation*. London: Sage Publications.
Yuval-Davis, N. and P. Werbner (eds). 1999. *Women, Citizenship and Difference*. London: Zed Books.

3

Speaking Violence: Pakistani Women's Narratives of Partition

Furrukh A. Khan*

And now the voyage ended, and the vessel
Was worn from travel, and they came stepping down
To their own shores, and Tereus dragged her with him
To the deep woods, to some ramshackle building
Dark in that darkness, and he shut her in there,
Pale, trembling, fearing everything, and asking
'Where was her sister?' And he told her then
What he was going to do, and straightway did it,
Raped her, a virgin all alone, and calling
For her father, for her sister, but most often
For the great gods. In vain ...

But Tereus did not kill her; he seized her tongue
With pincers, though it cried against the outrage,
Babbled and made a sound something like 'Father,'
Till the sword cut it off. The mangled root
Quivered, the severed tongue along the ground

*I would like to thank Dr Itty Abraham and Malini Sur of the Social Sciences Research Council, New York which provided me with a junior fellowship under the aegis of the South Asia Fellowship programme and which made available financial support for the completion of this paper; the Lahore University of Management Sciences (LUMS); Dr Navnita Chadha Behera of the University of Delhi; students past, present and future of my 'Literature of Conflict' class at LUMS; Ayesha Nadir Ali, Sarah Hameed, Rabia Kamal, Maria Omer and Faisal Khan who helped with the research for this paper; and Tamkin Hussain for proofreading and offering her insights.

Lay quivering, making a little murmur,
Jerking and twitching, the way a serpent does
Run over by a wheel, and with its dying movement
Came to its mistress's feet ...

And a year went by
And what of Philomela? Guarded against flight,
Stone blocks around her cottage, no power of speech
To help her tell her wrongs, her grief has taught her
Sharpness of wit, and cunning comes in trouble.
She had a loom to work with, and with purple
On a white background, wove her story in,
Her story in and out, and when it was finished,
Gave it to one old woman, with signs and gestures
To take it to the queen, so it was taken,
Unrolled and understood. Procne said nothing—
What could she say?—grief choked her utterance,
Passion her sense of outrage ... (Ovid 1955: 146–48).

When Philomela imagines herself free to tell her own tale to anyone who will listen, Tereus realises for the first time what would come to light, should the woman's voice become public. In private, force is sufficient. In public, however, Philomela's voice, if heard, would make them equal. Enforced silence and imprisonment are the means Tereus chooses to protect himself from discovery. But as the mythic tale, Tereus' plot and Ovid's own text make clear, dominance can only contain, but never successfully destroy, the woman's voice.

When Philomela begins to weave over the long year of her imprisonment, it is not only her suffering but a specific motive that gives rise to her new use of the loom: to speak to and be heard by her sister. As an instrument that binds and connects, the loom, or its part, the shuttle, re-members or mends what violence tears apart: the bond between the sisters, the woman's power to speak, a form of community and communication. War and weaving are antithetical not because when women are weaving we are in our right place, but because all of the truly generative activities of human life are born of order and give rise to order. But just as Philomela can weave any number of patterns on her loom, culture need not retain one fixed structure (Klindienst 1984: 51).

Language forms the critical basis of articulation of not just individual, but collective and national, experiences, which in turn provide a basis of narrating a nation's history and its ideology. A nation-state most often sets down its own version of selective history, which is expected to be accepted in order to consolidate and further its collective identity. As it has already been highlighted by the extremely influential discourse of the Subaltern Studies Group[1] that such a meta-narrative is almost always a history of the elites, focusing more on their heroic deeds which are supposed to have been singularly responsible for determining the road-map for the creation, governance and future of a nation-state. In such histories, voices which challenge this meta-narrative are side-lined at best and totally ignored at worst, so that alternative histories and per-spectives that might break the selective linearity of the state's version are institutionally marginalised. One of the primary aims of this paper is to provide some examples of such ignored voices that are of citizenry doubly marginalised: women who belong to the lower economic strata of Pakistani society. Even though there are significant differences be-tween the stories which were narrated during the interviews, there is a distinctive individualised perspective, especially a woman's perspective, that is completely absent from the state's version of history. The violence of Partition, especially that directed at women, is replicated by the state's perspective that aims to exercise control through a hierarchy of selection of events and personalities that are represented in such a discourse. Individual stories on the other hand are more often than not glimpses of the lived experience of people's lives, as aspect that is lacking in the official version of events. Women's stories, as will be illustrated in this paper, offer an insight into the individual and hence subjective experi-ence as memories of Partition are recalled. These stories are in complete contrast to the official version of history, which fails to take into account the utter devastation suffered by countless individuals, especially women.

This paper aims to delve into the interconnections between violence, memory and cognition of events of women's' lives during Partition. It is believed that only through explication of the combination of experi-ence and memory of Partition can one possibly arrive at the lingering effects of that traumatic period and how it continues to shape victims' present outlook. Their deep-seated detestation of the 'Other' (Hindus and Sikhs) is still intense, primarily because of personal experiences, as well as the state's deliberate efforts to carefully cultivate and foster certain fears and apprehensions among its populace.

The partition of the Indian subcontinent in 1947 serves as the foundation of the modern history of Pakistan.[2] This event divided the hitherto united and colonised India into two independent countries: India and Pakistan. In the ensuing bloodshed and forcible dislocation, by some estimates, over 14 million people moved from one part of the country to the other, the largest human migration in history. The exact figures of those wounded and killed have never been known, and as a result there is a wide range of numbers which are used to describe the casualties. The numbers of those killed vary from 200,000 to 2 million and about 750,000 women were kidnapped or raped, and to this day most of them remain unaccounted for (Butalia 1998: 4). As has occurred on numerous occasions in civil, ethnic or religious conflicts, women bore a significant brunt of the violence and brutality directed by the members, mostly men, of warring communities. Stories of these women do find a place in the meta-narrative of the narrations, but are rarely considered of any significance other than as illustrative examples of the violence and maliciousness of the 'Other.' Narratives used in Partition-inspired fiction or those historians' accounts, which are considered and legitimised as authentic by the state authorities, are always imbued with a patriarchal perspective and signify the violence carried out on women as almost always more important than the victims' subjectivity. There are very few instances of women actually talking about their experiences, especially so if they belong to the lower economic strata of rural or urban populations. In India a considerable amount of work has been done by social and literary researchers like Urvashi Butalia, Ritu Menon, Kamla Bhasin, Gyanendra Pandey, Ashish Nandy and Veena Das, who have explored and developed discourses to comprehend the events of Partition. On the other hand, apart from some exceptions like Nighat Said Khan and Neelam Hussain, no sustained effort has been undertaken from the Pakistani side to collect and catalogue women's stories of Partition, hence leaving out a pivotal dimension from what is perceived to be the collective discourse.

My research for this paper entailed interviewing over fifty women from various economic and social backgrounds, with a particular focus on the lower and lower-middle economic classes. The interviews took place in a number of cities including Rawalpindi, Islamabad, Sialkot and Lahore, as well as in smaller cities like Narowal and Shakargarh.[3]

The theoretical model for this paper is inspired by the theorisation of the establishment of discourse as articulated by the French poststructuralist theorists, and Gilles Deleuze and Felix Guattari's seminal work *A Thousand Plateaus* (1987). Arboreal and rhizomatic models of thought seem to dominate their understanding of cultural, social and historical discourses. Even though their work is not specifically about the partition of India, I strongly feel that the ideas they have espoused can be used to encapsulate the conflicting versions of the historiography of this event and how subsequent questions of identity, ideology and idealism are expressed.

Arboreal thought, according to Deleuze and Guattari, is linear, hierarchic, sedentary and full of segmentation and striation, which makes it a convenient and classic mode of discourse employed by the state. It is unbending and unrelentingly vertical in structure, hence providing no space for 'diversion' or debate. In contrast, rhizomatic thought is non-linear, anarchic, and almost itinerant. As John Lechte (1994) very rightly posits, 'Deleuze's thought is radically horizontal'. Rhizomes, as outlined in Deleuze and Guattari's work, create a smooth space, and cut across boundaries imposed by vertical lines of hierarchies and 'order' imposed by the state. Such a thought is multiplicitous, moving in many directions and connected to many other lines of thinking, acting and being, hence cutting across borders. It also builds links between pre-existing gaps between nodes that are separated by categories and the order of segmented thinking. According to Deleuze and Guattari, '(a) rhizome ceaselessly establishes connections between semiotic chains, organisations of power, and circumstances relative to the arts, sciences, and social struggles' (1987: 7).

Women's stories of Partition are denied any mode of 'official' transmission beyond their 'private' space, and issues of violence, especially sexual brutalisation, are rarely allowed to be passed on to the next generation. Implied in their coerced silence is the usurpation of their right to speak by the patriarchically-inspired state's meta-narrative. This particular practice is an apt example of 'deterritorialisation', as used by Deleuze and Guattari, to refer to a 'minority' discourse that is denied a public forum. This discourse is not one written or spoken in a 'minor' language, rather it refers to the revolutionary condition of all literatures at the heart of what one calls major or established languages. However, I feel that Deleuze and Guattari's model can be developed to refer to 'minority' or 'majority' influences, sources controlling the discourse of, in this case, Partition. The state's meta-narrative, as has been described earlier, is inspired and controlled by patriarchal sensibilities, and the 'minority' discourse, in this case oral stories by women, is seen as a disturbing influence on the grand narrativisation. However, as originally outlined by Deleuze and Guattari, the 'minority' discourse does interact through subversive ways with the 'influential' discourse, and the resultant is a more realistic and complex narrative.

The blood-stained artificial lines drawn on the body of Mother India are replicated with gruesome regularity on the bodies of women from all religious groups. These bloodied bodies are forced into assuming the gruelling task of carrying ideological messages of each warring community. Both the newly sovereign states became mangled national territories inhabited by equally devastated women. The ensuing situation was made worse by the social and patriarchal obsession with silencing the voices of these literally broken spirits and bodies. The concern in such undertakings is always less about the women than the acknowledgement of their scarred bodies as evidence of violation by the hated 'Other.' Thus women's bodies, which had suffered their subjection to deliberate acts of brutality as a 'geographic' territory, were expected to hide the manifestations of their violation as otherwise it would 'shame' their respective communities. It is the struggle taking place during the violence of Partition that leads one to concur with Gillian Rose, according to whom the female body is 'geopolitically' placed: its location marked with a matrix of specific historical and geographical circumstances (Rose 1993: 29–30). The discourse of nations, especially during times of conflict, requires blank spaces in the shape of women's bodies to assert and display the physical dominance of the ideology of different groups.

A state's narrative obsessively revolves around 'dates' as this particular insistence provides a 'coherent' packaging of historical events that may be read and interpreted with a particular bias. In individual interviews, these same dates are not so politically and historically loaded. The strategically essentialist mode of 'one' history of a nation requires selective placing of chronological events and clearly defined protagonists, usually the political leaders, and in the same vein, a block compartmentalisation of the 'villains' and victims. Individual memory, on the other hand, offers a much less clinical separation of dates; one of the most significant descriptions that occurred in almost all the narratives was the incessant rain and the flooding of the river Ravi. The state's arboreal narrative has no mention of the characteristics of the daily events and conditions that were faced by people who were caught up in Partition's forced uprooting.

In order to highlight the lack of women's self-representation in the national ideology of Pakistan, I feel that it is pertinent to talk about the 'nation' and its discourse. Ernst Renan was one of the first theorists to actually write about the nation and its constructs, and contrary to the widely held belief that the nation was a 'modern' concept. Twentieth century theorists like Eric Hobsbawm and Ernest Gellner defined the 'nation' as one of the most potent forms of collective identity. The formation of a nation did not depend so much on the geographical boundaries of land as a group or community's identification with a shared sense of beliefs and traditions, and the resultant culture. Following them was the influential *Imagined Communities* (1983) by Benedict Anderson, who talked about the perception of connection between a particular group of people, who even though would never meet one another, yet form a bond to collectively 'imagine' a nation. Post-colonial cultural theorists like Homi Bhabha and Partha Chatterjee have challenged and furthered the discourse of what constitutes a 'nation' and the constant re-negotiations of identity that had not been taken into account by Anderson. The Subaltern Studies Group highlighted the absence of the voice of the marginalised, who form a numerical majority over the elite group whose deeds had, in the traditionalist mode of discourse, resulted in 'history' and were responsible for determining the future of the nation.

The experience of trauma suffered during Partition represents a theoretical and political preoccupation with the lived and witnessed reality of women—the position to articulate them is constantly challenged not just by the community, their exclusion is institutionalised by the state. It was felt that interviewing them would evince the multiplicity of their narratives not just for themselves, but to add even a discordant voice to the parochial, patriarchal and elitist meta-narrative of the experience of Partition. Their deliberate assertions fill the gaping holes not just in the social, but also in the political, construction of the recent past of Pakistan. The forcibly denied space to talk about their experience in their own voices is expected to push their lived experience into the unconscious and imaginary realm of the victims. However, by expressing individual perspectives, these women take the first tentative steps to bridge a hitherto missing link to the collective imaginary.

A community's past plays a categorical role in the construction of present identity, with different sections of society recalling various components of the jigsaw past to come up with a comprehensible picture. This collective memory may not always produce a result that is collectively agreed upon. One of the best definitions of 'collective memory' has been put forward by Barry Schwartz, according to whom it '[I]s a metaphor that formulates society's retention and loss of information about its past in the familiar terms of individual remembering and forgetting' (1991: 301–19).

The strain of the interviews conducted was always the tension between the horror of atrocity and the controlled suppression which had very rarely been allowed to surface. It was apparent how this sustained pressure had accentuated the chasm that ironically separated a number of women from their own experiences. They repeatedly raised questions about the legitimacy of their own witnessing and suffering. While conducting these interviews, I had to constantly grapple with a moral dilemma: at what point does recording the borne and witnessed traumatic experiences of human suffering cross from documentation of the critical memory to the manipulation of the survivor for cold academic dramatic effect?

Oral history has enriched the process of remembering and recording events of the past because of its ability to include voices that are, as Perks and Thompson describes, 'hidden from history' (1998: ix). This particular methodology has resulted in a comparatively more democratic portrayal of social and political events. Oral narratives of Partition are circumscribed within two major emotional boundaries, which are explained by Dipesh Chakrabarty as:

> ... the sentiment of nostalgia and the sense of trauma, and their contradictory relationship to the question of the past. A traumatised memory has a narrative structure which works on a principle opposite to that of any historical narrative. At the same time, however, this memory, in order to be the memory of trauma, has to place the Event—the cause of the trauma, in this case, the Partition violence— within a past that gives force to the claim of the victim. This has to be a shared past between the narrator of the traumatic experience and the address of the narration. Yet it cannot be a historicist version of the past, one that aims to diffuse the shock of the traumatic by explaining away the element of the unexpected (1996: 2143–151).

The erratic and disjointed memory confronts the linear meta-narrative of the state, whose collective suffering is harnessed or ignored to produce a chronological arrangement of events with clearly defined victims and villains. Such categorisation is rather simplistically cast along religious lines, as each state's discourse aims to present a more linear and selective version of events, especially with stereotypes that perpetuate the myth of the 'Other'. On the other hand, individuals, because of the comparative proximity and experience of culturally mixed existence, offer versions of events that are rarely as unsophisticated as that of the state. As a result of such shared experience, the narratives presented by individuals are more complex and because of their traumatic nature are that much more difficult to recall. Janet Walker points out the recurring personal struggles which are fought by the survivors in their mental exertion of remembering and forgetting their agonised past:

> History of trauma, a history of events that are forgotten in their experiencing. The historical power of trauma is not just that the experience is repeated after its forgetting, but that it is only in and through its inherent forgetting that it is first experienced at all…. For history of trauma means that it is referential precisely to the extent that it is not fully perceived as it occurs (1997: 803–26).

The events of Partition are enshrined in the sudden and explosive repercussion of political events which were taking place outside the domain of the rural everyday social and communal sphere. When these events are recalled, the survivor's trauma re-ignites its fiery glow in the dark recesses of her/his mind, where it had been locked away except for private confrontations, as well as creating an altered, and what may appear as an exaggerated, notion of what was witnessed. These narratives are presented in a spasmodic chronological linearity, their personal rendition of the events is '… marked by repetition, and centred on an event it calls attention to and deflects attention from'. These are events which are not fully grasped at the time, even by the very participants as they unfolded (ibid.). The helplessness and the humiliation of the past is one of the most significant aspects of individual narratives, an aspect that is deliberately erased from the state's version of events. Women's voices are able to raise the spectre of the menacing past that has been neutralised of its potential to affect an individual and a community's psyche as a result of the state control and simplification of the narrative of what happened during the Partition. Theirs are memories without memory, retained in their narratives are scars of traumatic events, which if one were to believe the state's version of events, have never taken place.

Hajra Bibi, who was a 17-year-old girl living in Gurdaspur in Punjab (India), and now relocated to Lahore, recalls that fateful time:

> In August 1947 the *Thanedar* came and warned our family to leave the village as it was going to be attacked with machine guns (*Aethe machine phairi jaaey gi*).[4] The river (Ravi) was very close to our home, with one side touching Pakistan. That night women quickly cooked some food for the short journey. People used to think we were only going away for a short while and would be coming back soon. We had to spend one night at the riverside, as it was not easy to find enough boats to carry all the people across. The sound of gunfire was heard clearly and scared us. Eventually, a huge crowd gathered there. My husband jumped into the river and swam across back and forth and spent the entire night arranging for boats to take us across.
>
> Things became chaotic. I remember one woman who allowed her infant son to flow away with the river as she was unable to carry him and run. Her own father said to her 'Save yourself and don't fall into the hands of Hindus and Sikhs' (*Apni jaan bachaa, kafiran dey hath na aa*).
>
> ... I still remember how we left our home in a hurry at the time of Partition. The milk containers were still filled with fresh milk, our cows, hens and all our belongings had to be left behind.

For individuals such as Hajra Bibi, the sudden rupture of her from the place that she was most comfortable with, is captured not just by understanding the violence, instead, there is a desperate attempt on her part to maintain some grip on a semblance of reality as the whole social structure has been blown away by the violence taking place around her. Veena Das and Ashis Nandy have carried out extensive research on the language and discourse of violence, of the different ideologies which explain its use. The one which is directly related to Partition is the 'language of feud', which is:

> ... [S]tudied intensively by anthropologists in the context of tribal societies. Despite variations between cultures and societies, feud may be defined as a pact of violence between social groups in such a way that the definition of the self and the other emerges through an exchange of violence. Whereas the victim of violence in sacrifice is the means by which the moral community is established and hence bears

a close relation to the sacrificiant, the victim of feud is simply a bearer of the status of his group. He is the means through which the pact of violence may continue to be executed (Das and Nandy 1986: 177–95).

Both authors are very critical of most of the written literature of Partition, because of what I had stated earlier in this paper: that it entails an essential and often deliberate attempt to form a simplistic and stereotypical portrayal of a character along particular religious lines. Once this form of characterisation takes place, the authors' need to create a balanced view invariably results in a predictable tit-for-tat plot, in which his/her own religious community is always less guilty than the others. Writing about such literature, Das and Nandy state that:

> The experience of the partition produced a large volume of literature, much of which was autobiographical in inspiration. Most of this literature remained inauthentic, because it tried to reduce the violence to the language of feud in which violence from one side was equally balanced with violence from the other. Thus the description of violent, inhuman acts perpetuated upon those travelling by a train coming from Lahore would be matched by another description of similar gruesome acts to which travellers coming from Amritsar would be subjected. If a prostitute gave shelter to two women whose bodies had been mutilated by rioters then one could be certain that one of these women would be a Hindu and the other, a Muslim. Similarly, the language of self-sacrifice was often used to describe events, but inevitably degenerated into a glorification of self-mutilation without exploring the generative capacity of suffering. In some ways, these representations were the same as using ordinary language to convey an extraordinary and traumatic experience to someone who has not shared it.... It is precisely the use of the same context or phrase which sums up the unbridgeable chasm in understanding (ibid.: 189).

Orality provides a counter-balance to the rather artificial and 'closed' narratives in written literature. It allows the narrators much more freedom and space to bring in issues and events which, if not impractical, would weaken the written narrative. One of the most distinctive features of orality is the lack of pressure to include 'matching' scenarios, to somehow justify or to provide a 'balance' to a particular narrative.

As described in Veena Das's research regarding women's stories during Partition, I had similar experiences with women I interviewed. The actual moment of dislocation is very sudden, denying the subjects any time to comprehend the violent intrusion of the physical aspects of public discourse into their private space. The abruptness of this event denies the 'normal' mode of moving from one place to another, in which case one would pack one's belongings, meet one's neighbours and take care of any pending commercial or monetary matters. Das outlines the trauma of 'disruption' of the 'private' lives of women:

> The forms of representations that emphasise the disruption of every-day life and violence to the women's world of cooking and feed-ing and decorously covering the body are also not idiosyncratic expressions—they represent forms through which disruption of life through a sudden announcement of death is traditionally represented in personal narratives of women (Das 1991: 65–77).

As these 'normal' activities are brusquely terminated, women, relegated to private spheres of their homes, are suddenly and literally thrust into the vulnerable, public and open space without the 'protection' they had been socially guaranteed. The emotional and physical threat of brutal violence manifests itself repeatedly in the narratives of women and men who had to undertake the journey from East to West Punjab and vice versa. Because women were pushed into a new, dangerous and almost alien domain, their reaction of incomprehensibility may well be under-stood. However, men still find it hard to come to terms with the fact that they, who had grown up with the belief that they could always 'protect' their women, failed, albeit against forbidding odds. These emotions of impotence seem to have been internalised or were mani-fested in the particularly gruesome acts of these 'refugees' into Pakistan, as they took 'revenge' on those (Hindus and Sikhs) who were still in West Punjab.

Sakina Bibi, of village Dalla Bora, recalls one such disruption of her family's lives:

> My mother was baking bread. We were urging her to get up, for a (Sikh) *Jatha* had come. She said that she would not leave until they had had something to eat. My brother removed the *tawa* (frying pan) and said 'get up, do you want to be left behind?' And then we left our home.

The violent transition from the private to public space is made even more difficult by the events taking place all around them. Large numbers of people fleeing violence around them gathered into groups, in some cases numbering 100,000, denied access to social amenities of the private space as might have been expected in 'normal' times. Privacy, it seems is the first casualty of such an entrance into the public domain and it was particularly bewildering for the women. Sakina Bibi continues:

At the crossing (of the river Ravi), there were just so many people. At that place, Hindus and Sikhs started killing people. I saw so many bodies of men and women who had been murdered. There were so many corpses; one was overcome with fear by seeing such a large number of bodies. It was time to beg for forgiveness (from God). There was nothing to eat, no way to sleep or go to a toilet. We had left with only the clothes we were wearing. We stayed on the river bank for six days before we were able to cross over to Pakistan.

When one remembers that time, one still gets goose bumps, what kind of a time was that. One asks for forgiveness. One's heart is fearful. It was a terrible time. Mothers were not able to look after their infant sons. Many of the children were thrown in the river so that the mothers could escape the Hindus and the Sikhs. There was chaos, just like *qayamat* (the day of judgement). No one cared for anyone else. They just wanted to escape from their attackers.

Many survivors' accounts convey a sense of personal confusion (following the rupture of the old life), loss of identity and an increasing focus on the minutiae of life on the move, a state of alertness to the particular which alone might contribute to survival. A number of subjects said that they became much more aware of their surrounding, factors like the presence of sugarcane plantations and the direction of the wind assumed critical importance in order to escape detection. They had to be very vigilant of water wells, for a number of them had been deliberately poisoned.

Allah Rakhi who now lives in Oorah, a village near Sialkot, talked about her experience during Partition:

I lived in Jindera Pind in Riasat Jammu. I had been married for five years when Pakistan came into being. Our village was fine until the night when it was attacked and someone came and warned us and said we should run away (*nassan waali ghal karo*). I remember running away at night along with many other women. We came to Jammu and then by train to Meera Sahib. From then onwards, all I remember are the killings. So many were killed.

My husband and his elder brother had already left for Pakistan sometime earlier. That is how they were able to survive. After we were attacked, no Muslim (man) remained to defend us women and we were abducted. They locked all of us in a school-like place for two or three days and teased us and misbehaved with us. Then I was taken to a house and had to live there. I was treated very badly. They told other people in the house not to let me get away to Pakistan. The border wasn't very far from that place (*Kehnde si raakhi karo, tur na jaye Pakistan*).

I lived like this for six years. I gave birth to two sons in this time. I had no idea of what had become of my family. The military used to come and enquire about abducted women but the villagers would lie and tell them there were none. One day, the military came and forced their way into our courtyard. I came out and told them that I had been abducted; they said that 'we have come to get you.' I got into the military car with my 10-month-old son. My captors would not let me bring my other son with me. He was two-years-old and I had to leave him behind. I remember they followed the military car all the way to Jammu. We arrived at a camp full of abducted women. A number of other women had not brought along their children, they had left them behind. We were eventually brought to Lahore. I remember one woman who kept trying to run back to Jammu.

Of course I remember that horrendous time, even to this day. It is impossible to forget. I still miss the son I left behind with my abductors. We did try to get him back but were unsuccessful.

A sense of immediate panic and utter confusion is apparent even when the events are narrated after such a long time. The instinctive reaction is to save oneself (*Nassan waali ghal karo*) and the focus is to get as far away as possible. There is an immediate break-up of the social mode of behaviour which had till then governed women's lives, for at the particular moment of attack, they had to fend for themselves.

Allah Rakhi, throughout the interview, never referred to people by their names. Even when she was asked the name of her 'husband' (whom she continued to refer to as an abductor) and the son that she left behind, she refused to acknowledge the question.

The injuries that seemed to crystallise Partition's violence were mostly inflicted on women of 'Other' groups. For it was through their bodies that 'Self' and 'Other' were defined as diametrically opposed notions of differentiation. In this binary opposition however, groups brutalised their own women because they thought that it was the best way of saving their honour. The most potent example of this notion manifested itself through the intensity with which women of each group were guarded from the 'Other'. There were numerous occasions in which the interviewees had been eye-witnesses to the savagery inflicted on women from one group by men from another, which included amputation of breasts, mass rape, parading them naked through public and religious places, cutting open the wombs of pregnant women, and tattooing their bodies with nationalistic and religious slogans. Ritu Menon and Kamla Bhasin explain this particular form of violence and the reasons behind it as actions that would last for much longer than the Partition itself. According to them:

> Marking the breasts and genitalia with symbols like the crescent moon or trident makes permanent the sexual appropriation of the woman, and symbolically extends this violation to future generations who are thus metaphorically stigmatised. Amputating her breasts at once desexualises a woman and negates her as wife and mother; no longer a nurturer (if she survives, that is), she remains a permanently inauspicious figure, almost as undesirable as a barren woman. Sudhir Kakar, in his exploration of how communities fantasise violence, says that sexual mutilation figures prominently: the castration of males and the amputation of breasts 'incorporate the (more or less conscious) wish to wipe the enemy off the face of the earth' by eliminating the means of reproduction and nurturing (Menon and Bhasin 1998: 44).

Women's bodies become markers of the violence of exclusionary nationalism and destructive communalism, which were the two major ideologies operating during the upheaval of Partition. Nusrat Maqbul, who worked as a volunteer nurse in Lahore, described the horror that people crossing from one side of the border to the other had to face:

> There was one train which came from Amritsar to Wagah in three days. Everybody, when I say everybody, I mean every adult was killed on that train. Most of the girls had been abducted. For three days there were some babies ... their mothers tried to protect them, many had died. We had to clean those children, bathe those children, feed those children. And the smell of blood. (She starts to sob, then apologises for becoming emotional). Young girls, 20-, 16-years-old, one breast chopped off, the other cut into such small pieces as if it was minced meat. I am sorry I have to tell you these gruesome stories. Women refugees told us that two men would get hold of their legs, open them up and with *kirpans* they ... Oh God ... they cut the private parts as if they chopped off a piece of baked meat. This was the condition. And it went on and on and on. Probably I was too young ... I could not take it after sometime and on doctor's orders I had to stop working there. But I can never forget the whole thing.

Most of such graphic details are never part of any written history, be it by the state or the individual. Oral literature, on the other hand, is how most of the population of Pakistan remembers the collective ordeal it went through. This form of articulation of memory of Partition has been marginalised for long enough, and has suffered because of the post-colonial nations' obsession with the colonial version of collecting and articulating a national history, which has always been in a written form. Orality demonstrates the complexities of remembering that cannot be captured in written literature and hence adds a dimension missing from the otherwise linear narrative. These collective voices need to be tapped into in order to create new, hybridised forms of national autobiography. Gyanendra Pandey has pointed out the need for inclusion of a variety of voices, some of which could construed as offering contradictory perspectives. He posits:

> Ultimately, too, we shall have to return to the question of the language of historical discourse and its ability to represent violence and pain and daily struggle. This refers not only to the vocabulary available to historians, but also the structure of their discourse. How do we structure or frame the histories that we write in order to allow some place for the bodies that carry the marks of these 'everyday'

(marginal, not so much lying outside as reworking the consequences of centralised production and representation) occurrences, and thereby often constitute the 'larger' events and processes of History? (Pandey 1994: 188–221).

Pandey's arguments are very pertinent to the urgent need of the collection of oral narratives of Partition if the subcontinent is to achieve a realistic understanding of what took place during that time. Historians and other academic scholars need to admit and understand that certain events involve such complexities and contradictions that articulating them might fall outside the realm of the tools that they might have at their disposal. It should not be such a difficult step if one acknowledges and appreciates the fact that in many cases, even the victims are unable to either comprehend or explain their traumas.

One of the primary aims of this paper was to avoid the rather unsophis-ticated tendency that state narratives have of generalising the experience of suffering. Instead, the idea is to give voice to various perspectives that assume the responsibility, and indeed accountability, as those who have experienced specific forms of human pain and are still able and willing to articulate their subjectivity, even when it is most threatened. Individual narratives, as Deleuze and Guattari's rhizomatic thought had outlined, make connections that are totally ignored by the 'vertical' and 'fact-based' discourse of 'official' history. These stories are rarely as single-mindedly simplistic as those employed by the state, whose meta-narrative chooses particular leaders, religious ideologies or a com-munity to cast as the entity solely responsible for everything that went wrong during Partition.

Women's narratives add a new dimension to the hitherto existing 'layer' of someone else describing their experiences. These narratives assert first steps, more than 55 years ago, to claim their subjectivity, to talk about their loss. How their 'private' domesticity was suddenly shat-tered by the events taking place in 'public' where they exercised little or no influence. These narratives are examples of how the convergence of individuals' memory constantly find ways to overcome state strictures in order to remember, recall and sustain the narrative that fosters a link with the past, which the state constantly attempts to make its own. It was felt that an awakened sense of self-awareness in these victims, through making their pain public, would go a long way in arousing similar feelings in the larger community. Women's sharing of private grief would add a human dimension to the sterile and reductive version of events which is expected to be accepted by the populace as the only 'authentic' version of what occurred during Partition.

Notes

1 The Subaltern Studies Group (SSG) or Subaltern Studies Collective are a group of South Asian scholars interested in the postcolonial and post-imperial societies of South Asia in particular and the developing world in general. The term Subaltern Studies is sometimes also applied more broadly to others who share many of their views. Their approach is one of history from below, focused more on what happens among the masses at the base levels of society than among the elite. Scholars associated with Subaltern Studies include Gayatri Chakravorty Spivak and Partha Chatterjee along with Gayan Prakash, Ranajit Guha, Shahid Amin, David Arnold, David Hardiman, Sumit Sarkar (later dissented), Gyanendra Pandey and Dipesh Chakrabarty.
2 The term 'partition' conjures up different meanings in the two countries. One can use terms like 'independence' or 'freedom' to describe the creation of Pakistan. However, I am using 'partition' rather unproblematically to describe the physical separation of India and Pakistan in 1947.
3 These interviews were carried out with the help of local informants. In a number of the interviews, the initial contact was made by a research assistant (RA) who then interviewed these women and wrote up a preliminary profile. On almost all the occasions, a female RA was used as it made the task of gaining access comparatively easier, and allowed the subject to feel more relaxed.
4 The firing by a machine gun is described by using an agrarian metaphor of a machine that mows down and evens out the crops. It could also describe a machine used for cutting hair. The over-riding image is of people either killed in large numbers, or of them crawling to escape indiscriminate firing.

References

Anderson, Benedict. 1983. *Imagined Communities: Reflections on the Origin and Spread of Nationalism*. London: Verso Publishers.

Butalia, Urvashi. 1998. *The Other Side of Silence: Voices from the Partition of India*. New Delhi: Viking Penguin.

Chakrabarty, Dipesh. 1996. 'Remembered Villages: Representation of Hindu-Bengali Memories in the Aftermath of the Partition', *Economic and Political Weekly*, 31(32): 2143–151.

Das, Veena. 1991. 'Composition of the Personal Voice: Violence and Migration', *Studies in History*, 7(1): 65–77.

Das, Veena and Ashis Nandy. 1986. 'Violence, Victimhood, and the Language of Silence', in Veena Das (ed.), *The Word and the World: Fantasy, Symbol and Record*, pp. 177–95. New Delhi: Sage Publications

Deleuze, Gilles and Felix Guattari. 1987. *A Thousand Plateaus: Capitalism and Schizophrenia* (trans. Brian Massumi). Minneapolis: University of Minnesota Press.

Klindienst, Patricia. 1984. 'The Voice of the Shuttle is Ours', *Stanford Literature Review*, 1: 31–51.

Lechte, John (ed.). 1994. *Fifty Key Contemporary Thinkers: From Structuralism to Postmodernity.* London: Routledge.

Menon, Ritu and Kamla Bhasin. 1998. *Borders and Boundaries: Women in India's Partition.* New Jersey: Rutgers University Press

Ovid. 1955. *Metamorphosis* (trans. Rolfe Humphries). Indiana: Indiana University Press.

Pandey, Gyanendra. 1994. 'The Prose of Otherness', *Subaltern Studies*, 8: 188–221.

Perks, Robert and Alistair Thompson (eds). 1998. *The Oral History Reader.* London: Routledge.

Rose, Gillian. 1993. *Feminism and Geography: The Limits of Geographical Knowledge.* Cambridge: Polity.

Schwartz, Barry. 1991. 'Iconography and Collective Memory: Lincoln's Image in the American Mind', *Sociological Quarterly*, 32: 301–19.

Walker, Janet. 1997. 'The Traumatic Paradox: Documentary Films, Historical Fictions, and Cataclysmic Past Events', *Signs*, 22(4): 803–26.

4

VIOLENCE AND HOME: AFGHAN WOMEN'S EXPERIENCE OF DISPLACEMENT

Saba Gul Khattak[*]

Introduction

This paper depends upon a collection of over 50 qualitative in-depth interviews with Afghan refugee women that were conducted during 2000–01.[1] The purpose was to investigate the gendered effects of conflict upon women. The interviews were conducted in the Pushto and Dari languages, and later transcribed and translated. We changed the names of the respondents for reasons of their personal security. Quotations in this paper are from the translated interviews.

The women we interviewed came from diverse backgrounds and experiences. A majority of them lived in and around Peshawar (Pakistan) in camps as well as in different neighbourhoods of the city. The interviews reveal multiple concerns and interpretations. Of course, these are class-bound and connected to the number of years/total time the respondent has spent in Pakistan, i.e., the stage she is at with regard to migration and change of location. The distance or immediacy of the violence that women encountered as well as the intensity of their loss also coloured the interviews.

There are several themes that emerge from the interviews we held with the Afghan refugee women regarding violence, peace, displacement, loss, death and hope. Of these themes, I chose to concentrate

[*]A shorter version of this paper appeared as 'Floating Upwards from History: Afghan Women's Experience of Displacement', in *Development*, 45 (1): March 2002: 105–10, *www.sidint.org/development*.

upon their conception and representations of home, as it captured several of the themes that we investigated and provided a lens with which to get a view of their myriad realities. Instead of allowing grand theory to categorise and guide, I made a conscious effort to let the women's voices speak and derive my analysis from their words rather than any preconceived ideas.

To facilitate further discussion, I divided their ideas into two broad schemes pertaining to their conception of home as a social and psychological space, and as a specific geographic location and structure. This is not to imply the binary division between mind and matter, or the material and sublime; the conceptions of home in the present context merge into one another and are simultaneously present at multiple levels in the discourses of refugee women. As the different representations of home in women's discourse simultaneously contain ideas of identity, culture, creativity, happiness and sadness, the past and the future, and security and insecurity, I have not attempted to segment them into neat categories. The ideas merge and emerge out of one another, and it is best to let them stay that way.

The next section discusses why it is important to examine the nexus between conflict, home and women in the context of international relations. The third section provides a brief summary of the Afghan conflict as a background to understanding Afghan women's experiences of conflict and insecurity. The fourth section is entirely devoted to women's voices as they talk about home with reference to conflict, and this is followed by the conclusion.

International Politics, Conflict, Women and Home

This paper discusses the constant disruptions in the uniform meanings of home for Afghan refugee women due to the direct impact of war upon their lives. To do so, we look at the different ideas that are contained within, and that underlie, the concept of home. In this regard, we take home to be more than the binary division of public and private, though this concept is at the root of the idea of home since it serves to include, as well as exclude, more or less like a state or a nation.

The constitution of private and public space is fundamentally an ideological divide that keeps shifting in accordance with changes in economic and social realities. This divide is also a gendered divide as men are associated with the public spheres of politics and work, and women associated with the private sphere of home and family. The state is identified with the public sphere, but its incursions extend into the private sphere as it legislates for the protection of the latter and by so doing continues to erect boundaries and separation between the two spheres. However, there is a definitional shift when one looks at the state in the context of international relations. The state as an entity among a polity of nations identifies itself with the home/the private sphere when it comes to issues concerned with internal policies. This is why it is possible to talk about domestic policy. However, the connection between the home (in its actual form) and the state in the context of violent conflict remains unseen. While a declaration of war is seen as an attack upon the greater home (the state), attacks on actual homes in the context of armed conflict is not taken into consideration at all and does not even emerge as an issue of concern.

As discussed earlier, while some of the functions of the home are similar to the state, one seldom comes across any mention of home in the context of international politics. This is so because the home is not accorded any importance or attention in international relations theory. In fact, one may criticise international relations (IR) theory as being limited in that it does not look at home as a construct that is integral to state formation and its continuation. In IR theory, the basic unit of analysis is the nation-state; even extra state actors such as parastatals and international organisations also constitute its subject matter, but the micro construct of home upon which the edifice of social life in a state is built/constructed is not part of international relations theory.

One associates wars with battlefields and with men, whether they ride horses, tanks, jeeps or helicopters and planes. Wars are associated with wide open spaces, public spaces, and not with homes. Homes are associated with women and with the family, hence they belong to the private sphere. International law regarding war and armed conflict re-inforces such dichotomies by making a difference between combatants (soldiers) and non-combatants (civilians), going into great detail about the areas that can be attacked or bombed, such as airfields, and areas that are outside the purview of war, such as homes and communities. Many of these laws have been ineffective and widely challenged by women's groups and victims of wars over the past decade, and before that by warring parties contesting the definition of combatant and non-combatant due to the involvement of entire populations in war efforts. Women's rights groups and other like minded groups question the public/private dichotomy and insist that sexual violence must be recognised as an instrument of war. Such groups have recently been successful in having rape declared as a war crime.

The recognition of rape as a war crime admits the fact that women constitute an integral part of war not only because women are women, but also because their bodies and beings have representational and symbolic value. Although rape and other forms of corporeal punishment and humiliation leave deep scars and are therefore of immediate concern, the destruction of homes and villages is also debilitating and is also used as an instrument of war to spread fear and intimidation. The tendency of marauding armies in the past to murder, loot and burn that which they could not carry with them resulted in the destruction of entire villages and communities. While this has been widely documented, very few people have looked at the issues that emerge out of these acts of violence.

The destruction of home and community has implications that go beyond the physical being of these places. These range from ideas of self, of identity, creativity, interpersonal relations and one's worldview. Some of these issues have been addressed and analysed by anthropologists in the context of recent conflicts. However, these accounts are generally restricted to documenting and observing changes in human relations in the context of individual violence such as murder, rape, ritualistic violence and so on. One seldom comes across accounts that make the connection between the violence of war and conflict in conjunction with the dislocation of people from their homes. This kind of violence is rarely discussed.[2]

In conjunction with the absence of home, the subject matter of IR theory and security studies is also devoid of the presence of women for the most part. This has been more than highlighted over the past two decades by feminist readings of international and security studies. Although a handful of women authors have brought women into the ambit of security studies, their work continues to be regarded as marginal by mainstream analysts (Elshtain 1987, 1990; Enloe 1983, 1989, 1993, 2000; Grant and Newland 1991; Peterson 1992, 1993; Reardon 1985; Tickner 1992). The paucity of writing by women and about women in IR texts leave intact gaps in our knowledge about the role of women in security, i.e., how they interpret security and how they require it. These limitations make it imperative to write this paper, as well as difficult to research since there is little to frame it in.

While there is little about the home in IR texts, feminist theory has addressed the issue of violence in the home effectively. Home is predominantly viewed as sacred because it is a fundamental unit of the private sphere and therefore outside the purview of the public sphere. The women's movement, spearheaded by feminists in the 1960s and 1970s, looked upon the home with suspicion as they exposed the myth of home as a nurturing sacred space and drew attention to the brutality and oppression women face when they question family values and challenge male authority.[3] The home, because it is the symbol of the private sphere, assured of privacy by the state due to the social contract, is guarded by patriarchal traditions as a space that cannot be questioned with the result that violence (predominantly perpetuated by men) can continue to go unquestioned so long as it does not result in murder. At times, even murder is condoned in the name of tradition or narrowly enforced morality. It was thus an important step forward to focus on the abusive aspect of the home—an aspect long accepted and seldom addressed to the advantage and protection of women.

Bringing domestic violence out of its centuries old closet is a critical contribution. In conjunction with other studies coming from the field, it appears that women continue to face violence in the home more intensely as they become refugees.[4] However, such a focus, crucial for understanding women's multiple oppressions, serves to divert attention from other equally important connections that revolve around the home in the context of violent conflict. In this regard, it is also important to view the relationship from other angles if we are to understand the complexity of women's experiences and the shaping of their relationship with home by war and conflict, especially when homes are targeted. In this context, home as the site for domestic violence becomes one aspect among others of women's complex experiences. It is these other aspects that are ignored by the dominant discourse, and that are not 'authenticated' by feminist or IR theory, which forms the crux of this paper.

Given these broad parameters, and given the gaps, this paper presents a women-centred analysis of a situation that affects both women and men deeply. The focus on women is particularly important as their voices are seldom included because of the assumption that these are represented by the so-called neutral social science that extends to everyone.

Afghan Women's Experience of Insecurity

There are several ways in which one can discuss the concept of home in the context of Afghan women refugees' lives. First, one can discuss it in the context of the most recent exodus, that of Afghans (mostly women and children) fleeing the American bombing of Taliban-held cities in Afghanistan starting 7 October 2001, following the events of September 11. This was preceded by an exodus of Afghans uprooted by drought and near famine situations. As the actors at the political helm of affairs changed, so did the refugees and their experience. To go back to the beginning then, one can talk about the initial phase of the conflict between the army of the former USSR and what may be generically termed the Afghan resistance from 1979 to 1992. This affected the lives of rural women as the source of resistance came from the more conservative sections of the population rather than the educated elite of Kabul. The second phase of the conflict began when the Mujahideen[5] took over Afghanistan from 1992 to1996. This phase affected the urban professional classes and resulted in their dislocation. This was also the beginning of the 'ethnic-isation' and 'sectarian-isation' of the conflict. The third phase of the conflict, with the coming of the Taliban in 1996, affected all women, irrespective of their class, sect or ethnicity.[6]

All of these changes have produced different types of refugees; additionally, there are many who repatriated and then returned to Pakistan as the violence and war did not subside. Although there have been different types of effects of the conflict upon the homes and lives of these different categories of women and refugees in general, yet there are some narratives that are common to all women. Over the course of the conflict, as bombs and rockets fell upon houses, people were forced to flee their homes as villages and cities became sites of fighting and terror. According to Trinh T. Minh-ha (1994: 12), the story of refugees 'exposes power politics in its most primitive form ... the ruthlessness of major powers, the brutality of nation states, the avarice and prejudice of people'. The story of Afghan refugees contain tales of terror unleashed by major powers and neighbouring states, as well as their own people. Their experience cannot be grouped under neat categories associated with exile, migration or refugee-hood. Indeed, their experience can be analysed in all these contexts and several others at several levels. Therefore, at one level, it does not matter whether the bombs are manufactured in the USA or the former USSR. What matters to the people is what the bombs do to them when they are dropped. As one Afghan woman in Pakistan, a recent refugee from the bombing, explained, *Jung sho— Kabul taa raalo* (Fighting erupted, and it reached Kabul) or as another woman put it in an understated way, 'The circumstances became unbearable', meaning that the bombing was horrendous. For the women then, what mattered was that they had to flee their homes in order to be secure.

This was the case much more for women than men who have some sensitivity to whose bombs are raining although many have learnt to distance themselves from the warring factions. For many of the poor displaced women and their children, the removal of the Taliban and the killing and looting carried out by the Northern Alliance is not tantamount to liberation, neither does the promise of democracy hold meaning. What they underscore is their need for peace (*qaraar-araami*). For example one respondent, when asked if her son would wage/continue the jihad (holy war), promptly emphasised that he would only work to establish peace. This is a contrast to the mother of 20 years ago who was willing to sacrifice her son's life for the war. The following section explains why such a phenomenon is possible today. The main focus is on women's relationship with home in the context of violent conflict.

Home and Afghan Refugee Women's Experience

The pain and suffering of Afghan refugee women indicate constant physical and psychological violence. This paper concentrates upon their experience of and relationship with home in the context of displacement. As discussed earlier on, we interpret home as a positive locus of identity for women rather than adhering to the feminist position considering home to be primarily the first site of oppression for women.[7] This is not to deny the validity of the feminist position, but to limit the parameters for the present analyses in the context of displacement.

The major themes that appear in the interviews pertain to the different associations with the idea of home in its physical as well as symbolic contexts. The leaving of home is not only about acquiring security, it is also symbolic of leaving behind a sense of identity, a culture, a personal and collective history. Indeed, the word 'home' has several connotations for women, hence, its leaving, its abandonment and its making are important. Women find it hard to grapple with the sense of danger and threat they associate with home as a result of the 21-year-old Afghan conflict. Instead of being a safe haven, home and homeland also represent a place of peril in the interviews. Displacement from home and country evoke a deep sense of loss and resentment as well as despondence. Simultaneously, there are constant attempts and thoughts of going back. These are accompanied by various recollections and depictions of home representing peace and plenty an important coping mechanism as there is hope that this memory can be revitalised sometime in the future. We thus find that there are several interpretations and representations of home—some of which are conflicting and paradoxical—that coexist in women's discourse of home and displacement.

Starting from the broader parameters of a conception of home, it is interesting to note that the word for country and home is used interchangeably: *watan*. When Afghan refugee women talk of going home, they talk about going back to their *watan* (there are obvious connections with the nation and nationalism to which we will return later). Home is thus intricately woven into the idea of belonging, belonging to a place and a community. In this sense, a person derives her/his sense of self from home, hence the saying 'to be at home'. Refugees and migrants are never quite at home in the countries and places that they live in since the sense of belonging and home is missing. This is because home also represents a way of life, a way of being, a culture, a way of thinking. Salman Rushdie, writing about refugees and migrants in his novel *Shame*, expresses their angst: 'We have come unstuck from more than land. We have floated upwards from history, from memory, from time' (cited in George 1999: 173). Leaving home is thus not a simple act of changing one's place of residence. It denotes a parting of ways with a life that one is familiar and comfortable with. This is so because one derives ones identity from one's sense of home.

Rosemary Marangoly George (ibid.: 19), giving an example of the equating of self and home, relies upon the psychoanalytical theory of Jung to demonstrate these connections. Jung, she writes, 'regarded an individual's home as the universal archetypal symbol of the self'. According to Jung the different rooms in a house represent a person's different selves and states of consciousness. This identification with the house is deeply embedded in the human psyche. George explains that this identification is a two way process whereby the home not only represents how one perceives one's self, but also stands for how others may perceive one. Therefore, the home is crucial for the perception of identity and many women consider it to be an extension of their selves. This is why there is so much emphasis upon teaching girls about house-keeping; they slowly learn to derive their identity and self-worth from the manner in which they keep their house clean and in order. There-fore, when they are forced to leave home—the space that they took great pains to build into a reflection of themselves, they suddenly feel bereft of an identity. The way one furnishes and decorates one's home—the furniture, the crockery, the cutlery and other material objects—have representational value as they reflect one's social and economic status. They are signifiers of a woman's personal talents as well. The following quote from an Afghan woman refugee named Rahila demon-strates this amply: '... Our family left our home just like that and didn't even carry a single spoon or a cup. We still don't have anything proper as we came to Peshawar with only the clothes that we were wearing at that time' (from SDPI Archive on Women, Conflict and Security, 2001).

Another woman refugee, Surraya, also stresses the paucity of material possessions that she could bring with her when she left home the first time and goes on to describe the second time she was forced to flee to Pakistan:

We left everything that we owned and came to Pakistan in the midst of a snowfall. With a broken heart we came towards Pakistan, leaving everything behind. All we had were just a few blankets.

The first time wasn't that difficult since I came alone. But this was the second time and I had my children with me. There was no end to the fighting so we came to Pakistan. We couldn't bring our belongings with us since there was no time to do that. All I had was a blanket and a basket that I carried in my hands.

It was a very difficult time. Some of us came here and others stayed back. All the assets that we had were left in Kabul. We just saved our skins and came here. When we came here, we received a tent at Nasir Bagh. Then houses were built for us. We lead a poor life here (from SDPI Archive on Women, Conflict and Security, 2001).

The story of another refugee woman, Farida, reproduces the same theme in a slightly different manner. Here she emphasises her helplessness and the complete absence of home as they had to live in a tent:

> In Pakistan we ended up in Nasir Bagh refugee camp, and at the time my son had pneumonia. I didn't know where to go, but God bless a Pakistani policeman who gave me a reference, due to which my child received medical attention. During our early days we were living in tents. Living in tents was very hard because it provided little protection from the harsh storms and summer heat. It took us a long time to get used to living in a tent. It was very hard for my children to live in a tent during the scorching heat of the summer. Due to such hard conditions we were forced to rent a house, but our neighbours kept bothering us because my husband had worked in the communist regime (from SDPI Archive on Women, Conflict and Security, 2001).

Farida also outlines the multiple problems connected with the location of a house. She was among the second wave of refugees who had fled Kabul after the Mujahideen took over; as such, first wave refugees who had fled the Russians and pro-communist regimes perceived her and her family as the enemy who were responsible for their plight. Thus the renting of a house did not ease her problems. Instead, her countrymen and women made her doubly uncomfortable in a second country due to her husband's job with the government.

The locale of home is thus not devoid of the larger politics of the country of origin. Since refugees either live in camps or tend to settle in similar neighbourhoods, they tend to reproduce the politics of their homeland in the host country. Sometimes families get enmeshed in such politics—a politics that can easily take a violent or threatening turn. The presence of friends and relatives in close proximity to the location of home is thus important for psychological security. Even on home ground, people often have contacts and relatives or friends upon whom they rely in times of crisis. As aliens without any reliable structures for protection, they rely much more heavily upon their informal networks of friends and relatives: 'We had a good life in Afghanistan when there was still peace. We had property and everything. Most importantly, we had relatives. Now we have no one. I lost my son ...' (SM from SDPI Archive on Women, Conflict and Security, 2001).

This demonstrates the sense of well-being and security associated with home, property, country and peace. For this respondent, the presence of relatives and her son are as important as the presence of property for a good life. Thus home is not only a structure, but is associated with a sense of security that is nourished through the existence of loved ones who will take care of one in times of need. Equally importantly, there is a sense of happiness connected with one's relatives as they are also a source of love and shared experiences of sadness and laughter. These are important relationships that provide a sense of identity and grounding due to shared values and shared lifestyles as well as experiences. For women more than men, these relationships that they have nurtured throughout their lives are an important resource and investment. Given their restricted mobility and limited knowledge of the outside world, their dependence upon these relationships is pivotal to their security.

While many women's experience of life was restricted to the home, this did not mean that the home was a prison. Even as they are physically restricted to the 'refuge of the father' (Minh-ha 1994: 15) they are able to transcend the confines of home through writing, imagination and storytelling. Home is thus a place from where the imagination can take off without fear—from where one can undertake several journeys that are inexhaustible in their scope and width. This is how many women are able to express their ideas and concerns and communicate with the outside world. For many women writing and creativity are possible only when there is a secure and settled life ensured through the existence of a stable unthreatened home. The forced retreat from home affects women's creativity. As one respondent explained,

> I was always interested in writing poetry, even when I used to live in Khanabad. When I came to Kabul I started writing for both Pushto and Dari magazines and newspapers. I even won a literary prize for my writings .... I was very interested in writing but due to the outbreak of war, things started to change. There was danger most of the time, as a result I worked occasionally but I kept writing and had contact with the papers. I saw the bad effects of war; people were recruited by force into the army, and girls faced problems going outside. (Wajia, from SDPI Archive on Women, Conflict and Security, 2001).

The disruption of peace through violent conflict affected women's creativity in other ways as well. In a bid to save their lives and their loved ones, they were preoccupied entirely with escaping into safety. Under such circumstances, as one respondent poignantly said, 'I was in such a hurry that I cannot remember the way I came through here from Afghanistan. I was anxious. How could I remember the poetic collection? I was not sure of survival here' (Nausherwan, from SDPI Archive on Women, Conflict and Security, 2001).

Given the fact that war creates fundamental anxieties about existence and survival, it embodies insecurity in the form of the rupture with home. Leaving home becomes symbolic of the larger insecurity where one is unable to guard against the outside and is therefore forced to abandon the most sacred of places—the home.

This is so because this space for refuge—the home—is protected in patriarchal societies by the figure of the father. This is why the physical leaving of home implies entrance into uncertainty as one crosses into unprotected terrain. This is why it is often assumed to be acceptable if women are harassed outside their home as the underlying logic is that they should not have left the refuge of the father. In other words, they are assumed to have 'asked for it' (Minh-ha 1994: 15). In much the same way, the loss of country is also synonymous with the loss of home, and in the case of refugee women, both occur simultaneously. The deep psychological insecurity therefore exists at multiple levels. As they leave their home, they leave behind various familial relationships; as they leave their country, they leave behind the larger familial metaphor represented by nation, culture, history and identity. As they enter a new country, the sense of exposing themselves to the danger of the unknown, to harassment in a male domain for which they were neither prepared nor trained, takes on frightening proportions. The patriarch who protects, the interchangeable father and the state, is absent and unable to protect. Displacement is thus not a simple fact of changing one's place and country of residence. It has deep-seated psychological repercussions.

The psychological sense of security associated with home is not only turned on its head, but the home which provides nourishment becomes the very place that leads to death. It becomes a metaphor for the grave. Furthermore, the constantly changing forms of the 'enemy' (ranging from the Russians to the Soviet-supported governments to the Mujahideen, the Taliban, the Northern Alliance and now the Americans) make it hard to single out one identifiable phenomenon and associate it with insecurity. In the case of Afghanistan, there are multiple enemies and one does not know which one is worse or which one will strike. A Freudian analysis might lead one to assert that this

coming together of the grave and place of security is symbolic of harken-
ing back to the mother's womb, which is both a space for security as
well as a watery grave. Of course, such a notion of home is not applicable
across cultures, but in the present context it might make an interesting
interpretation that may be well worth exploring further. One may begin
by asking if home, in the context of violence, pushes a person back to a
helpless fetal state in which danger may come from any direction, including the mother's body itself. Thus the inability to identify a clear
enemy on the one hand, and the possibility of the government/state/
patriarch being the enemy on the other, results in deep trauma.[8] The
following quote, where the respondent could not tell whose rockets
and bombs were killing the people, makes this very clear:

> Missiles came and landed. What was it! It was a kind of war. Our
> home was down the mound. On one side was Tina Pass mound and
> on the other side we had the Bala Hisar, and on another side the
> Special Guard … we were surrounded from all four sides. Bombs
> from all sides landed on our area. Many people died in our area. In
> every home, if there were four persons, all four died; if there were
> five, five died; if there were six, six died; if there was one, that one
> died. People lost their assets as well as lives.

> Day and night the planes kept coming and conducted bombardments
> which destroyed our homes. Nothing was left. Wealth and property
> was destroyed. We were left with nothing, not even enough to cross
> over to Pakistan. There were also children. On one occasion, the
> bullets would come from the Mujahideen while on the other from
> the government's soldiers. There was heavy war … (Roshan SR,
> from SDPI Archive on Women, Conflict and Security, 2001).

The inability to identify one single enemy makes the experience of
displacement harder. When everyone becomes the enemy, 'othering'
for peace becomes increasingly difficult so that practical/implementable
options are hard to visualise. Under such conditions, women are unable
to provide or envision strategies for peace and reconstruction. Thus,
the possibility of an indigenous feminist or women-centred formula
for peace remains non-existent or latent.

Indeed, the Afghans whose hopes of achieving their objectives
for peace have been destroyed due to having fled from their country
twice, and sometimes thrice, demonstrate why their visions of peace

are singularly unimaginative. It would be very hard to go through the
devastating experience of violence over and over again and still stay
optimistic about the future. The following is a moving account, and
I include it here not because it is a solitary voice but because it is representative of many other similar voices. This particular narrative is about
the double trauma of going back to Afghanistan only to find out that
conditions did not change with a change in government and hence the
respondent's decision to come back:

We went. When the Islamic government took over, our whole family went back. Our home was in Kabul. We had been punished enough.
We had seen many hardships during our refugee life and gone through
helplessness and loneliness. We thought perhaps we would find peace
in our homeland. But when we went, rockets were launched on the
very first day. Our father had told us that there would be peace but
there was fighting everywhere. Not for a single day did we have
happiness. We spent the whole night in fear as rockets were being
launched constantly. These were Engineer Sahib's rockets. At that
time they were known as 'Engineer Sahib's rockets'.[9]

… One day rockets were launched constantly and towards the late
afternoon my cousin came and told my mother that my uncle had
been martyred…. All our family has been destroyed in this revolution … we were all frightened. My father was left with small children and we were so grief stricken that we didn't know what to do.
When they left my brother and we (three sisters) remained in the
house. Toward the afternoon our houses and our whole colony
was put under siege. When we inquired we were told that war had
broken out between Shoravi (the pro-Russian government) and the
Hizb-Islami. This is what our neighbours said. We were surprised
and confused about the war. What if it never ended? If they broke
into our house what would we do? We used to buy bread from the market and that day there was not a single piece in the house. We didn't
know what to do, especially with the small children. We were having
feelings of regret. We wished that we had gone back and had not
stayed here. We stayed hungry in the house with the children for
two days and two nights. Rockets were constantly launched. No
one could go out nor could anyone come in from outside. We had
no hope for life. We always thought that any time a rocket would
fall and hit our heads. After two days the siege was over. They went

away after satisfying themselves. Many people died or were injured. We told our father that it was better to be without a homeland than to be living in such a homeland. So we came back to Pakistan. (Rahila, from SDPI Archive on Women, Conflict and Security, 2001).

The sense of being trapped and the wish to leave one's home and homeland makes Rahila equate the security of home with 'un-homeness', so that by rejecting the physical edifice of home and the territory of a country one can achieve security. Rahila (ibid.) goes on to describe the final event that convinced her father to return to Pakistan once again as a refugee:

I told my father that we wanted to go back to Pakistan but he did not agree. He said that the war would be over one day. When he did not agree with us, we prepared ourselves to combat the rockets and stay ... when I was coming back [from my uncle's house] towards my house, which was located on a roadside, a rocket fell and hit a bus and then a taxi. Both burst into flames.... I have a habit that I always wear white clothes. When I looked at my clothes they had shreds of human flesh on them. They looked like raindrops.

... I could not tolerate it anymore and I ran towards my house when another rocket came and hit our house. I was injured again. I was very seriously injured because when I regained consciousness I was in a hospital in Peshawar in Pakistan.

Rahila's experience of displacement is not an ordinary one if we compare it to non-refugee populations. However, for the Afghan refugees, such stories have managed to acquire 'normalcy' due to their repeated occurrence. Connected with the double trauma of going back and returning to the country of refuge is also the constant shifting and wandering of the refugees within the host country. Shifting from camps to homes and from there to other cities, in search of safety and livelihoods, is an inhospitable experience as the host population looks upon the refugees as anathema.

We migrated from Afghanistan for the first time 15 years ago because the Russians bombed our home. My uncles were mujahideen and had their own front. Therefore, it was difficult for us to live there. So we migrated to Pakistan and lived in a camp. My family moved

to Quetta to live there ... for the second time when the Najib government collapsed, we went to our country. We went there with the
hope that our country would be free, women would be free and that
we would live in peace. None of our dreams came true. When we
went there, the situation was worse for women. There was war,
rockets and rocket firing. It was the game of jihadis.[10] They fought
for the seat of power. They did not care whether people lived or
died.

... After one or one-and-a-half years, we came back, because conditions for education were not suitable. There was no school. Schools
were closed. There was a war going on. Girls were abducted, it happened in broad daylight. We came back. (S J, from SDPI Archive on
Women, Conflict and Security, 2001).

While there were those who shifted back and forth in the hope of
settling back in their country eventually, there were others whose villages
were completely destroyed and who are unable to relate to a country to
go back to. These are the people who are extremely poor and have no
home and nowhere to go. After the destruction of their village and
their way of life they live life as if they are outside the state. The sense of
belonging is absent and there is no grand narrative, either of the state
or of peace, to relate to.

But that [Afghanistan] is also not our country (*watan*). We are not
only refugees here [in Pakistan] but also there [in Afghanistan]. We
have no village (*watan*) anywhere. Today we are here and tomorrow
there. Now the landlord has asked us to vacate this place but we
don't have money to shift. (Fareeda, from SDPI Archive on Women,
Conflict and Security, 2001).

Although the Afghan refugee women are unable to 'make sense'
and narrativise[11] their collective experience at present, this does not
preclude a common theme of a golden past that they would like to re-
create. They usually begin with emphasising how good life was in
Afghanistan. In fact, all respondents underscore this view. It comes
repeatedly, irrespective of whether they were rich or poor. This is often
done in great details: descriptions of meals—breakfasts, entertainment
when guests arrived—images of plenty. Very few talk of other aspects
of well-being. This past associates home with happiness and plenty,

and is basically dependent upon a dreamlike memory of the homeland. To the question as to how life was in Afghanistan, the following is a fairly representative sample:

Life was good there. Nights were good. One's own country is always beautiful. Have you not heard the Pashto couplet that nobody leaves his/her country (*watan*) with their own consent but either because they become poor or out of grief for his/her beloved. Our country and houses have to be built again. At the moment our houses are destroyed and this is the life we face day in and day out (Roshan, from SDPI Archive on Women, Conflict and Security, 2001).

The present inability to imagine a future is poetically explained as a mistake in having forgotten to ask God for peace:

What we regret mostly is that we wish to God that our visit to Afghanistan had brought us happiness and we could see what our country was like ... what did we see in our country? War and bloodshed! We only saw bloodshed and war in our homeland and we returned to Pakistan with these images in our minds.

We had forgotten what happiness was. We prayed to God to give us our homeland but we did not ask for our peace and security there. Perhaps we had asked Him to give us our country but forgot to ask Him to grant peace along with it. This was a mistake that we made. (Rahila, from SDPI Archive on Women, Conflict and Security, 2001).

Conclusion

This paper addresses how women fare during times of conflict on the home front, and why there are ruptures in the meaning of home as the result of war, and tries to highlight the depth and extent to which the multiple meanings of home impact women.

While some studies indicate that in fact wife abuse increases in refugee situations, the focus of the present analysis is on the meanings of home. Among these meanings, home becomes a symbol of violence when it comes to a woman's relationship with a man and patriarchal authority. However, her own relationship with the house/home is different in that it represents a sanctuary—even if it is a patriarchal one. Home is the source of primary identity for women not only because both are associated predominantly with the private sphere, but also because home is the locus of self, culture and belonging. This is true for men as well as women; however, due to the historical role that women play in the making of home, they identify much more with it.

Women's understanding and representations of home involve multiple themes that relate to both the physical as well as imagined and intangible aspects. Aside from being a reflection of self, social and economic status, home represents the space where women can be happy and secure, where they can be creative and where they enjoy familial support. At the same time, due to the extreme degree of violence and destruction that has been perpetrated due to the war, home and country are no longer symbols of protection and security. Both mirror the peril they contain for the very people they need to shelter and protect. This peril has been experienced several times, leading to double and triple trauma as the Afghan refugees keep fleeing back from their country and their homes in the face of constant bombings and fighting. This process has also rendered some women completely homeless so that they are unable to conceptualise the presence of a place that may be called home.

The themes that emerge from the interviews are about the destruction resulting from war and deaths due to rocket attacks and the yearning to go back to the place that was home and that now lies destroyed. Many talk about the double trauma of returning under the Mujahideen only to find the same destruction and senseless war continuing and that they were as insecure as they had been previously. There is thus a sense of betrayal that is not alleviated by the sense of alienation in Pakistan. Their house is not 'home'—it is a place, a mud house, a rented house, a camp or a tent. It is not home. There are constant thoughts of returning home and this prevents them from coming to terms with the present. Their refusal to accept their move as final (something their hosts also do not want them to do) makes them feel that the present is 'temporary' even though it has affected their lives very deeply and permanently.

We also conclude that displacement, whether within one's country or outside of it, has implications not only about physical security but also anxieties about non-material aspects that form the basis of our identities, of who we are. These issues involve shifting identities, ruptures in their meanings and our perceptions of ourselves and others' perceptions of us. These identities also have to do with being men and women. For many women memory is an important coping mechanism. Memory serves to preserve their class and social identities, and also their national identities and association with their country as something beautiful. However, simultaneously the memory of violence prevents them from narrativising their individual experience into collective history or collective consciousness.

I do not wish to end on a note of pessimism. As a social scientist, I would like to see new spaces being created by Afghan refugee women in the midst of the tremendous violence they face. I am confident that these spaces and a new politics will eventually be formed; however, for the time being, we need to recognise that having undergone multiple traumas at multiple levels, they require respite and some breathing space—a space and time for personal and collective healing to take place and for creativity to be able to take off. For us to expect towering narratives of courage and indigenous exotic wisdom and survival is to begin to impose a new colonising idea and discourse upon them.

Notes

1 These interviews with Afghan refugee women were conducted as part of an SDPI project entitled 'Women, Conflict and Security in Pakistan'. They constitute the SDPI Archive on Women, Conflict and Security, 2001.
2 There are some excellent accounts though; e.g., Carolyn Nordstrom (1997) Patricia Lawrence (2000) and Pamela Reynolds (2000).
3 See O'Toole and Schiffman (1997: 243–304) for a comprehensive history of the issue as well as other issues related to domestic violence in section 3.
4 I am grateful to Urvashi Butalia who pointed out that studies of women in Kashmir indicate that as the struggle for autonomy from India intensified, so did domestic violence. In Kashmir some studies also indicate that many women have also become immune to violence and become perpetrators in the home context as well as the public sphere.
5 The Mujahideen (literally freedom fighters) were a coalition of seven Pakistan-based Afghan political parties that took over from the Najibullah regime. The coalition of extremely conservative and middle of centre religious parties could not last long as there was internal dissent over who would exercise power.
6 The Taliban (literally students of religion), supported and trained by the Pakistani Inter Services Intelligence (ISI) agency, occupied more than 80 per cent of the country until their fall in early 2002 and had imposed a very conservative (mis)interpretation of Islam upon the country. Afghan women have been impacted in the most disastrous manner by these policies that restrict them to the home and deny them the right to earn a livelihood or acquire education.

7   I am grateful to Farzana Bari, Women's Studies Center, Quaid e Azam University, Islamabad, who pointed out that I was looking at the home in a very positive way, whereas the home is not always a positive space in women's lives. While I acknowledge that even in the present context Afghan refugee women feel that the home has become a place of confinement and imprisonment for them, there are also other over-riding aspects of the issue that are generally neglected and therefore not a part of the dominant discourse. Also, because I have let women's voices guide me rather than imposing my own narrative upon them, I have tried to analyse the themes that surface in their interviews.

8   Similar comparisons of the home with the grave occur in several interviews, e.g., a later description also highlights the same feeling of being caught in a space from where escape becomes impossible in the face of unpredictable and long periods of rocket attacks.

9   The reference is to the then Mujahideen Prime Minister, Engineer Gulbadin Hikmatyar. Thus the implication is that, ironically enough, the government itself was attacking and destroying the Afghan people.

10 The word jihadis, meaning those who wage jihad (holy war) is being used here interchangeably with mujahideen.

11 I borrow the usage of this word from Katherine Pratt Ewing (2000: 251) who writes about the denial of a narrative and women's inability to narrativise Turkish Muslim womanhood.

References

Elshtain, Jean Bethke. 1987. *Women and War*. New York: Basic.

Elshtain, Jean Bethke and Sheila Tobias (eds). 1990. *Women, Militarism and War: Essays in History, Politics and Social Theory*. Savage: Rowman & Littlefield.

Enloe, Cynthia H. 1983. *Does Khaki Become You? The Militarization of Women's Lives*. London: South End press.

———. 1989. *Bananas, Beaches and Bases: Making Feminist Sense of International Politics*. Berkeley: University of California Press.

———. 1993. *The Morning After: Sexual Politics at the End of the Cold War*. Berkeley: University of California Press.

———. 2000. 'The Prostitute, the Colonel and the Nationalist', in Cynthia H. Enloe, *Maneuvers: The International Politics of Militarizing Women's Lives*, pp. 49–107. Berkeley: University of California Press.

Ewing, Katherine Pratt. 2000. 'The Violence of Non-recognition: Becoming a "Conscious" Muslim Woman in Turkey', in Antonius C.G. Robben and Marcelo M. Suarez-Orozco (eds), *Culture Under Siege, Collective Violence and Trauma*, pp. 248–71. Cambridge: Cambridge University Press.

George, Rosemary Marangoly. 1999. *The Politics of Home, Postcolonial Relocations and Twentieth Century Fiction*. Berkeley: University of California Press.

Grant, Rebecca and Kathleen Newland (eds). 1991. *Gender and International Relations*. Indianapolis: Indiana University Press.

Lawrence, Patricia. 2000. 'Violence, Suffering, Amman: The Work of Oracles in Sri Lanka's Eastern War Zone', in Veena Das, Arthur Kleinman, Mamphela Rampheles and Pamela Reynolds (eds), *Violence and Subjectivity*, Berkeley, Los Angeles and London: University of California Press.

Minh-ha, Trinh T. 1994. 'Other than Myself/My Other Self', in George Robertson, Melinda Mash, Lisa Tickner, Jon Bird, Barry Curtis and Tim Putnam (eds), *Travellers' Tales: Narratives of Home and Displacement*. London: Routledge.

Nixon, Rob. 1994. 'Refugees and Homecomings: Bessie Head and the End of Exile', in George Robertson, Melinda Mash, Lisa Tickner, Jon Bird, Barry Curtis and Tim Putnam (eds), *Travellers' Tales: Narratives of Home and Displacement*. London: Routledge.

Nordstrom, Carolyn. 1997. *A Different Kind of War Story*. Philadelphia: University of Pennsylvania Press.

O'Toole, Laura L. and Jessica R. Schiffman. 1997. *Gender Violence, Multidisciplinary Perspectives*. New York: New York University Press.

Peterson, V.S. 1992. 'Introduction', in V.S. Peterson (ed.), *Gender States. Feminist (Re) Visions of International Relations Theory*, pp. 1–29. Boulder: Lynne Rienner Publishers.

Peterson, V.S. and A.S. Runyan. 1993. *Global Gender Issues*. Boulder: Westview Press.

Reardon, Betty A. 1985. *Sexism and the War System*. New York: Teachers College Press.

Reynolds, Pamela. 2000. 'The Ground of All Making: State, Violence, the Family, and Political Activists', in Veena Das, Arthur Kleinman, Mamphela Rampheles and Pamela Reynolds (eds) *Violence and Subjectivity*. Berkeley, Los Angeles and London: University of California Press.

5

MIGRATION/DISLOCATION: A GENDERED PERSPECTIVE

Urvashi Butalia

I

This paper is part of a longer work-in-progress, and basically presents an initial set of questions that have arisen for me in the course of that work. In the main, these relate to issues to do with the gendered nature of migration, more specifically migration caused by violent conflict, a phenomenon that is becoming increasingly common all over the world today. My attempt is to unpack the meanings of words such as 'migration', 'dislocation' and 'displacement', their relationships with the ways in which political and geographical spaces are constructed, and to try and understand some of the differences, as well as the overlaps, that they encompass. As well, I would like to understand how migrants and dislocated people are received and perceived, and how they perceive themselves, in different contexts, and what notions of belonging, nation and citizenship come to mean for them, more specifically in terms of gender.

As a first step, I would like to begin by tracing the trajectory that has brought me to this work. Several years ago I published a book on the partition of India, a set of oral histories of those who had lived through the violence of the partition. My attempt was to focus specifically on the experiences of women, children, the aged, and those on the margins of society, particularly Dalits. One of the things that research and writing on Partition foregrounded at the time—and mine was not the only such work, there were, and continue to be others (Das 1995; Kaul 2000; Menon and Bhasin 1998)—was the experience of the thousands of women who were abducted and raped, or sold into slavery and prostitution, or forcibly married to their abductors. The history of the rape and abduction of women is by now well known, and I do not need to rehearse it afresh here. But let me just briefly outline some of its key aspects.

The scale of women's 'disappearances' (for which read abductions) became clear within a few months after Partition, as family after family began to report the loss of their women. A unique, and completely unexpected, problem now confronted the new fledgling states and forced them to act. They did so by setting up search committees—made up of police and women social workers—who were allowed to go into the 'other' country (barring certain sensitive areas) and seek out the women who had been abducted. (Interestingly, in India, while there were rapes and abductions in both the west and the east, and search parties sought out women as well, on the eastern side these did not have official, that is, state, sanction. Rather, they were set up by women's groups and others.) But how were the search parties to decide on who had been abducted and who not? A workable rule of thumb that was followed was that if a Muslim woman was found living with a Hindu man in India, or if a Hindu woman was found with a Muslim man in Pakistan, after a certain date, it was assumed that the relationship must be a forcible one, and the woman therefore abducted. Thus, the majority of abducted women found in India were Muslim, and therefore it was assumed that they belonged now to Pakistan, just as the majority of abducted women found in Pakistan were Hindu and Sikh and it was therefore assumed that they belonged to India.

The fate of the large numbers of women who were thus abducted became a matter of concern to the state once their families began to file complaints, and once a well known and influential woman, Mridula Sarabhai, swore an affidavit in India testifying to the terrible conditions in which abducted women found themselves. Her class and influence ensured that she was given a hearing, and, as a result, the governments of Pakistan and India came together to discuss the problem. They arrived at an understanding (later given legal shape) to set up search parties made up of women social workers and the police, authorised to look at reports and go into clearly demarcated 'interior' areas, in search of abducted women. Women thus located had to be brought back to what was defined as their 'home': Hindu women were to be brought back to India and Muslim women to Pakistan, no matter that this might not correspond to their real homes. It was a curious paradox for the Indian state, for India perceived itself as a secular, rational and modern nation, and religion was not what defined its identity. Yet women, theoretically equal citizens of this nation, were being defined in terms of religious identity. Thus the 'proper' home for Hindu and Sikh women presumed to have been abducted was India, home of the Hindu and Sikh religion, and for Muslim women it was Pakistan, home of the Muslim religion. In neither case was the home these women might actually have chosen a consideration, for the notion, and indeed the space, of home had changed. No longer was it the boundary of the domestic that defined home; rather, it was the boundary of the nation. But even here, choice was not so easily defined. At Partition, every citizen theoretically had a choice as to which nation he or she wished to belong: it was a choice unavailable to women. Although accurate figures are hard to come by, the assumption was that about 100,000 women had been thus abducted on both sides of the newly formed borders. By the time the Central Recovery Operation, as it came to be known, came to an end in 1954, the numbers of women who had been 'recovered' were 7,981 in Pakistan (these were Hindu and Sikh women) and 16,168 in India (these were Muslim women) (Butalia 1998; Menon and Bhasin 1998).

The Central Recovery Operation came to an end for a variety of reasons, key among which was the fact that many 'recovered' women found that by the time they came back, or were brought back, to their natal families, they were no longer acceptable and the families refused to take them back. In the rare case that the family did accept the woman back (often after she had been made to undergo a purification, or *shuddhi*, ceremony to cleanse her of the pollution she had been subjected to, through sexual contact with a man of the 'other' religion), her children, if any, were totally unacceptable. As the boundary of home opened up beyond the domestic space to encompass the national space, the boundary of family closed in to become a 'pure' space, which then did not allow for any 'external' influence to enter it.

II

The mass movement of people as a consequence of the British decision to partition the country has been called the 'largest human migration known to history'. It took place on the western border of India over roughly a three-month period, and then it tapered off, with small groups of people or individuals crossing over from time to time. On the eastern border, which remained much more porous, the crossings were spread out over a much longer period. Initially, many Hindu families chose to stay on in East Pakistan (later Bangladesh) but with each political upheaval, and as the country became more Islamised and less comfortable for minorities, migrations took place. The number who crossed over on both sides was counted in several millions.

In the past, and even today, like many others, I too have used the descriptive phrase 'the largest human migration known to history' often, when speaking of Partition. And yet, I have wondered about it. What was it about that movement of people that made it a 'migration' as opposed to a 'dislocation'? While much literature on this mass movement does speak of the dislocation of entire communities, in common parlance, the word that is used to describe the phenomenon is 'migration'. What exactly are the meanings these two words carry? Does one, in some way, imply an element of choice and the other an element of coercion? Discussions on migration also often make use of the associated/related terms 'refugees' and 'displacement'. A recent UN document makes the distinction between these two terms as follows: 'Those who move within their own countries are known as displaced, those who leave their countries and cross borders are designated as refugees' (UNRISD 2005). Yet, as we will see, the distinctions are not so easily made, particularly when people of the same or similar ethnicities move across borders. The use of the word migration also implies a movement from somewhere, to somewhere, and yet, the 'from' and 'to' of migration become real when places get demarcated in political terms, for example, and borders are drawn to separate them—as happened with Partition and the drawing of new national boundaries.

Whenever Partition is spoken about, there is another ambivalence that comes up: the longer-drawn out move at the eastern border of India is somehow seen to be less devastating, less 'serious' in its consequences, than the movement across the western border which basically lasted three months (although, as we shall see below, periodic migration continued here too for a long time afterwards). This is evident even in the responses of the state: refugees or migrants from the west, for example, received and were entitled to much more compensation than refugees or migrants from the east. Somehow, both the brevity or length of time, and the fact that people moved, theoretically of their own free will, invest this move with a different kind of importance than other kinds of moves. If brevity or the length of time is one consideration, another is the collective nature of certain migrations—for the mass movement of people is usually taken to be of a more serious nature than individual movement.

The context in which people moved during Partition was one of terrible violence and fear. And yet, in some ways, 'choice'—a choice made and exercised largely by men—also entered the picture somewhere. In the small village of Dinanagar in what became Pakistan, Sikh families fearing attacks from Muslims decided to leave en masse. This decision, however, did not include the women who were seen as being vulnerable and weak, and therefore open—more so than the men—to sexual assault, rape and conversion. Their 'choice' therefore, was between death and sexual violation—death at the hands of their 'own' men, and sexual assault at the hands of the 'other'. These would-be 'migrants' therefore faced death, and many families were guilty of killing their own women, ostensibly in order to prevent them from getting raped, converted and/or impregnated. While many such incidents took place in Punjab, thereby preventing large numbers of women from 'migrating', on the eastern border we have very different examples of the exercise of male choice. In the aftermath of Partition, Sealdah station in Calcutta, for example, was flooded with women, who had been forcibly sent away—by their men—from East Pakistan where they had their ancestral homes, because the men felt East Pakistan was no longer secure (Chakravarty 2004: 46). How do we explain these different choices, both on the part of men—the one to keep (and kill) their women, thereby raising them to the level of martyrs, the other to 'send' their women away, and therefore presumably ensure their safety (although of course such a move begs the question of how 'safe' the women would have been at Sealdah station, a public place no doubt, but with all the attendant dangers)? In neither case was women's agency the principal one. In theory, everyone had a choice to move or to stay, but in practice, staying on was virtually impossible, and most people therefore 'chose' to leave, or had this 'choice' forced upon them. Within that broad realm of choice, there were many layers. Where women were concerned, the 'choice' of whether to move or to stay, or to return (as in the case of recovered abducted women) were constantly choices that were being made for them, the assumption being that they were incapable of making these choices themselves. There are no records, and barely any anecdotes, that tell of women exercising a choice about where to migrate, when to leave, often even what to carry—although here they did have some autonomy. It is also important to note that men's fears for women's safety were not unfounded: women are particularly vulnerable at such times and the widespread rape and abduction of women shows exactly how much danger they were in. But the question remains: why were women not allowed, by and large, to be party to discussions about their own, and their families', fate? In exercising the choice to move, people headed to places where they felt they would be safe, with their own kind, leaving behind people who were now, by virtue of belonging to the same community or religion, also safer because they were with their own kind. Both of these assumptions, of course, proved completely untrue. Violence has marred the lives of many migrants into India, and indeed those who left from India, just as it has marred the lives of those who stayed on. For the women who turned up in their thousands at Sealdah station, for example, while they may have fled one situation of insecurity, the new 'home' had little to offer, at least initially. Many had nowhere to go, and the station became their home for long periods of time, during which they were vulnerable to all kinds of violence and attack, and many were lured away into prostitution (ibid.).

The gendered narrative of partition migration thus rehearses the age-old pattern of males as actors and decision-makers and females as passive accepters. The silences in this meta-narrative about women, the absence of their voices in the narrative itself, and in history writing generally, has ensured that this remains the most prominent representation of women. The stories of abducted women, however, rupture this narrative and throw into question the whole notion of migration, not only in a collective form but also individually, just as they question notions of choice and its gendering. When we begin to ask, for example, what this mass migration of five to six million people meant for women, we are immediately confronted by the narratives of raped and abducted women. Abducted women crossed the border between the two countries twice—and other borders perhaps many more times—and at neither time was this of their own free will. In the larger context of the 'migration' of Partition, how do we view these women? Were they too 'migrants', or were they 'dislocated women', and victims of history? Unlike the majority of Partition migrants, women who were abducted did not choose to go where they were taken (although an element of 'choice' may have entered their lives at a later stage when they were being 'recovered' and many refused to leave), nor did many of them choose to be brought 'back' to their 'homes', or the newly

defined spaces of the nation (with which they were probably quite unfamiliar). What then does this enforced movement make them? There
are further complexities here. A recent study on women refugees in
post-Partition Bengal throws some light on this question, and shows
that the experience of women migrants/refugees/abductees/dislocated
women was extremely variable, and in some cases also led to their involvement in political activism (ibid.). In examining this aspect, this
study points to a crucial dimension of the process of migration, which
is the aftermath. The process of migration/dislocation is the actual process of movement, but it does not end there, for movement has to be
followed by some kind of settlement, which, in turn, can and usually
does lead to social change. For many migrants, this is the most difficult
moment for it is when settlement begins to lead to social change that
the initial welcome that migrants may (and they do not always have
this) have received turns to concern and resentment. Literature on migration to Assam, one of the most conflicted states in north-eastern
India, where the question at the root of the conflict has been the authen-
ticity of the 'indigenous' peoples as opposed to that of migrants, shows
how the initial waves of migrants were welcomed and even encouraged by political parties who stood to gain in the form of votes, and it
was only when their presence began to put pressure on land that the
tide began to turn against them. Tensions are apparent among communities who settled in different places in the aftermath of Partition as
well, the most notable of these being the migrants (mohajirs) in Sind
in Pakistan. Similarly, it was only when abducted women actually came
'back' that problems arose about their 're-integration' into society. As
Ranabir Samaddar so aptly puts it, 'The act of redrawing the boundaries
is ... only the beginning: its life—or larger than life—begins thereafter'
(Samaddar 2003: 25). But these are well known and I would like to
turn to a different kind of story to look at quite other dimensions of
the question.

In the aftermath of Partition the courts in India and Pakistan were
required to adjudicate on a large number of cases and disputes relating
to property, savings, jobs, nationality, and so on. Among these were the
cases of abducted women—those who refused to return to their 'own'
families, those who wished to stay on with their abductors. The majority
of such cases, especially in the early days of the Central Recovery Operation, were decided by the special tribunals set up to look at them. But
as time wore on, and issues became more complex, some of these cases
came up before the courts, and because the decisions in them had to

do with border crossings, and the element of choice and/or coercion was always unclear, and questions of nationality, citizenship rights, rights of residence and property rights were at issue, some matters did come up before the courts. I would like now to turn to one of these.

Just as the history of rape and abduction of women is well known by now, so also is the history of their resistance to being forcibly recovered. The law gave them no real rights in this, assuming that women could not think for themselves and were not really capable of making independent decisions. Officers of the police and social workers had the right to decide whether or not a woman was abducted, and if they felt she had been abducted, they could take her into what was called 'protective custody' and keep her there till her fate was decided. If the woman, or someone else on her behalf, disputed her status as an abducted person, the case came up before a tribunal whose decision was final. This is illustrated in the case of Ajaib Singh vs the State of Punjab,[1] described below.

On 17 February 1951, Major Babu Singh, an officer of the No. 1 Field Company in Faridkot, reported that one Ajaib Singh had three abducted persons, all women, in his possession. The officer was convinced that these were abducted women and he used the extraordinary powers the law gave him, to go into Ajaib Singh's house, where he found only one of these women, and to take her into custody. The girl he took into custody was called Mukhtiar Kaur (alias Sardaran) and was believed to be some 14 years old. The police took her away, theoretically until her fate could be decided. Fearing that the police would use their powers to send Mukhtiar Kaur to Pakistan, Ajaib Singh filed a writ of habeas corpus in the Division court, asking that the girl not be removed from Jullundur, where she was being held, until the disposal of his petition. He got an interim order from the court that Sardaran would not be removed from the High Court to whom the case had been referred.

When the case came up before a tribunal, they were convinced that Sardaran had indeed been abducted and therefore recommended that she be 'returned' to Pakistan. However, when the petition came up for hearing, the judges took a number of other issues into consideration, and finally referred the case to a full bench. The full bench argued the case on the basis of questions of fundamental rights, citizenship, questions of movement and residence, and the troubled question of how and why a person who was not a criminal, could be held in custody by the law without his/her being informed of their supposed 'crime'.

Mukhtiar Kaur/Sardaran's case was not very different from the many others that came up at the time, which had to do with other abducted or presumed-to-be-abducted women who were awaiting decisions about their future. The key question was: where, and to whom, did these women belong?

The question of belonging is a deeply troubled one and one that most migrants confront all their lives—do they belong to the land they left behind, or the one in which they find themselves, or somewhere else altogether? The choice afforded to most people after Partition was not available to some women—so Sardaran, for example, found herself in India, but did she belong there? Not in the eyes of the state, which had located her belonging in Pakistan. Abducted women lodged in camps in Punjab and Bengal were Hindu women, presumed to belong to India, but for many, their families had now rejected them, so this 'belonging' was not much good. For many women, denied agency and the rights of ordinary citizens all their lives, the categories of 'nation' and 'family' can and do, at such times, overlap. Leaving spaces rendered unsafe by the violence of conflict or war, women refugees and migrants often report feeling insecure in, say, refugee camps that are, in many ways, meant to replicate the conditions of home to instill a sense of security and stability. The offer of return to the 'nation' then, can suggest a certain kind of security, just as the hint of re-entering the family fold can. Yet, often, neither structure nor institutions are able to offer belonging in quite the same way—for a variety of reasons.

For Sardaran/Mukhtiar Kaur, the question of belonging was crucial, but it was not one she was allowed to answer—we never hear in the case proceedings about what she had to say. After all, a 14-year-old is quite capable of recounting a history and a past, but the courts and the representatives of the newly-formed state did not consider this at all and so, instead of turning to Sardaran, the courts turned to everyone else, including her 'abductor', to determine who the girl really was and where she really belonged. Given the blurring of lines between choice and coercion, the difficulty of recovering the voices of those who were abducted, the question that arises is: was Sardaran/Mukhtiar Kaur a migrant? Or a refugee? Or a dislocated person? Or all of those? How do we understand her experience? And where, if at all, does this experience enter into the meta-narratives of the 'mass' migration of people across the newly formed borders? I have no easy answers to these questions except to say that the more deeply one begins to address the question of migration, and in particular of its gendered nature, the more difficult and ambivalent become the issues of nation, belonging, home and family, especially for women.

The thousands of women who were abducted and who either married their abductors, or were sold into slavery, were dislocated once by the act of abduction, being taken forcibly from their homes, and dislocated a second time when the recovery police came to search for them. When some of them protested, or refused to return to their natal families, the state took it upon itself to decide for them where their proper home was. In other words, when they chose to exercise choice and agency about where they wanted to live, the state was of the view that because they were in a coercive environment, any choice they exercised could not have been fully free. Here, we are confronted with the question of how to place these women in the meta-narrative of the state. The dominant narrative of Partition is one of mass migration—the pictures of large columns of people on the move in both directions are almost iconic by now. And it is this narrative that lends itself to the accompanying narrative of the making of the nation-state: here were millions of 'the nation's' people making their way out of a violent situation into a new home, a new country. The newly formed nation state responded as a parent does to their suffering, with care, and by offering rehabilitation, relocation, jobs and compensation. But within this narrative lie the stories of those who do not quite fit in—the abducted and forcibly recovered women. Their narratives question, resist and sometimes disrupt the meta-narrative and help us to unpack the seemingly unproblematic category of migrants. In their refusal to return to their families, some abducted women further complicate the meta-narrative by refusing to accept, and own, the borders that now separate the two nations.

The women's refusal posed an even greater problem for the newly formed nation-state in its attempt to legitimise itself. It was important, at the time, that all those being dislocated, *believe* in the project of the new nation, *see* it as a safe haven and *accept* its legitimacy. Among those who were seen to be questioning this, were the women, and their 'chosen' mode of questioning was through questioning the institutions of the family, the community, the nation. Where, many asked, were their families or the functionaries of the state when they were being abducted? A young woman, prior to being 'recovered' posed the following question of Mridula Sarabhai: 'You say abduction is immoral, and so you are trying to save us. Well, now it is too late. One marries only once—willingly or by force. We are now married. What are you going to do with us? Ask us to get married again.... What happened to our relatives when we were abducted? Where were they?' (Menon and Bhasin 1998: 97). How could the parent-state accept such questioning by its children, in particular those it saw as being unable to exercise independent choice or agency? Further, when such questioning was born out of what was generally seen as an illegitimate arousal of women's sexuality through contact with the 'other', it became even less acceptable. All signs of such illegitimacy needed to be erased, and forcible recovery was part of this enterprise. This is also why children, who were further tangible evidence of the sexual transgression of women, had to be separated from their mothers—a development not dissimilar with that of Bangladesh, where the raped women of 1971, termed *bironganas*, were not allowed to keep their children born of the violation of their bodies.

III

Let me now turn to another aspect of this complicated history. I have said above that the Partition in the west and the migration from there is somehow assumed to have been of a more serious nature because it took place within a short, compressed space of time, while on the eastern border the slow trickle of migrants and refugees took place over a much longer period. However, nothing is ever as simple as the dominant narratives would have us believe, and even on the western border, more than half a century later, sporadic migration continues to take place. This adds a further complication to the kinds of questions our discussions are attempting to address, for how do you understand the slow, sporadic, individual movement of people that relates to a conflict, or a situation of violence that is in the past, but whose repercussions are felt even today? Let me explain by giving some examples.

As is well known, at Partition, a small number of Hindus stayed on in the interior districts of Pakistan. For the most part they continued to live peacefully and did not face any particular violence, although the status of being a minority is always marked by different kinds of discrimination and violence that are sometimes difficult to give a name to. However, each time relations between the two countries went downhill, things became bad for Pakistan's minority Hindu population, and the fear of their getting worse made many people migrate. Although the slow, sporadic, individual migration of individuals and families has been going on for some time, there were two major moves which involved large numbers of people, and these took place in 1965, at the time of the India–Pakistan war, and later in 1971, after the Bangladesh war of liberation. Generally, according to members of the groups in Rajasthan, most moves—other than the individual ones—took place at moments when relations between the two countries were really at a low ebb, and the fear was that they would get worse. As often happens at such times, vulnerable groups such as minorities are targeted and Hindus in Pakistan also faced such targeting. Many of the people who migrated were the original inhabitants of the undivided region of Thar, and they crossed over into Rajasthan. Between 1965 and 1971 the number of 'refugees' living in the border districts of Gujarat and Rajasthan increased from 10,000 to 90,000.[2] The migrants belonged to all caste groups, and many were nomads and poor peasants. Citizenship status, rights and privileges remain an issue for this group of people even today. Many belong to nomadic communities—one might even say they are eternal migrants—but in order to get citizenship they have had to settle in one place, something that further complicates the issue.[3]

After the influx of 1972, the government set up refugee camps in Barmer district of Rajasthan to house these migrants. Used to living and moving about freely over vast spaces, they found this atmosphere difficult to adjust to. This problem echoed what was felt by Bengali migrants at Partition, who were suddenly forced to live in cramped surroundings in India. There were other problems: in Rajasthan, a limited number of tents were set up in the camps and were assigned to families, with ration cards being issued to the head of the family. It does not take much guessing to see who the head of the family was always assumed to be. The process of regularising the status of 'refugees', however, was so long drawn out and tedious that some people gave up and went back to Pakistan.

What of the women, however? When the larger group of people crossed the border in 1965 and 1971, they took care to choose their moment and to learn from the experience of Partition, as well as to move in an organised fashion. Young boys were trained to carry arms for self-defence, the day they chose was the day of the Eid festival, and women were sent in advance with men to guard them, so as to avoid the possible danger of rape and abduction. But no matter that women may have crossed over safely, and that over half a century had passed since the original violent conflict that pushed people into migrating, such a move is always fraught with other kinds of problems, and I outline some of these below.

Ram Singh, a Hindu from Pakistan who had migrated to Rajasthan, went back to his home in Pakistan to marry his present wife, Tara, also a Hindu, who lived there. He brought Tara back. She continued to hold a Pakistani passport, although she was now married to an Indian (Ram Singh had by then become naturalised). She applied for Indian citizenship, and continued to live in India with her husband while her application was being processed, her status remaining uncertain. A number of visits to the Pakistan embassy, money being paid out for various formalities, all of this yielded nothing. In 1999, the Central Home Department sent her a letter asking for renunciation of her Pakistani nationality, but when she went to the Pakistani embassy to do what was required, they sent her back to the Indian officials. This to-ing and fro-ing went on for some time. Tara's fault was that she remained ignorant of, or did not pay attention to, the mapping of national borders that had happened as long ago as 1947, for it was these that now dictated the shape her personal life could take. Today, Tara continues to live in an uncertain state, not sure where she belongs,[4] a victim of a decision that would, without these borders, have been a 'normal' happening, but with their existence, became an instance of transgression, an unsanctioned and unsanctionable migration.

Tara is not the only member of Ram Singh's family who has faced this problem. His sister Dhan Bai, who was married and had crossed into India in 1984, but without any legal documents, applied for Indian citizenship, and she too is still waiting to hear about her status. Meanwhile, she has had children who also remain in a sort of limbo.

Government rules regarding who does and does not have the right to stay in India (these relate only to people from Pakistan) are as follows:

1. Member of a minority community in Pakistan (Hindus and Sikhs).
2. Pakistani women married to Indian nationals and who have been staying for a long period in India.
3. Indian women married to Pakistani nationals and returning to India due to widowhood, public divorce and having no male member to support them in Pakistan.[5]

The displaced Pakistani Hindu population I refer to above has formed itself into an organisation to demand citizenship and recognition from the Government of India. The Pak Visthapit Sangh has been active in taking up cases and helping people to get settled, and Hindu Singh Sodha, their leader, is a tireless worker. One of the key aims of their advocacy is to seek naturalisation and citizenship, and with that, to seek a piece of land—property—where they can then establish themselves. In other words, they are seeking a home, a sense of belonging and a nation (symbolised also in the desire to have an identity as established by a state document, the Indian passport) to call their own. But for many of them, these notions keep shifting. Is 'home' where they now are, or where they have spent much of their lives? Is the 'nation' where they have now set up camp or is it the country whose passports they continue to hold? For many migrants, while they may be located in a new state, home remains elsewhere, the land they left behind. For the members of the Pak Visthapit Sangh, this is no different, and many hold on to notions of home in Pakistan. While this narrative of the migrants, whose history is seen as an adjunct to the 'main' history of Partition, questions the making of the dominant narrative, it is in itself questioned by narratives of the women from this group. For within the Pak Visthapit Sangh, the women who crossed over from Pakistan continue to live in *purdah*, and continue to remain silent on their experiences, and any privileges that are granted to this group in terms of land, compensation, jobs, etc. have so far been in the name of men. Citizenship, too, as always, remains mediated through men and the family. And yet, women are not totally lacking in agency. There is much anecdotal evidence that brings to light stories of women's agency. Key among these stories is one that recounts how women members of the Pak Visthapit Sangh decided to help improve their family incomes by taking the step of crossing the border back into Pakistan, travelling to their villages where many older Hindu women had stayed behind, and learning the skill of embroidery from these older women. This skill was then put to good use once the women were back within Indian territory, where they made and sold embroideries on a small scale and earned some money to contribute to the family income. This kind of criss-crossing of borders is not uncommon, but once borders are in place and rigidly defined, these movements, which are otherwise normal, become tinged with a different significance. They come to be seen as migration and sometimes dislocation. If the women of the Pak Visthapit Sangh had been picked up on their return to Pakistan, for example, what is the word that would have best defined them? Holding Pakistani passports, hailing from villages inside Pakistan, they were nonetheless now resident in India and awaiting Indian citizenship, but marriages still went on across borders, except that they took place between ethnically contiguous peoples. In which narrative do these experiences then fit?

When these histories—whether of the recovery of raped and abducted women, or of the crossing over of Hindus from Pakistan in recent years—are written, they will be written as histories of the achievements of state, the meta-narrative of numbers, houses built, citizenships granted, plots of land regularised. All of this touches on women's lives of course, but the deeper losses and ambivalences we see reflected in the stories of either Sardaran, or Tara, or the many nameless abducted women I have spoken of, do not find a place in this meta-narrative. Within this meta-narrative, a violent displacement is seen as more deserving of attention, because it suggests a sudden pulling out of roots. And yet, the forced migrations and displacements that take place in what is seemingly a moment of peace—as has happened with the women from Bhutan, for example, where those who have been ousted are said to be 'voluntary' migrants, which at least forces a recognition that they can be involuntary migrants as well—go as deep and represent as much of a loss and are therefore equally deserving of attention. In India, we are all aware of what is happening in Kashmir and of the migration of Kashmiri Pandit women from their homes in the Kashmir valley. Seemingly, displaced families who have been rehoused in Jammu or Delhi or other places, are now living in conditions that may be described as conditions of peace. Yet what does this peace—and the afterlife of migration, settlement—really mean for women? All over, whether it is in India or elsewhere, we find examples of women who are caught in situations such as these. In Punjab, for example, women who were once valorised because they chose to marry militants, or to give birth to children born of unions with militants, for the cause, have been forced to leave their homes and live in villages close to the border, ostracised from 'normal' society. Theoretically, they can be said to be living in conditions of peace, and yet, peace has very different meanings in their lives than it does for, say, the men—both militants and members of the security forces—who were involved in the struggle in Punjab.

IV

In recounting these few histories, I have touched only the tip of the iceberg. There is much to be learnt about the ways in which the experience of forced transfers of population, particularly following violent conflict, are gendered, and their meta-narratives, largely male and often only majoritarian, are ruptured by the stories and experiences of those on the margins, particularly women. Yet, these experiences continue to remain liminal, partly because we have so little information on them, and also because if we are to take the case of abducted women during Partition, even though the scale of the event was not small, the experience remained, by and large, at an individual level, and therefore consigned to a deeper silence. Here, a contrast with the experiences of another marginalised community, the Dalits, may provide a useful example. Partition narratives of the mass migration of people across both borders are largely articulated in terms of Hindus (and Sikhs) and Muslims, the two major communities who were pitted against each other. Yet, there are stories of large groups of Dalits migrating as a community, from Sindh and other areas, and migrating as a community to specific areas. There is evidence of the allocation of plots of land, houses, jobs to the community—we may question such allocations which replicate the caste hierarchies inherent in Hindu society, but we need to accept that the experience of the Dalit communities is visible in ways that were different from that of women, largely because the community was politically organised, and therefore had a 'collective' identity which the women lacked. This further means that the valuable lessons and insights that women's experiences may have to offer in helping us nuance the broad brush-strokes of the meta-narrative of migration and displacement, may be lost to us. There is no gainsaying the importance of carefully unpacking the meanings these concepts carry so that we understand not only the gendered dimensions of migration, but also the complexities and ambivalences that lie within it, especially when it is looked at in connection with the making of the nation-state and gender. Clearly, we need a set of new tools altogether to begin to understand the many meanings these words—migration, displacement, movement, choice, coercion—carry for women.

I want to end this essay by using another example, not of one story, but of several. In the course of my research I came across a book entitled *List of Non Muslim Abducted Women and Children in Pakistan and Pakistan Side of the Cease Fire Line in Kashmir*. Compiled in 1954, this book contains a district-by-district listing of Hindu women and children who were presumed to have been abducted by Muslim men. The 21,809 names in this book were compiled specifically so that they could be supplied to the Pakistan Recovery Organisation to help in their work of recovery. One of the interesting things about this volume is that it lists women according to the place where they are found to be living, in many instances several years after they were abducted. Often different from their places of origin—home—these places were sometimes at a considerable distance away from where the women originally lived. But in all probability, they had become home; no matter how harsh the conditions, and how difficult their lives, for abducted women whose families were now across the borders, these new places of residence were home. Migrants or refugees, citizens or aliens, they were now in places that they had to call home for there was nowhere else. Until, that is, the recovery police arrived to take them away to places where the state believed they should be, where they should belong. A second migration, a different location, another story, another beginning and another end. For me, the stories of these women are the ones that provide the underside of the meta-narrative of Partition migration, these are the stories that we need to turn our attention to, for these are the stories that cross not one, but several borders, that question both choice, and coercion, and home and state.

Notes

1   Criminal Appeal No. 82 of 1952. The State of Punjab–appellant vs Ajaib Singh and another–respondents, 182, 1953, *Criminal Law Journal*: 1319.
2   Figures provided by the Pak Visthapit Sangh, Barmer, Rajasthan.
3   My knowledge of these communities is based on extensive discussions with Hindu Singh Sodha, their main leader, who has been actively fighting for their rights in Rajasthan.
4   Report of the Pak Visthapit Sangh by Hindu Singh Sodha, prepared for Aman Public Charitable Trust, March 2004.
5   Ibid.

References

Butalia, Urvashi. 1998. *The Other Side of Silence: Voices from the Partition of India*. New Delhi: Viking Penguin.
Chakravarty, Gargi. 2004. *Coming Out of Partition: Refugee Women of Bengal*. New Delhi: Shristi.
Criminal Appeal No. 82 of 1952. The State of Punjab–appellant vs Ajaib Singh and another–respondents, 182, 1953, *Criminal Law Journal*: 1319.

Das, Veena. 1995. *Critical Events: An Anthropological Perspective on Contemporary India*. New Delhi: Oxford University Press.

Kaul, Suvir (ed.). 2000. *The Memory of Partition*. New Delhi: Permanent Black.

Menon, Ritu and Kamla Bhasin. 1998. *Borders and Boundaries: Women in India's Partition*. New Delhi: Kali for Women.

'Report of the Pak Visthapit Sangh' by Hindu Singh Sodha. March 2004. Prepared for Aman Public Charitable Trust. Barmer.

Samaddar, Ranabir. 2003. 'The Last Hurrah that Continues', in Ghislaine Glasson Deschaumes and Rada Ivekovic (eds), *Divided Countries, Separated Cities: The Modern Legacy of Partition*, pp. 21–35. Delhi: Oxford University Press.

United Nations Research Institute for Social Development (UNRISD). 2005. *Beijing Plus Ten*. Geneva: UNRISD.

6

WOMEN AFTER PARTITION: REMEMBERING THE LOST WORLD IN A LIFE WITHOUT FUTURE

Anasua Basu Raychaudhury[*]

Memory 'is the engine and chassis of all narrations' (Hazra 2002). Memories are objects that tumble out unexpectedly from our mind, linking the present with the past. 'A traumatised memory has a narrative structure which works on a principle opposite to that of any historical narrative' (Chakrabarty 1996: 2143). A historical narrative, after all, concentrates on an event, explaining its causes and the timing, but what it perhaps cannot explain is whether the subjects belong to the 'marginalia of history' like 'accidents' and 'concurrences' or not. Perhaps that is why one sociologist has rightly pointed out that 'Memory begins where history ends' (Bose 1997: 85).

But can memory really capture the truth of violence? One may ponder over this question while exploring the minds of those few surviving people who attempted an escape from the violence of the partition of the east—partition of their homeland, partition of their soul and partition of their identity. The truth may elude a person more when she/he delves deep into the minds and memories of women who had a tryst with the violence of partition or the trauma associated with that violence. The way Amiyaprova Debi, Surama Debi or Sarajubala Debi (the three protagonists of this paper) would narrate their tales of dispossession—dispossession of their childhood, womanhood and parenthood—and

[*]Many Partition-refugees in the east were kind enough to share their painful memories with the author, who interviewed them while working as a researcher for a project on 'Reconstructing Lives' sponsored by the New Delhi-based CSDS. The author has learnt a great deal through her interactions with Ashis Nandy. The author is also grateful to Rita Manchanda for her valuable comments on an earlier draft of this article.

narrate the incidents of violation of their basic human dignity, or the way they would like us to know how Partition-related violence changed their identity over a period of time may really put us in a fairly difficult position.

It is known that narratives are always related to some sense of the self and are told from someone's own perspective 'to take control of the frightening diversity and formlessness of the world' (Kaviraj 1993: 13). Through the narrative, the self finds a home, or it would perhaps 'describe the process better if we say that around a particular home they try to paint a picture of some kind of an ordered, intelligible, humane and habitable world' (ibid.). Here the self tells the story to an audience—in this case the author—and thereby creates a kind of relationship with the listener (ibid.: 33). In the process, 'the historical self configures memories differently from the way the ahistorical self does' (Nandy 2003: 117–18).

Most of us are familiar with writings on the suffering of people because of the partition of the west. Both social scientists and creative writers have extensively and touchingly highlighted such sufferings of human beings. Compared to that, the experiences in the east have been discussed in very few books and articles.[1] Jasodhara Bagchi and Subhoranjan Dasgupta have rightly pointed out in their recently published edited volume entitled *The Trauma and the Triumph: Gender and Partition in Eastern India* that, while 'the Partition of Punjab was a one-time event with mayhem and forced migration restricted primarily to three years (1947–50), the Partition of Bengal has turned out to be a continuing process'. They add: 'Displacement and migration from the East to West, that is from former East Pakistan and Bangladesh to West Bengal, is still an inescapable part of our reality ...' (Bagchi and Dasgupta 2003: 2).

Against this backdrop, we shall try to look back in this paper at the sufferings of a few women who were uprooted in the context of the partition of the east in 1947. For this purpose, we shall cite the life-experiences of three women still languishing in the refugee camps of West Bengal that exist till today. But before we come to the narratives of these three women, let us briefly take note of a few facts of the camps that exist in different parts of West Bengal. This would perhaps help us to understand the situation of these women in a proper perspective.

As the cross-border influx continued interminably during the second half of the 1940s and early 1950s, the helpless, uprooted people reached the reception and interception centres at the Sealdah station. From there they were subsequently sent to the transit camps and permanent relief camps. The host government decided not to send the refugees straight to the rehabilitation camps mainly due to the magnitude of the influx. Moreover, many of these refugees were supposed to be sent to other parts of the country and instant arrangements could not be made possible for their travel. Therefore, the relief and transit camps were established in different parts of West Bengal to provide immediate help to these people.[2]

Initially Cooper's Camp was one of the major transit camps in Ranaghat in West Bengal where displaced people stayed for 10–15 days before their permanent resettlement. (Das 2000: 7–10). Later on, the camp was converted into a permanent relief camp.

On 30 November 1952, the population of these camps and homes was 34,000, including the population of the orphanages. The number soon increased to 37,000. In fact, the number of persons in the Permanent Liability camps (PL camps) in West Bengal was quite high. Now, even after 58 years of independence, approximately 837 inmates of these refugee camps are PL members. Of these 837, 243 are in Chandmari, 121 in Dhubulia, 11 in Titagarh, 141 in Habra, 44 in Bhadrakali, 45 in Bansberia, 146 in Chamta, 43 in Cooper's Camp and 43 in Ranaghat.[3] Over time, a major portion of these PL camps have been transformed into rehabilitated areas. However, there are still 9 PL camps in West Bengal, out of which 7 are located in Nadia district alone.

In most cases, camps for the refugees were established in military barracks and tunnel-shaped huts made of corrugated iron sheets and originally constructed for Allied soldiers during World War II. Thousands of refugees were placed in these camps, the displaced persons arriving either by train or by truck from across the border. As some of these camps became overpopulated and the government could not provide any more space in the makeshift military barracks or huts, the additional refugees were given tents to live in. Each refugee family comprising four members got one tent, and a bigger family (exceeding four members) got two tents to live in.

As a result, camp life was not always satisfactory, but rather sometimes sub-human in nature. Even in the dormitories of those barracks, each refugee family was allotted a little space. Each family marked its occupied area with pebbles and stones. Sometimes, the allotted area was so inadequate that it could only provide sitting space and not even sleeping space for the members of the refugee family. Under such circumstances, there was absolutely no question of privacy. The refugees definitely got shelter far away from their home and communal hatred, but scarcity of water, lack of proper healthcare and irregular supply of dry rations made their lives unbearable. In such a situation, many children died of dysentery in the camps. The dead bodies of children were sometimes buried, but very often were simply left in the jungle for paucity of funds. The government used to pay Rs 16 for the cremation of a body. This has now gone up to Rs 250.

Let us note that we shall frequently use the term 'refugee' in this paper, and that by 'refugee', we shall mean a person who has been up-rooted from his or her *desh* ('homeland', or what Dipesh Chakraborty would translate as 'foundational homeland'). Let us also make it clear that we shall not use the term 'refugee' as it appears in the UN Convention of 1951 or the UN Protocol of 1967. Rather, we are more concerned here about the human sufferings of a forcibly displaced woman, and not much about her legal and juridical status. The memories of three elderly dispossessed women, Amiyaprova Debi, Surama Debi and Sarajubala Debi, will help us realise how they faced a violent situation in their familiar surroundings and how they still carry the trauma they experienced at some point of their lives. Their memories may be subjective in nature, but these selective memories could help us to understand how the displaced women may become both victims as displaced persons and victims as women.

We are familiar with the fact that the partition of the Indian sub-continent displaced millions of people from East Pakistan (or East Bengal as it was known prior to Partition). Whereas people fleeing with precious belongings could reconstruct their lives on the other side of the border in a relatively easier way, for those belonging to the lower middle class, it was not at all easy, and sometimes almost impossible. Many such displaced persons had to spend years and years in refugee camps before they could even think about a decent life and living. Many of them could not even return to their original occupations and, therefore, felt a sense of alienation and irreparable occupational loss even after partial rehabilitation.

The refugees who have been surviving in the camps in West Bengal for the past five decades and have not yet been rehabilitated are, in a sense, prisoners of the past. It seems that the life and times of these people have been frozen within the boundaries of the camps. In our paper, we shall try to find out whether the women among those displaced faced a double jeopardy in such a situation—first as refugees, and then as women. We shall attempt to share the feelings, experiences and trauma of the contemporary displaced women, and try to look at their life and times through their own eyes. In fact, we shall accept their own perspective of victimhood and reconstruction of their own lives in an alien land. After all, these displaced women were not and are not aware of today's feminist perspectives. Therefore, looking at them through a sophisticated conceptual lens may not always capture the reality of their own struggle and survival.

The camp life indeed thrust upon a fixed identity on these refugee women. But, that was not the end. As their escapades from violence compelled them to negotiate with various new choices, their identities were forged through their macro-level struggles. But as we look into the lives of these women, we shall realise how their self-identity quite often challenges their ascribed identities.

When these women left their respective homes on the other side of the border, they started their uncertain journey along with other members (in most cases with the male members) of their families. But along their route to West Bengal, many of them not only lost these near and dear ones, but also their own dignity and womanhood. Even when they were given shelter in camps, with other women as well as men, their private space became merged with the public space. Whatever privacy they had enjoyed in their ancestral homes, seems to be a sweet memory of another life.

From *Janmo-Bhite* to Cooper's Camp

Amiyaprova Debi (not her real name), a 75-year-old woman and a resident of the refugee camp in the Cooper's Notified Area, still collects her rations as a refugee. She is originally from Muladi town of Barishal district in East Bengal. She left her *desh* after the Hindu–Muslim riots in Muladi (Jolisha) in the year 1950. Her father owned a grocery shop. She grew up in a more or less well-to-do traditional Bengali joint family. Her family possessed a small piece of land as their property where the Muslim *projas* (tenants) of her own village used to work. She can still remember her *janmo-bhite* (ancestral house), her *desher bari* (the original home) and the *khelar math* (playground) where she used to play her favourite game *dariabanda* (a traditional sport of East Bengal, particularly popular among young girls) with her elder brother, sisters and younger cousins. She especially remembers the days of the Durga puja when she used to receive new clothes and had fun with her cousins. She even remembered distinctly their *pujar ghor* (room for worshipping) where her mother used to worship Radha-Madhav. She spent the happiest moments of her life in her village, Jolisha, when she was a child. When she was only 13 years old, she was married off to a farmer from Patuakhali, also in Barishal district. But unfortunately she became a widow within two years of her marriage and came back to her paternal house at Jolisha again.

In Jolisha, a riot took place on the day after the Shib Choturdashi.[4] In Amiyaprova Debi's own words:

Oh God! They were chanting Allah-ho-Akbar and were rushing towards us. Streams of people on the road! Bhuban and I left for the Shib temple. Bhuban is my distant relative. He came to visit us for an outing. He was small. I had eight or ten other people from our locality with me. In such a situation they suddenly pounced upon us. They had swords, sticks, my God! Oh! What a riot took place! In front of my eyes! They snatched Bhuban from me and stabbed him. My dress got drenched in blood. I didn't have the strength to flee then. I was just screaming and calling for my elder brother. I don't know what happened—one of them suddenly said, my God! She is the sister of Radhika Ranjan Dutta. What have you done? Ultimately, those people must have returned me home. I don't really remember what happened. I can't remember how long I was in that bloodstained dress. I could not sleep for next three months, could not eat also, I had a nauseating feeling …

The riot continued for seven to ten days, something that made it clear to them that their *desh*, their homeland, was no longer a safe place for them to live in. She blamed the *Musalmaan*s or Muslims coming from outside for the riot. She said:

The Muslims of our locality were nice enough. They were our subjects. For them, even after the partition, we did not have to leave our *desh*. The people who came from outside were behind the troubles—they were Biharis.[5]

The growing sense of insecurity ultimately forced Amiyaprova and her family to leave their home in 1951. She left home for Barishal town along with her younger brother and niece. Her mother had gone with her second brother. After staying a few days at Barishal town, Amiyaprova crossed the international border and reached Bongaon in India and took shelter at one of the transit camps there. She also got her refugee identity card from the Government of India. Thus Amiyaprova Debi became a 'refugee', and started her journey of searching a new home.

For the past five decades, the Cooper's Permanent Liability camp in Ranaghat has been Amiyaprova's address. She was already a widow when she left home. By the time she got shelter in the PL camp at Ranaghat she was estranged from her near and dear ones—while trekking to the relief camp on the Indian side of the border she lost her younger brother and niece. Therefore, she did not have any scope of setting up a home outside the camp and becoming 'rehabilitated permanently'. Perhaps that is why in her loneliness she looks back to her *desh*, where she had everything. For her, the present only means a fixed amount of irregular cash dole and rations from the camp authorities and tears. She not only lives with her past, she also lives in her past. Her nostalgia for her *desh* is always with her.

An Interminable Journey

The Bansberia Mahila Sadan or Bansberia Women's Home is located on the bank of the river Hooghly in Hooghly district. It falls on the way to Tribeni from Bandel. The PL camp is not as large as Cooper's camp, the Dhubulia camp and the Ranaghat Mahila Shibir. Like at Ranaghat and Bhadrakali, the inmates of this home comprise only women. Out of a total 45 inmates living in the camp, at least 10 camp-dwellers are physically as well as mentally disabled.

When one enters the home through its big, heavy green-coloured gates, one may meet Surama Debi, an elderly camp-dweller. Surama Debi (not her real name) is a widow aged about 90. She is thin and fair, with a face full of wrinkles. She has the typical aged Bengali widow's short hair, and wears white *than* (a piece of unstitched cloth). She has recently become paralytic due to rheumatic arthritis. She stays at the

camp dormitory, where each PL member has been allotted a little space
that they mark out with pebbles.

Earlier, when this home was full of refugees, the allotted area per
person was so small that it could not even provide sleeping space for all
the members of the camp at a time. Now the dormitory is almost deserted. But old habits die hard. Therefore, Surama Debi does not feel
the urge any more to move beyond her demarcated territory. Like other
invalid camp-dwellers, she also gets cooked food from the camp administration on an aluminium *thali* or plate.

Surama Debi is also from Barishal district. Her father had a small
piece of land, which the Muslim *projas* (subjects) used to cultivate. She
can vaguely remember her childhood days at her village of Jhalokathi.
Surama Debi had grown up in a joint family. Her father was the youngest
of four brothers, and Surama Debi had a total of 20 cousin brothers
and sisters.

She got married at the age of 13. Her husband was also from the
same district but from a different village. Now she cannot recollect the
name of her in-laws' village. Her husband used to look after the land,
which was Surama Debi's in-laws' property. She had a son but unfortunately lost him when he was just six. Within a few years of her son's
death she lost her husband too. After being widowed, Surama Debi
once again came back to her parental house like many other widows.

Then one day a riot broke out. In her own words:

The riot began on the day of Shib Choturdashi. So far I can remember it started immediately after the Muladi riot. The outsiders created trouble. I lost everything. They chopped everyone. Burning
our houses, they killed my elder uncles. Dada (elder brother), bhai
(younger brother) got separated from us. Who knows where they
had gone. They never returned. My parents and me only stayed
back for a little more.

But then one day Fakir Mollah and Rafiq, two good men from her
village, advised them to leave. So they came away.

Surama Debi did not have to directly witness the brutality of killings. She, along with her mother, was inside their house. In those days
the married women used to stay inside their homes. They very rarely
came out of their *andarmahal* to meet the male guests of the family.

The male guests (other than close relatives) and neighbours did not have access to the *andarmahal* of these women, Surama Debi explains:

> I was not only a married woman, but also a widow. I rarely came out of the room. Me, my mother and other girls and married women of our neighbourhood also shut themselves up inside the premises. What a terrible situation outside! We could peep through our windows and see that the houses nearby were aflame. We understood that we would not be spared. We fled. So many people of our village ran away from their own ancestral land!

Surama Debi's eyes are now full of tears. She is silent and bows her head. She looks very exhausted and tired. She may not have witnessed violent attacks. Her silence probably speaks of her trauma of the violence and her sense of unbearable loss.

Taking a deep breath she continues:

> So many people came. We came by steamer and then by train. Before we reached Dorshona my father died. My mother and me knew nothing as to where to go. After reaching the border we registered ourselves as refugees. They sent us to the Dhubulia camp. We stayed there for two years. After that, they brought us to Bhadrokali at Uttorpara. I cannot remember the exact date.[6]

From the World of Senses to a World of Insanity?

A corridor of the Camp Office at Cooper's camp is now the makeshift residence of Sarajubala Debi (not her real name). Everyone around her dismisses her as being insane. This 'insane' lady of 75 may very humbly and repeatedly request you to listen to her. Whether she is 'normal' or not is difficult to say. As a trauma survivor she lives not with memories of the past, but with an event that continues into her present and is current in every respect. She presents a collage of events where the past and present very often get juxtaposed, sometimes belying chronology and sometimes defying the senses and sensibilities of a world of sanity.

Sitting with her earthen *chulha*, saucepan, *thali* and glass, she may show you the official papers of her land that was given to her as an allotment for rehabilitation within the camp area and a photograph of her along with her very dear cow. She has two pieces of baggage tied with a rope and a *chatai* (cot) as her own.

Sarajubala Debi too is from Barishal. She comes from the village of Rajapur, near Bauphal police station. Though she grew up in a joint family, her family had their own house. She was the only child of her parents, and never went to school. Sarajubala Debi's family had nearly a hundred acres of cultivable land. 'I grew up in a more or less well-to-do family,' she says. Their home was made of tin. They had one large room surrounded by a balcony. In those days they, like the other *paramanik* (barber) families of their village, used to live in one corner. Though they had quite cordial relations with the Muslim villagers, their family never allowed these people to enter inside their home.

Sarajubala Debi can remember clearly their *pujor ghor* (room for worshipping). They used to celebrate Kali puja, Monosha puja and Shitola puja, and Durga puja in Rajapur village. They had to go to the other village to see Durga puja. In her childhood, she loved to play with dolls. Within her extended family there were many cousin brothers and sisters. Their cousins were like her friends and they used to play together. This was the happiest part of her life.

Sarajubala Debi lost her father when she was only 7 years old, and was married off at 10. Her in-laws were from Dulia Gobindopur village of Barishal. Her husband, who was a pharmacist, worked with a doctor. He used to stay near the doctor's dispensary at another village called Madanpur. Before her marriage her father-in-law and mother-in-law died. So she used to live with her parents even after her marriage. Sarajubala Debi gave birth to a daughter. When her daughter was only six months old, her husband also died. Her uncles were jealous of her deceased father's property. Though her husband died of diarrhoea, she believed that her uncles were responsible for his death.

Like many other villages in Barishal, there was tension between the Hindus and Muslims in their village too following the riot at Muladi. But Sarajubala and her fellow villagers did not witness the riot directly. In her own words:

We heard that the Hindus and Muslims were killing each other and were approaching our village. Aged men of our village guarded the houses. We used to hide in different orchards. At night, we went to the house of Kala Miyan, a rich Muslim in our village. He had a two-storied house. The Muslims of our locality were good people. Our Muslims did nothing wrong with us.

However, the Brahmin and Kayastha areas were very badly affected in that riot. All the men there were killed and their heads chopped off. Sarajubala Debi saw pools of blood. The rioters also tortured the women of the Brahmin and Kayastha areas. To avoid such torture, a few women preferred to hand themselves over to the rioters. But not all of them survived. Everything in Sarajubala Debi's village of Rajapur became normal after seven days of unrest. But they realised that their village was no more a safe place to live in. So they ultimately followed many other villagers and left Rajapur forever. She says, 'Putting on all lights we came out of our home through the back door. We left everything in our room. We were able to send a few things to our relative's house—but the remaining we lost …'.

After leaving her *desh*, Rajapur, Sarajubala Debi with her mother, daughter and son-in-law came to Barishal town in an over-crowded boat. From Barishal they took a steamer to reach Khulna, and from there caught a train to cross the India–Pakistan international border. After reaching Bangaon in West Bengal, India, they enrolled their names as 'refugees' in one of the transit camps. In this transit camp they got their 'refugee tickets' and rations. Later Sarajubala Debi and her family members were shifted from Bangaon to Cooper's camp at Ranaghat in Nadia district of West Bengal. When they reached Cooper's camp they had to stay on the platform for one day and the next day they were sent to another place within the camp itself.

Sarajubala Debi and her family got one tent to live in. Each refugee family comprising four members got one tent, and a bigger family got an extra tent. Sarajubala Debi lived there in this way for almost a year. When their tent developed many holes, they were again shifted to a thatched hut located at another part of the camp. They had definitely got shelter far away from their home and communal hatred, but their lives remained uneasy due to scarcity of water, lack of proper healthcare, and irregular supply of dry rations and cash doles. The women did not have any privacy. During those days many children died of dysentery in the camps. There were also hyenas around their camp. Usually the hyenas appeared after sunset and sometimes took away children from the tents or huts of the overcrowded refugee camp.

When Sarajubala Debi crossed over the border, she was still young. The money that she got from the government as a cash dole was not sufficient for the survival of the whole family. So she took a job in a small iron-cutting company at Tollygunge in Calcutta, and there she fell in love with a fellow-worker.

Sarajubala Debi lost her mother in Cooper's camp. After her mother's death there was a devastating storm that destroyed their hut again and displaced them from their temporary shelter once more. But this time Sarajubala Debi and her family got a one-room concrete house. They had to live with other refugee families in that room itself. Finally, the Government of India rehabilitated Sarajubala Debi, her daughter and son-in-law in 1962: they received 5 cottahs of land, tin sheets and Rs 2,200 in cash for constructing their house within Cooper's camp.

Since then it has been Sarajubala Debi's new home. She set up a small grocery shop in her house. She bought a cow also, which gave birth to a calf and was a source of plenty of milk. Her son-in-law set up a make-shift saloon near their house.

But they became homeless once again after an influential neighbour illegally grabbed her property. According to her, they allegedly killed her son-in-law in broad daylight. They killed her cow and calf too. After the death of Sarajubala Debi's son-in-law, her daughter became mentally disturbed for a while. Later, slowly but steadily, she came back to her normal self after going through rigorous psychiatric treatment.

After recovering, her daughter became a maidservant in a neighbour's house who was a *swajati* (a person from the same caste) of Sarajubala Debi. But the person took that opportunity to ruin her life. She became pregnant more than once due to the relationship her neighbour forced upon her and had to undergo several abortions. Sarajubala Debi made several futile attempts to stop this, but the man ultimately succeeding in creating a gap between Sarajubala Debi and her daughter, and finally, with the help of some local goons, forced her to leave her 'home' once more. She again became a refugee.

How a few people managed to kill her son-in-law, exploit her daughter (who now lives separately in the same camp) or grab her small plot of land——her new shelter——is difficult to understand from her partially incoherent utterances. She mentions two names—that of the local physician, and of a local thug. But one is not sure whether her allegations are true or not. The camp officer indicates that her version is largely true. Perhaps too many shocks in her life have disturbed her senses. Names and events, therefore, become merged. The difference between her past and present becomes blurred. She appears to be an insane person to the civilised world. Nobody cares to listen to her story any more. And so life moves on.

Sarajubala Debi's present address is now a corridor of the camp office. She has this to say:

> As I speak out all these nuisances prominently, they call me mad.... Once what a position I enjoyed—what a huge property my father possessed—coming from that background I am on the street. How much suffering can a person cope up with? Am I really a mad?[7]

Her silent sobs make the atmosphere heavy. Who is interested in listening to her tales of woe and to what end? She has a past, a violent and terrible past, which no one would like to live through. History does not care for her story. She is simply one of those many millions who crossed over to India during a time of turbulence.

Andarmahal to *Barmahal* (outer part of a house/the outside world)—A Long Walk

Amiyaprova Debi, Surama Debi and Sarajubala Debi, and thousands of other women like them, became refugees due to the riots accompanying the Partition of 1947. They were displaced from their land, from their 'foundational home' (if this term at all makes one understand the feeling for one's *desh*), to which they could never return. They lost everything they had—home, friends, relatives, all their material belongings—and had to start their lives afresh. Their displacement changed their perspective toward life. Partition converted these housewives of yesteryear—the wife of a farmer, a landowner and a pharmacist respectively—into uprooted refugees leaving a deep impact on their whole psyche.

Amiyaprova Debi, Surama Debi and Sarajubala Debi left their home in view of the riots of 1950. Before these riots, the female members of their families used to live in a private space, known as the *andarmahals* of their respective houses behind veils and were mostly ignorant of the outside world. All of a sudden, the riots placed them out on the streets, in the midst of the public sphere. Growing up in traditional Hindu patriarchal families, as young girls these women, our three protagonists, like many other girls at that time, never had the privilege of socialising with any males from outside their own families.

In spite of living in male-dominated households, these women were apparently secure from outside interventions. But when the country was partitioned and the riots broke out in Bengal, men and women alike were on the streets. All hell suddenly broke loose. History brought the women out of their *andarmahals*. When the patriarchs themselves were at risk, these women perceived themselves as insecure. Newer insecurities and uncertainties engulfed their lives when some of them got detached from the male members of their families. The self-proclaimed guardians were no longer present to play the role of protector, and traditional values imposed by the patriarchal society started to become irrelevant. Patriarchal dominance became meaningless, at least for the time being, due to the forces unleashed by Partition (which was primarily an outcome of an almost all-male politics) that were beyond the powers of the patriarchs. Therefore, when these women began to reconstruct their lives in an unknown territory on the other side of the border, the boundaries between the public and the private sphere had already become blurred for them (Weber 2003: 64).

Communal riots and pogroms ruptured the lives of these women in many ways. Some of them as women faced abduction, molestation or rape, and even murder on many occasions. On a few occasions these displaced women were forced to convert to Islam and marry Muslim men. However, most of these displaced women preferred to remain silent about the physical violence if they had to face any.

Most of them say that they were aware of such incidents in other villages, but that they themselves never faced that kind of a situation in their villages. Amiyaprova Debi mentions the name of the Brahman *para* or locality where women were physically tortured by the rioters. According to her, the Muslims abducted many young girls and in one case, the Muslims abducted two young sisters from the same family who later committed suicide. Like Amiyaprova Debi, Sarajubala Debi also specifies that the women of Brahman *para* were badly traumatised by the Muslims. She remembers a case where the daughter of a farmer agreed to go with the rioters just to save her father's life. Similarly, Surama Debi tells us that she was aware of a few incidents where women were physically tortured, but that she cannot specifically remember any incident.

In their later life, the women refugees, as trauma survivors, live not only with memories of the past but also the reality of an uncertain present. This present seems to have no ending. From their perspective it is very much real—the harsh reality they cannot escape and a bitter past they cannot forget. Even their selective memories carry those bitter moments with an unbearable subtlety.

The future is always a distant dream for the refugees, who have survived in the camps for more than five decades and are yet to be rehabilitated. The elderly and infirm PL members therefore nurture memories of happier days in their traditional homeland, and agonise over losing their friends and relatives during communal tensions and riots. Their stories of abundance may be imaginary. All the displaced families could not have had so much property in East Bengal. Indeed, being dispossessed from everything they had, at least some of these people have a tendency to exaggerate the size of the property they had. Similarly, as a communally surcharged atmosphere forced them to leave their traditional homeland, many of them seem to still live with a fear of communal holocaust, often without a substantial reason. As the present implies very little for them, the past seems to envelop their entire existence. The present only means a fixed amount of irregular cash dole and ration from the government. As they reconstruct their past, they idealise it. Their reconstructed past is based on both bitter and sweet memories. They remember their childhood days, their belongings and their violent past—a past marked by riots, homelessness and uprootedness. The memories of their past are a montage of sweet nostalgia and the bitterness of being 'un-homed'.

The childhood memories of these hapless, displaced people are usually sweet. The memories of their *desh* are associated with an idea of beauty and sacredness, and with that of cultural value. Amiyaprova Debi clearly remembers the game of *dariabanda*, the names of her childhood friends, the *pujor ghor* of their house, everything that she lost during the riots following Partition. Sarajubala Debi, despite her apparently incoherent utterances, and despite appearing insane, can clearly remember the names of her close childhood friends.

While portraying the picture of their *desh* these displaced women do not nurture any deep-rooted grievances against the local Muslims. They usually recall these local Muslims as a few good men who helped them in many ways during the riots. But, the reminiscences of these uprooted women indicate that the Bengali Hindu's traditional ideas of cultural values faced a major blow due to the violence accompanying Partition. Their past is marked by violence, and violence 'is seen here as an act of sacrilege against everything that stands for sanctity and beauty in the Hindu Bengali understanding of what home is' (Chakrabarty 2002: 121).

Past as Present and Past as Future

Thousands of women got separated from their family members when they were on the move after the partition of the east. The suddenness of the event and the magnitude of the forced migration came as a bolt from the blue to the displaced women. In many instances the male members of the families were lost in the journey towards seeking shelter beyond the border. In a few cases the rioters killed them. The women from more affluent families could later on reunite with their near and dear ones. The women from not so affluent and influential families were not so fortunate. With or without other members of their fleeing family they had to take shelter in the refugee camps. They had another kind of experience.

Life for the displaced persons, irrespective of their class or caste, got disoriented. Those few families who had relatives in West Bengal had, at least for a few days, a temporary foothold. The remaining mass of people tried to survive in the refugee colonies that sprung up in the far-flung suburban areas of Kolkata or in the camps set up near Sealdah Station. Those belonging to the middle class and lower middle class families could hardly find any ostensible means of livelihood immediately, and took shelter in the overcrowded relief camps by default. People with a little bit of land and other kind of property in East Bengal, who were not affluent but could survive without much problems, could not at all imagine that some day they would have to seek shelter in camps.

This 'un-homing' tore apart the traditional family structure prevalent in the villages of East Bengal. The patriarchy also crumbled, at least for a while. Amiyoprova Debi, Surama Debi and Sarajubala Debi, the women of the *andarmahal*s, had to put aside their veils, both literally and figuratively, and, all of a sudden, found themselves out in the hustle and bustle of the public sphere. The family patriarchs, who once did not allow them to go out of the house without a responsible male companion, were taken over by the events of the time. They did not have a choice. As everyone had to come out onto the street, the distinction between the public sphere and the private sphere became meaningless. The refugees had to renegotiate with various new choices, and women refugees were no exception to it. In fact, the communal violence that occurred during and after Partition always made women the victims of double jeopardy. The displaced women were victims both as displaced persons and as women. For them, the economic uncertainty associated with a life beginning almost from scratch spelt disaster, and they faced different kinds of atrocities, in the form of sexual abuse and violence—atrocities that usually only women face. Their unfamiliarity with the world outside also made their life quite vulnerable. The narratives of the three elderly refugee women make this point.

Amiyaprova Debi and Surama Debi were already young widows when they left their homeland. Subsequently, they found shelter in the camps and turned into 'permanent liabilities' of Cooper's camp and Bansberia Mahila Sadan respectively. They did not get any chance of being rehabilitated permanently. Their loneliness and their state of complete dispossession make them look back to their *desh* where they had 'everything'.

For them, the present only means a fixed amount of cash dole and rations (sometimes irregular) from the camp authorities. Amiyaprova Debi now has a separate room of her own within the camp, something she craved for much earlier. Now that space has very little meaning for her. She has become used to staying and even sleeping in a public space. Surama Debi still lives in a dormitory—in a huge hall with her broken cot, dirty sack and small containers. They, therefore, live in and with their past—with their trauma as well as their childhood memories. Amiyaprova Debi and Surama Debi have no means by which they can distance themselves from the past any more so that the present would be made the present in their consciousness (Das 1992: 359).

Sarajubala Debi was rehabilitated one day and ceased to be a PL member. But misfortune stuck to her. She lost her home, her daughter, her son-in-law, her cow—everything. The magnitude of her loss over time may have taken away her senses. Today she jumbles up her the past and the present. The names and events she mentions now are confusing to others. Was Harendra the doctor who poisoned her son-in-law and used to sexually exploit her daughter on a regular basis, or was it her son-in-law who set up a small barber's shop in front of their newly constructed house? Nobody knows. Perhaps nobody will know. After being 'un-homed' more than once, and being on the streets for many years of her life, Sarajubala Debi has created a new home within her where she hides her secrets. She may wish to share her sorrow, her story of dispossession, with a few sensitive souls, but she will not allow anyone to peep into her mind. So she lives with her closely guarded secrets and memories of the past.

Sarajubala Debi, Amiyaprova Debi and Surama Debi might have treaded different paths after the partition of their homeland in 1947. Life had different things to offer each one of them. But, whatever be their fate, they all lost their home—their world—which could not be re-crafted like it was before Partition. Perhaps life after Partition can never match the one before Partition—more so for the women who bear the brunt of changes in a completely different way than their male counterparts do. The vulnerability of women increases suddenly. Women so far confined to homes find themselves in a much larger and almost entirely unfamiliar world. In such a situation of increased vulnerability, a few women may escape the dark side of life. But not everyone is that fortunate. Whatever fortune has to offer them, they primarily tend to live in the past, as the future remains elusive to many of them.

Notes

1   One can only mention works like those by Prafulla K. Chakrabarty (1990), Ranabir Samaddar (1997), Pradip Kumar Bose (1997), and more recently, Jasodhara Bagchi and Subhoranjan Dasgupta (2003). There are a few important publications in Bengali, apart from a few articles written in English and Bengali. Barring a few literary figures in West Bengal, and exceptional filmmakers like Ritwik Ghatak, others have hardly paid any detailed attention to this phenomenon.

2   In fact, different types of camps were set up in West Bengal to deal with the unprecedented refugee influx into the state. The government set up mainly three types of camps: women's camps, worksite camps and Permanent Liability (PL) camps. The inmates of the women's camps were also PL members, comprising mostly women and children with no male member of their family to look after them. No males were allowed to enter the camp premises without permission from the camp authority. Here lies the difference between the general PL camps and the women's camps. The Bhadrakali and Bansberia women's camps in Hooghly district, the Ranaghat Women's Home and Rupasree Pally in Nadia district, and the Titagarh Women's Home in the North 24 Parganas district were such women's camps (for details see Anil Sinha 1995: 20–21). At present, Rupasree Pally is no more a camp. It has now become an area for permanent resettlement. As time has passed many inmates of

these women's camps have been permanently rehabilitated along with their family members in and around the camp area.

Second, in order to counteract the demoralising effects of prolonged stay in camps, the government introduced a system of keeping able-bodied men engaged in useful work for the development of the area where they were supposed to be rehabilitated. Accordingly, 32 such worksite camps were set up in West Bengal. Bagjola camp in the North 24 Parganas and Sonarpur R5 scheme in the South 24 Parganas are examples of such worksite camp. However, a large number of displaced persons who have been staying in these camps for decades are yet to be rehabilitated.

Finally, the PL camps are for those refugees who were considered unfit for any kind of gainful employment with which they could be rehabilitated. These were the old, infirm, invalid and orphan refugees. Unlike women's camps, in these general PL camps male and female inmates could stay together. These PL camps were located in Dudhkundi in Midnapore district, Bansberia in Hooghly district, Chandmari in Nadia district, Cooper's camp (partially), Chamta and Dhubulia in Nadia district, and Habra, Ashoknagar and Titagarh in the North 24 Parganas district.

3 Based on author's interview with Nirmaledu Das, Superintendent of Chamta camp in Nadia district, on 22 December 2001.
4 A Hindu festival, common among the followers of Lord Shiva.
5 Based on an interview with the author on 13 December 2001.
6 Based on an interview with the author on 28 November 2001.
7 Based on an interview with the author on 15 December 2001.

References

Bagchi, Jasodhara and Subhoranjan Dasgupta. 2003. 'Introduction', in Jasodhara Bagchi and Subhoranjan Dasgupta (eds), *The Trauma and the Triumph: Gender and Partition in Eastern India*, pp. 1–14. Kolkata: Stree.

Bose, Pradip Kumar. 1997. 'Memory Begins Where History Ends', in Ranabir Samaddar (ed.), *Reflections on Partition of the East*, pp. 73–86. New Delhi: Vikas Publishing House.

Chakrabarty, Dipesh. 1996. 'Remembered Villages: Representation of Hindu-Bengali Memories in the Aftermath of the Partition', *Economic and Political Weekly*, 31(32): 2143–151.

———. 2002. *Habitations of Modernity: Essays in the Wake of Subaltern Studies*. Delhi: Permanent Black.

Chakrabarty, Prafulla K. 1990. *The Marginal Men: The Refugees and the Left Political Syndrome in West Bengal*. Kalyani: Lumiere Books.

Das, Samir Kumar. 2000. 'Refugee Crisis: Responses of the Government of West Bengal', in Pradip Kumar Bose (ed.), *Refugees in West Bengal: Institutional Practices and Contested Identities*, pp. 7–31. Calcutta: Calcutta Research Group.

Das, Veena. 1992. 'Our Work to Cry: Your Work to Listen', in Veena Das (ed.), *Mirrors of Violence: Communities, Riots and Survivors in South Asia*, pp. 345–98. Bombay: Oxford University Press.

Hazra, Indrajit. 2000. 'A Time to Remember', *The Hindustan Times*, Kolkata.

Kaviraj, Sudipta. 1993. 'The Imaginary Institution of India', *Subaltern Studies*, Vol. VII, pp. 1–39. New Delhi: Oxford University Press.

Nandy, Ashis. 2003. 'State, History and Exile in South Asian Politics: Modernity and the Landscape of Clandestine and Incommunicable Selves', in Ashis Nandy, *The Romance of the State: And the Fate of Dissent in the Tropics*, pp. 110–31. New Delhi: Oxford University Press.

Samaddar, Ranabir. 1997. 'Still They Come—Migrants in Post Partition Bengal', in Ranabir Samaddar (ed.), *Reflections on Partition in the East*, pp. 104–14. New Delhi: Vikas Publishing House.

Sinha, Anil. 1995. *Paschimbanger Udvastu Uponivesh*. (Refugee Colonies in West Bengal). Calcutta: Book Club.

Weber, Rachel. 2003. 'Re (Creating) the Home: Women's Role in the Development of Refugee Colonies in South Calcutta', in Jasodhara Bagchi and Subhoranjan Dasgupta (eds), *The Trauma and the Triumph: Gender and Partition in Eastern India*, pp. 59–79. Kolkata: Stree.

7

BETWEEN TAMIL AND MUSLIM: WOMEN MEDIATING MULTIPLE IDENTITIES IN A NEW WAR

Darini Rajasingham-Senanayake

We are in a no-war no-peace process. Much has changed and yet nothing has changed. People are not dying, that is good, and we can move about now, but the conditions are the same. Displaced people still can't go home because of high security zones, and military occupation.... You ask about women's roles. How have they changed after the ceasefire? They have not because ... because we do not have real peace in any case. They say there is the peace process and all the international community has promised funds for reconstruction, but nothing has changed, we are doing the same things.

—A women's NGO activist during an interview in Jaffna, northern Sri Lanka, in August 2003, 18 months after the ceasefire between the GoSL (Government of Sri Lanka) and the LTTE (Liberation Tigers of Tamil Eelam)

Introduction

Sometimes whole cities and towns may be displaced in a matter of hours. 'New wars' in Asia, Africa and Europe are increasingly being waged in multicultural urban spaces and neighbourhoods. Unlike the previous generation of wars, the post-Cold War wars in the global south tend to be fought not in rural battlefields distant from civilian life, but rather they pit those who once were neighbours of different ethno-religious or linguistic communities against one another, and often reconstitute historically hybrid and multicultural families, communities and identities amidst competing ethno-religious and cultural nationalisms. The new wars also result in the purging of diversity and the invention of mono-lithic and fictional national unities out of plural and complex identities.

One of the characteristics of 'new' or 'post-modern wars' in the global south is the targeting and forced migration of civilians, men and women alike, some of whom have become perpetrators and victims of violence and displacement seemingly in equal measure. A second char-acteristic of such wars fought for ethno-religious 'liberation' is that they often morph into self-sustaining dirty wars that pay diminishing returns to all, while the best and the brightest young men and women from all affected communities leave. As such, the new wars where civil-ians are deliberately targeted and displaced by armies and paramilitaries often result in ethnic cleansing, as well as the elimination of dissent, diversity and difference within ethnic or religious groups. Modern nationalist violence results in forced migration of individuals, families and whole communities sometimes due to generalised fears and at other times due to the destruction of livelihoods, identities and life worlds. After decades of war what remains are mono-ethnic enclaves and ghettoes while a culture of shared poverty is buttressed by a hidden economy of terror and taxation. In short, the new wars tend to being about radical transformations in the cultural geographies of historically multicultural societies as well as in gender roles and identities.

This paper contrasts and analyses representations, realities and dis-placements of women living among competing nationalisms in the post-conflict zones of north-east Sri Lanka. It focuses on how war has affected Tamil and Muslim women who share public space, history, language and matrilineal inheritance patterns, but belong to different faiths in the historically diverse and culturally hybrid north-east of the island. The matrilineal Kudi system of land and property inheritance is common among Tamil and Muslim communities in the east. Based on ethnographic study of the two decade long armed conflict and patterns of forced migration that began in 1983, as well as the three year old peace process (2002) between the GoSL and the LTTE, the paper ex-amines how the return of peace may affect Tamil and Muslim women's roles—particularly those who were forced to migrate internally and/or overseas and took on various new and unaccustomed roles such as principal income generator or the head of a household during the two decades of armed conflict in the north and east of the island. I suggest that the conflict, which has generated its own internal political economy, has also restructured society and generated new forms of social suffering, even as it has subtly but often irreversibly transformed gender roles and identities.

Based on previous analysis I suggest that the structure of the 'new war' in Sri Lanka is such that a return to a pre-war gender status quo may not be possible—contrary to nationalist imaginaries and a significant literature on women in war (Rajasingham 1999). Simultaneously, this paper traces how the conflict has also resulted in new gendered patterns of (forced) migration and the 'ambivalent empowerment' of Tamil, and to a lesser extent Muslim, women. Whereas previous labour migration had tended to be male-led, there appears to be a growing tendency for female-led overseas labour migration out of the conflict zones, partly as a result of the economic impact of the war as well as changes in international labour markets. The case of Muslim women who have found employment as domestic aides in the Muslim Middle East, despite the fact that they have traditionally tended to be the least likely to venture out of the household for work, is a particularly striking example how conflict may impact and transform gender roles and relations in a culturally conservative community. On the other hand, a generation of Tamil men and women have sought work and asylum in the Euro-American world.

In a comparative study of patterns of displacement and migration as a result of over two decades of armed conflict between the GoSL and the LTTE in Sri Lanka, Oivind Fuglerud has suggested that there is a marked difference between how Tamil and Muslim communities affected by violence have responded. He notes that while Tamil refugees have 'secured residence in countries from Finland to South Africa and on continents from Europe to Australia ... among the Muslims of the eastern province an opposite dynamic seems to be working. There is no international refugee flow and no internal displacement to Colombo or other areas outside the war zone. Rather than people moving out, Muslims towns have themselves become destinations for Muslims displaced from rural areas' (1999: 45).

While Fugelrud correctly identifies cultural differences in patterns of out migration and displacement, his analysis implicitly privileges male strategies for coping with conflict, and elides the large-scale overseas migration of Muslim women from conflict-affected areas to the Middle East. This paper then foregrounds Muslim and Tamil women's changing roles and routes of migration, including nationalist, in the past two decades, focusing particularly on inter-generational transformations in gender roles and identities in the Tamil and Muslim community affected by war in north-east Sri Lanka as a result of conflict and migration—forced or otherwise. The paper will compare how a younger generation of Tamil and Muslim women have sought to negotiate their rights within transforming economic, legal, political and social structures at individual, familial, community, regional, national and global settings, in the context of armed conflict and militarisation. It will ask why young Muslim women who have sought employment in the Middle East, and with far more education and mobility than their mothers and grandmothers who did not veil themselves, prefer to wear *hijab*? Does veiling or *hijab* enable or disable women's mobility?

I suggest that the social disruption caused by conflicts have tended to open up new forms of migration and spaces of economic agency for women, even as greater cultural control over women's bodies and sexuality is exercised by the community in the name of national honour. Of course, different communities and groups tend to react in different ways to violence and transforming gender roles, and a double discourse that simultaneously celebrates women's new role, while curtailing their sexual freedoms, may be apparent as with the LTTE's brand of Tamil nationalist feminism. In this paper I suggest that the shift in gender patterns of migration is both a result of the structure and form of the new wars in the global south where civilian populations are increasingly victimised and related economic depravation, as well as the restructuring of labour markets as a result of economic globalisation. This paper then traces gendered patterns of (forced) migration and displacement in north-east Sri Lanka, while suggesting that the resulting patterns of social transformations have also impacted on gender relations in conflict affected communities.

The changes that war has wrought on women's lives and the social and cultural fabric of family and communities in the conflict zones give us clues towards developing a creative strategy to 'empower' women and enhance their position and capacities for leadership and peace-building in post-conflict societies. Studies of women in conflict situations have only recently begun to address the deeper social and economic transformations that armed conflicts entail, and their implications for political empowerment in post-conflict settings. This paper then explores how conflict has opened up new spaces for women's agency and leadership within changing family and community structures, even as it has destroyed others and placed a double burden on many. It is hence that I trace the transformations that the armed conflict in Sri Lanka has wrought on many civilian women in small but significant ways by thrusting them into positions of power and decision-making within their families and communities in war affected regions.

The 'No-War No-Peace Process': Women's Agency and Movement

South Asian women generally have greatness thrust upon them. They are rarely born great though they may be born of great families, and they rarely achieve greatness without great men. The phenomenon of women from powerful political dynasties being displaced from the home to become public figures—president or prime minister—literally over the dead bodies of their husbands or fathers, is also a telling reflection and indictment of the gendered realities of political power and violence in the subcontinent. For, while post-colonial South Asia has had the highest regional concentration of women heads of state in the world—Benazir Bhutto in Pakistan, Khalida Zia and Sheikh Hassina in Bangladesh, Sirimavo and Chandrika Bandaranaiyake in Sri Lanka, Indira (and possibly Sonia) Gandhi in India—they are all widows and/ or daughters of male presidents and prime ministers. These women while in power have rarely succeeded in stemming violent trends in South Asian politics, or in chalking out an alternative vision and course for their conflicted countries. By and large even women heads of state who once had an alternative secular vision of communal and ethnic peace, such as President Chandrika Bandaranaiyake, remain captive to the violent political forces, structures and processes that in the first instance thrust them to power—a metaphor of women's ambivalent agency in the new wars. In short, South Asian women rarely appear to be agents of their destinies—a situation that may require rethinking frames of representation of gender roles and women's agency and victimhood that are often deployed when talking of women in conflict in South Asian societies.

With a two decade long armed conflict and much better social indicators (like literacy, health and education) for women in the South Asian region, Sri Lanka has had more widowed heads of state and widows contending for the post of head of state than any of its larger neighbouring countries. Family, motherhood and widowhood have been the symbols that women seeking political power, as well as women activists, have mobilised in their struggles for and ascent to political power in a country ravaged by multiple political conflicts and violence. In Sri Lanka, where widowhood bears a stigma in Hindu, and to a lesser extent Buddhist, culture, this has been powerfully reconfigured by the Bandaranaiyakes (both mother and daughter), and other widows of presidents and/or party leaders, such as Mrs Jalani Premadasa and Gamini Dissanayake. Notably, it was Chandrika Bandaranaiyake who took the unprecedented step among politicians of distancing herself from playing ethnic politics and Sinhala majoritarian chauvinism by calling for peace with justice for the minorities as a means to ending the armed conflict between successive Sri Lankan governments and the LTTE fighting for a separate state. She has as yet remained unable to fulfil that promise, caught up as she is in a violent game of political survival, and unable to transcend it—a metaphor for women's ambivalent achievement in a period of social and political turmoil that has cast women in new roles in the subcontinent. Other widowed women such as Sarojini Yogeswaran of the moderate Tamil United Liberation Front (TULF), who became the first elected woman mayor in 1998 in local government elections in the northern capital of Jaffna and was shot dead by militants at her residence (May 1998), have not survived the violence.

This contradictory scenario of women's agency partly explains why, despite that fact that images of child soldiers, women suicide bombers and women in battle fatigues and handling guns have become signifiers of how new wars in the global south blur gender roles as well as conventional distinctions between military and civilian actors, women living in conflict situations in South Asia continue to be represented, if not explicitly then implicitly, as doubly victimised. Not only are women living in conflict situations in the region regarded en masse as victims of patriarchal structures that are found in most societies in the world, but patriarchy is also seen to be exacerbated by caste and religious practices peculiar to the subcontinent. Additionally, after several decades of silence, an important and growing feminist literature on India's partition has traced the extent to which women and girls were the targets of rape, communal mutilation and humiliation in nationalist violence in South Asia (Butalia 1998; Menon and Bhasin 1998). Thus despite women's active roles as combatants as well as civilian women taking on new roles as the head of households in post-colonial armed conflicts in Sri Lanka, Nepal and Kashmir, the double victim image of women in South Asia's war zones remains compelling.

The almost two decade long armed conflict (1983–2000) in the northeast of the island resulted in the death of 65,000 people (officially) and the displacement of over a million people overseas and to other parts of the country at different times during that period. During the war years, a number of women took on new roles as principle income generators and heads of households, but the question remains—will they be pushed back into the kitchen with the return of peace? For, as a generation of feminist studies of women in conflict has suggested, the return to peace is often signified by a return to the pre-war gender status quo.[1] That analysis was however based on studies of an older generation of conventional inter-state wars between militaries in Europe, as well as de-colonisation struggles and revolutions in Asia (Vietnam, China). Rather, I suggest that the 'new war' in Sri Lanka that has been sustained and subsidised by a network of local-global actors—developmental, humanitarian, criminal and diaspora—and thrust women into new roles, has also enabled women to subtly and creatively craft their identities and destinies, often manipulating the 'victim' identity that is thrust upon them in the humanitarian and post-conflict policy discourse as they are displaced or widowed.

With the exception of the Australian wife of the LTTE spokesperson (Anton Balasingham) who has been present at the Track 1 negotiations between the conflict parties, namely the GoSL and LTTE, women have been excluded from the official peace process. The Track 1 negotiations overseen by international mediators, in this case Norway, continues to be carried on by men, despite the significant number of women combatants in the conflict, especially on the LTTE's side. On the other hand, the Sub-Committee on Gender had two meetings before the peace process was suspended. The result is an elision of how a truly gendered peace may be achieved. I draw on the work of Mary Kaldor (1999) who has suggested that new or post-modern wars in the Balkans and Africa that involve targeting and participation of large numbers of civilians and extensive international engagement presents a fundamental challenge to how we may conceptualise war—and peace. For in many parts of Africa and Asia, internationally brokered 'peace processes' and post-conflict reconstruction increasingly constitutes 'a no-war no-peace' situation.

Since the Norwegian-brokered peace process in the island in March 2001, the combatants (the LTTE and the GoSL) have observed a ceasefire, but many of the structures of terror, taxation, and displacement that sustained the political economy of war remain in place (Rajasingham, 1999). As such a 'real peace' or substantive peace remains elusive even as the Ceasefire Agreement (CFA) overseen and monitored by Scandinavian Peace monitors enables a minimalist or formalist peace. This paper then suggests the need to conceptualise a substantive peace that recognises women's agency in conflict situations and post-conflict reconstruction. It also suggests women's agency in war or peace, or to use a term more commonly found in development discourse, women's 'empowerment', is complex, non-linear and rarely un-ambivalent, and as such requires that we develop a new language to discuss gender identities and roles in peacetime.

On the other hand, the structure of migration/refugee policy in refugee/labour migrant receiving countries, as well as cultural ties between those displaced and the host countries/populations, appears to contour the migration strategies employed by individuals and communities caught in the new wars. It is hence often difficult to distinguish between individual agency and legal regimes in the (forced) migration patterns and strategies that communities affected by violence engage in. In turn, this difficulty poses a challenge to the increasingly contested distinction in international law—between refugees and internally displaced persons (IDP), or political migrants and economic migrants. In the new wars, reasons for forced migration are often simultaneously political and economic, and pose the need for a rethink of the international refugee regime, as well as the labour laws instituted in the aftermath of World War II and during the Cold War. This paper then suggests the need for an adequate emphasis on gendered analysis of the patterns and strategies of displacement and migration as a result of 20 years of armed conflict between the GoSL and the LTTE in north-east Sri Lanka.

The restructuring of war and peace challenges our conceptions of women's agency, or to use a term more commonly found in development discourse, women's 'empowerment', which is rarely un-ambivalent—in war or peace. Likewise, as Patricia Jeffery has argued, 'agency is not wholly encompassed by political activism' (1999). Yet it would appear that too many South Asian women's initiatives have neglected social structural transformations wrought by political violence. The overwhelming emphasis by women's groups, as well as by women in relief and development processes, continues to be on viewing women as victims who need to be brought into peace processes and positions of political leadership to foster women's participation in governance and on legal reforms beneficial to women. This has been the case despite the fact that, ironically, picture of women's advancement in the South Asian context seems also to show that women's rights are often advanced within an ethno-nationalist framework, as has happened with the

Bharatiya Janata Party's (BJP's) women leaders in India, and with the LTTE—an issue to which we will return.

This paper considers the changing shape of women's agency in the midst of armed conflict and its aftermath by exploring the new roles that women increasingly perform in their everyday activities in the north and east of the island where the armed conflict has been fought out bitterly and transformed social structures. Women from politically less powerful families than the Bandaranaiyakes have taken on many new and unaccustomed roles, such as heads of households and principal income generators, mainly due to loss of male family members and displacement arising from the conflict. At the same time many women and girls have been rendered barely functional after suffering the violence of bombing and shelling, the loss of family members, (extended) family fragmentation, and displacement. Moreover, due to the security situation and the fact and perception that men are more likely to be 'terrorists', civilian women from families affected by the armed conflict in the north-eastern war zone of the island have begun to play new public roles. Increasingly, women in the war zone deal with the authorities, from government agents to the military to humanitarian aid agencies. They file documents, plead their cases and implement decisions in public and private in the presence or absence of their men folk who are increasingly disempowered or have disappeared.

Women's agency/empowerment in war or peace is not a zero sum game achieved at the expense of men. War places different burdens on men. For it is the men and boys who are mainly targeted to fight and defend their nation, their community and family, and the honour of their women. Men are conscripted into paramilitaries to fight. Men and boys are more commonly perceived as a security threat if they are of the 'other' ethnic or religious community, and are also more likely to be killed. On the other hand, men who refuse to fight or who are forced to live off humanitarian aid in refugee camps feel de-masculinated because they often cannot support their families and play the socially prescribed role of protector and breadwinner of the family. The result is low self-esteem and a sense of failure that might lead to suicidal tendencies among men and boys. Reports from those living in refugee camps indicate that alcoholism is high, as is increased domestic violence. Clearly, there is a need for systematic studies of the impact of war and ensuing social and gender transformation on boys and men and the cultural construction of masculinity. However this is not within the scope of this paper, which mainly focuses on women's changing roles and lives due to the armed conflict in the Tamil dominated north-east of Sri Lanka.

I start from the premise that conflict affects women differently, depending on their religion, caste, class, ethnicity, location and political affiliation. But conflict also reveals a certain commonality in women's experiences. Women experience particularly gendered forms of violence, such as rape and the fear of rape, body searches and the fear of sexual violence, as well as social stigmas which dog women who have been raped. Moreover the fear of sexual violence that the situation of insecurity in armed conflict entails limits and inhibits most women's mobility, and hence their livelihoods, choices and realities. At the same time, women react differently to nationalist armed violence: some like the women cadres of the LTTE, or the women of the Sri Lanka Army and Air Force, have been radicalised and taken up guns and weaponry for their respective nationalist struggles. Others have become political and social activists for peace, seeking to build alliances across ethnic, cultural and regional borders (Mother's Front, Mothers and Daughters of Lanka, Mothers of the Disappeared, Women for Peace, Women's Coalition for Peace).

The paper then examines: (a) women engaged in peace and human rights work, and (b) women who have had to take on new roles as heads of households.[2] Hence the second part of the paper assesses the implications of women's transformed roles for humanitarian interventions and development work in war and peace time. The paper also attempts to map militant and civilian women's agency in moments of violent social transformation and cultural change, and to configure a more complex picture of women's agency, as well as their languages of resistance and empowerment in conflict. It also takes a critical look at how the construct of the Sri Lankan woman as a double 'victim' of war, as well as caste, culture, and society in peace time might obscure and indeed impede women's agency and empowerment in conflicts.

I draw from ethnographic field research conducted during several fieldwork stints over a number of years (1996–2000) among communities in the 'border areas' (both cleared and uncleared areas, as they have come to be termed in the media and popular culture). This border constitutes the shifting 'forward defence line' that demarcates land held by the Sri Lankan armed forces and the LTTE. Land held by the military is referred to as 'cleared areas' while land controlled by the LTTE is termed 'uncleared'. Roughly, the border runs from the main eastern town of Batticaloa in the east to Vavuniya in the central part to Mannar in the west. It encompasses most of the Eastern and North Central provinces of the island that have experienced cycles of violent armed conflict, including repeated bombing and shelling of civilian populations.

My observations on displaced women are drawn from interviews conducted with women living in three different settings of displacement:

- Welfare centres or refugee camps where people are housed in sheds, schools or other structures constructed by the UNHCR and other relief agencies working with the government.
- Residents of border villages who have been displaced many times by the fighting, shelling and bombing, but who chose to return to their villages rather than remain in refugee camps. These people live in constant fear of attack and displacement again, but since the majority of them are farmers they choose to return to their land.
- New settlements in the Eastern Province as well as the border areas of the Vanni district where the GoSL settles landless displaced families from the same province on new plots of land. These new settlements are part of the rehabilitation and reconstruction program in Vavuniya.

In particular, I draw from interviews with young women heads of households in Siddambarapuram camp, which is located just outside the town of Vavunia in the North Central province. This particular camp received a large number of displaced persons and families from Jaffna and the Vanni who had fled to India in the early 1990s and were subsequently repatriated. I also draw from interviews conducted with women heads of households in the new settlement scheme adjacent to Siddambarapuram camp.

The Victim and Her Masks

The tendency to view women as 'victims' in the armed conflict has been fueled by a number of popular and specialist discourses concerning several brutal rapes committed by the Sri Lanka Army, as well as the Indian Peace Keeping Force (IPKF) when they controlled the conflict zones (1989–90). Human rights discourse and humanitarian interventions have also significantly contributed to the tendency to view women as 'victims'. For the various and systematic forms of violence that civilian women experience at the hands of armed combatants, whether state armies or paramilitary personnel, in situations of armed conflict and displacement, was extensively documented and highlighted in the former Yugoslavia, Rwanda, and other parts of Africa and Asia. This process culminated in the UN resolution that established rape as a war crime and saw the appointment of the Sri Lankan lawyer Radhika Coomaraswamy as the first UN Special Rapporteur on Violence against Women in 1994.[3] Highlighting gross violations of women's bodies and lives in situations of conflict and displacement has been part of an important intervention by feminists and activists to promote women's rights as human right internationally.

The focus on women as 'victims' of war and patriarchal culture has also arguably resulted in the elision of how long-term social upheaval might have also transformed women's often subordinate gender roles, lives and positions in non-obvious ways. At the same time, in secular feminist analysis, women's political violence is often an uncomfortable black hole wherein women's agency, by being violent, becomes a male patriarchal project. The claim is often made that women who enter new spaces as militants in the nationalist armed struggle, such as the LTTE women, remain in the end pawns and victims in the discourse of nationalist patriarchy, and are hence pushed back into the kitchen after the revolution/war. Likewise, it is argued that civilian women who take on new roles such as head of a household, principal income generator and/or decision-maker in the absence of their men folk are really merely carrying a double burden. While there is little doubt that women in a war's interregnum carry a double burden, viewing women as merely victims of their culture, war and patriarchy elides women's agency in violence. Positioning women as victims might also mean that they are subject to secondary victimisation since victimhood also often entails carrying the burden of a social stigma. Women who are widowed and/or raped are particularly vulnerable to the double complex of the stigmatised victim.

On the other hand, the rise of Islamic movements and the fact that Muslim women in the north-eastern conflict zones have increasingly tended to adopt veils and other markers of Islamic cultural identity, often in response to Tamil nationalism and violence, also fuels the perception of women as doubly victimised by patriarchy, war and cultural practice. The fact that many of the women who adopt the veil in Sri Lanka do so upon their return from the Middle East where they have sought out work is often overlooked. It is indeed arguable that veiling may mask and legitimise a greater degree of economic independence and physical mobility. The veil may indeed be the mask of the victim who seeks to transcend her victimhood. As Yuvi Thangarajah has noted: 'Conventional analysis suggests that patriarchy and Islamisation exert pressure on women by restricting them to particular styles of dress and housing. My fieldwork suggests that women are using Islamic styles to renegotiate and expand rights and opportunities' (2003: 141).

But the construct of woman as 'victim' also draws from another genealogy. Anthropological, sociological and literary ethnography has tended to represent Tamil women as living within a highly patriarchal and caste-ridden Hindu cultural ethos, particularly in comparison to Sinhala women whose lives are seen to be less circumscribed by caste ideologies and purity/pollution concepts and practices. Muslim women have similarly been portrayed as subjects rather than agents of Islamic culture and tradition. The troubling figure of the LTTE woman soldier— the armed virgin—stands as one of the few highly problematic exceptions to the representation of women as victims of Asian patriarchal cultures, nationalism and war.

Of course the representation of Tamil woman in relation to caste and family is not entirely monochrome in the anthropological literature that is split on the subject. For many anthropologists have also emphasised strong matrilineal tendencies in Sri Lankan Tamil society, where women inherit property in the maternal line according to customary Thesavalame law and enjoy claims on natal families, in contrast to the rigidly patriarchal cultures of say north India where patrilineal descent and inheritance is the norm (cf Wadley 1991). Feminist ethnography, on the other hand, has emphasised the subordinate status of Tamil women in the Hindu caste structure, while frequently noting the split between the ideology of Shakti or female power as the primary generative force of the universe (also associated with the pantheon of powerful Hindu goddesses) and the reality of women's apparent powerlessness in everyday life (Thiruchandran 1997). Both schools however emphasise the generally restrictive nature of the Sri Lankan Tamil Hindu caste system on women and often tend to see caste and gender relations as culturally rather than historically determined. By and large, however, women have rarely been centred in debates on caste, and when they have been, they are more often than not constructed as victims rather than agents of culture.[4]

More recently, anthropologists have argued that colonialism permeated by British Victorian patriarchal culture eroded the status of women in the south Indian societies that follow the matrilineal Dravidian kinship pattern, where property is passed on in the women's line, from mother to daughter—a practice which usually indicates the relatively high status of women in society. They highlight how colonial legal systems might have eroded the rights and freedoms that women had under customary law, particularly in matrilineal societies, while emphasising the historically changing circumstances of family, kinship, caste and gender relations. In this vein, this paper explores how 17 years of armed conflict, displacement and humanitarian relief-development interventions might have altered the structure of the family, caste, land rights and the gender status quo among communities in the border areas affected by the conflict.

The Structure of Armed Conflict and Women as Nationalist Fighters

The figure of the LTTE woman soldier, the armed virgin, and the nationalist mother and/or queen of Sinhala legend who craved the blood of Tamils, and women in the armed forces stand as some of the few problematic exceptions to the representation of women as victims of war and their culture. The LTTE women have been portrayed by Adele Ann, wife of the LTTE spokesman, and Peter Shalk as 'liberated', and by Radhika Coomaraswamy as 'cogs in the wheel' of the male leadership of the LTTE. The reality of the LTTE women is probably somewhere in between. For while they may have broken out of the confines of their allotted domesticity and taken on new roles as fighters, it is indeed arguable that they are captive both to the patriarchal nationalist project of the LTTE leader Prabhakaran and the history and experience of oppression by the Sri Lankan military. However to deny these Tamil nationalist women their agency because they are nationalist is to once again position them within the 'victim' complex, where the militant woman is denied her agency and perceived to be acting out a patriarchal plot.

Arguably, the LTTE line on the women's question might have evolved beyond the first phase of the nationalist struggle when LTTE women seemed unable and unwilling to raise the question of gender inequality lest they be accused of fostering division within the Eelam nationalist cause. In the second phase of armed struggle in the 1990s when the LTTE maintained a quasi-state in the 'uncleared areas', non-combatant women played new roles, albeit in a highly war traumatised and transformed society. In 1987, in interviews with Dhanu (who subsequently assassinated the then Indian prime minister Rajiv Gandhi in a suicide attack) and Akhila (a senior woman cadre) at the LTTE headquarters in Jaffna, I was told that the most important struggle was the one for the liberation of Eelam and the Tamil people. The women problem would detract from focusing on the cause and could hence only be sorted out later. Subsequently, almost 12 years later in January 1999, on a visit to the LTTE-held 'uncleared area' near the north-eastern town of Trincomallee, I learned of the existence of a de facto LTTE policy on domestic violence. During a conversation with several members from a local CBO (Community-based Organisations), one young woman said that women who suffer domestic violence and are physically abused by their spouses could complain to the LTTE cadres who take appropriate action. At the first complaint the abusive spouse is given a warning, on the second he is fined, and if there is a third complaint he might end up in the LTTE's jail. There are also reports that women now sit at LTTE local courts and arbitrate local disputes in the 'uncleared areas'. What this suggests is that after the war, given the demographic as well as social changes that have occurred, if women are expected to return to the kitchen, rather than make policy on rehabilitation and reconstruction of the community, they might not do so willingly.

Displacement and Spaces of Empowerment:Displacing Gender and Caste Hierarchies

Since the armed conflict commenced in Sri Lanka the number of displaced people has fluctuated between half-a-million to 1.2 million, or between a tenth and a fifth of the country's population at various points in the conflict. At the end of December 1995, the Ministry of

Rehabilitation and Reconstruction in Sri Lanka estimated that there were 1,017,181 internally displaced people in Sri Lanka while 140,000 were displaced overseas (some of the latter have sought asylum status). Figures of displaced persons are however controversial. The University Teachers for Human Rights, Jaffna (1993) estimates that half-a-million Tamils have become refugees overseas. The decennial census of Sri Lanka scheduled for 1991 was not undertaken due to the conflict. Estimates are that 78 per cent of the internally displaced are ethnically Tamils, 13 per cent are Muslims and 8 per cent are Sinhalese. Many displaced people, Tamils, Muslims and Sinhalese alike, fled Sri Lankan Army and LTTE brutalities.

Displacement and camp life had also provided space for empowerment for several Tamil women who had taken on the role of the head of the household for various reasons. In this section I outline some of the processes of transformation in young, single and widowed women's lives with whom I met at the Siddambarapuram camp and in the adjacent new settlement. Siddambarapuram is located a few miles outside Vavuniya, the largest town in the north-central Vanni region. It had received a large influx of refugees from the north. In many ways the facilities, location and environmental/climatic conditions at the camp and the adjoining new settlement were exceptionally propitious. The relative prosperity of the locale and its residents was evident in the fact that the market in the camp was a vibrant and busy place, and had become a shopping centre for villagers from nearby as well. At Siddambarapuram the sense of independence, empowerment and mobility in many women heads of household was tangible and remarkable in contrast to other women I met in camps in less propitious settings. This can be explained in terms of the camp's location close to the town of Vavuniya where women could find employment, particularly in the service sector. This is, of course, not an option for displaced women in other less conveniently located camps.

The Siddambarapuram camp was initially constructed as a transit camp by the UNHCR for refugees returning to Jaffna from India in 1991, who were then subsequently stranded when the conflict started again in what is known as the second Eelam war. Many of the people in the camp had been residents for more than five years. One of the oldest refugee camps in Vavuniya, in many respects the camp was exceptionally well serviced. Several young Tamil widows I interviewed in the camp and the adjoining new settlement noted that while they had initially had a hard time adjusting to displacement, camp life and the burdens of caring for their young families, they also had gained freedom to work outside their households and increasingly enjoyed the role of being the head of the household and its principal decision maker.

Many women said that they had little desire to remarry, mainly due to anxiety about whether their children might not be well cared for by a second husband. Several women commented that previously their husbands would not permit them to work outside the household, even if they had done so prior to marriage. Of course one of the principal reasons for these women's newly found sense of control was the fact that they had found employment outside the household and the camp. Women in the service sector and the NGO sector had done well.

It is arguable that the erosion of caste ideology and practice, particularly among the younger generation in the camps, had contributed to women's mobility and sense of empowerment. For except for the highly westernised urban Tamil women professionals, caste has historically provided the mainstay of the Hindu Tamil gender status quo, since caste belonging often determines women's mobility and seclusion, particularly among the high castes for whom it is a sign of high status. Unlike in Jaffna where village settlement is caste and region based, in the camp it was difficult to maintain social and spatial segregation, caste hierarchies and purity/pollution taboos for a number of reasons. This is particularly true for members of the younger generation who simply refuse to adhere to caste inhibitions.

As one mother speaking about the disruption of caste hierarchies in displacement observed: 'Because we are poor here as displaced people we only have two glasses to drink from so when a visitor from another caste comes we have to use the same glass. Now my daughter refuses to observe the separate utensils and she is friendly with boys we wouldn't consider at home. Everything is changing with the younger generation because they are growing up all mixed up because we are displaced and living on top of each other in a camp'. This mother went on to explain how it was difficult to keep girls and boys separate in the camp situation. She thought that the freer mingling of youth meant that there would be more inter-caste marriages, and hence the erosion of caste. Presumably this also means that girls had more choice over who might be their partners.

The reconstitution of displaced families around women who had lost male kin curiously resonates with an older gender status quo: that of the pre-colonial Dravidian matrilineal family and kinship system where women remain with their natal families after marriage, and were customarily entitled to lay claim on the resources of the matri-clan, and hence enjoyed a relatively higher status in comparison with strictly patrilineal societies. As Bina Agarwal has pointed out in her *A Field of One's Own* (1996), the existence of matrilineal systems where matrilineal descent, matrilocal residence and/or bilateral inheritance is practised is usually an indicator of the relatively higher status of women as compared to the status of women in patrilineal groups. Similar observations concerning the status of women in matrilineal communities have been made by anthropologists who have studied the Nayars of Kerala, as well as the Sinhalas, Tamils and Muslims of the east coast of Sri Lanka, where matrilineal inheritance is the norm (Yalman). These are also societies where social indicators have been consistently good, with high levels of female literacy, education and health care in comparison to other South Asian countries.

During the colonial period in Sri Lanka there was however a general erosion of the matrilineal inheritance and bilateral descent practice, despite general provision being made for customary common law for indigenous communities (Thesavalame, Tamil customary law, Kandyan Sinhala law, as well as Muslim Personal Law). In the same period the modernising tendency towards the nuclear family, enshrined in secular European, Dutch and British law, also privileged male inheritance, thereby reducing the power of women within their families.

The switch from matrilineal and matrilocal to virilocal forms of residence and inheritance, where women take only movable property to their affinal household, might also be traced to various post-colonial land distribution schemes wherein title deeds for land were invested in male heads of household, with an injunction against the further division of land due to land fragmentation, which set a precedent for male inheritance of the entirety of the family's land. The result has been the tendency towards male primogeniture—with the eldest son inheriting the land and daughters being disinherited from land ownership. Unfortunately, the similar pattern of title deeds being invested in male heads of households is still evident in the new settlement and land distribution schemes for the landless displaced population which are taking place in Vavuniya under the rehabilitation and reconstruction project. In these projects it is only where the male head of household is presumed dead that title deeds are invested in women. Women whose husbands have left them or whose location/cannot be ascertained are not deemed eligible for land grants. Clearly in the case of Tamil inheritance patterns customary practices are more liberal than that of post-colonial development practices.

What all of this indicates is that cultural practices structure and direct changes in women's roles in situations of armed conflict. For while Tamil women have begun to play various unaccustomed public roles, the evidence from the war zones also suggest that conflict has also transformed Muslims women's mobility, and this transformation has a generational dimension. During a field visit to Akkaraipattu in the conflict affected north-east of Sri Lanka, I visited a Muslim household where there were three generations of women in residence. The grandmother wore her sari the traditional Tamil way, while the middle-aged mother loosely covered her head with the end of her *sari* as and when she left the household space. On the other hand the young daughter who had recently returned from the Middle East walked into the house covered from head to foot in the black cloak of a *hijab*. This young woman was far more conventionally dressed than her grandmother whose dress could signify Tamil or Muslim identity, while there was little ambiguity about the young woman's identity since her garb clearly marked her as Muslim. Yet she had travelled overseas, and had sent home funds to build the house. She seemed to assert that she was not *haram* (impure), even though she had travelled overseas, and had gone outside the home without a male escort, because she was veiled.

Rethinking Displacement:
The Changing Roles of Women in Conflict and the Humanitarian Challenge

Currently there is growing recognition among those involved in humanitarian relief and rehabilitation work that women frequently bear the material and psychological brunt of armed conflict, and that there is hence a need for gender sensitive relief and rehabilitation work. Yet few programmes have systematically explored how relief might aid recovery from individual trauma and social suffering, and facilitate women's empowerment in and through conflict. Thus many gender programmes organised by the government's relief and rehabilitation authority and by NGOs still remain within conventional development thinking rather than attempting to work out *culturally* appropriate and effective strategies for women's empowerment in the context of the social transformations that have occurred over years of armed conflict and displacement.

Popular romanticisations of home, as well as constructions of internally displaced people as victims (the Sinhala term *'anathagatha kattiya'* literally means 'the abandoned people', while the Tamil term *'veedu attavargal'* means 'people without a home'), like the victim discourse concerning women in conflict in the human rights field, often obscure the realities of living at home in conflict. There is growing evidence to suggest that despite the psycho-social traumas that displacement entails, long-term displacement has provided windows of opportunity to displaced people for greater personal and group autonomy, and experiments with identity and leadership, particularly for women (Sachithanandam 1995). Certainly this has been the case for many displaced Tamil women, many of who have lost husbands and sons in the conflict. It is time now for humanitarian relief efforts to be conceptualised in terms of: (i) sustainability, (ii) maintaining local orders of ethnic coexistence and empowerment between displaced people and their local hosts, and (iii) empowerment of women within community and family structures in dramatically different ways from the pre-conflict situation. In Sri Lanka this is particularly necessary if the ethnic conflict is not to spread to new areas where the displaced have found refuge and are often perceived to be in competition with the poorer local population.

Many internally displaced women who have given up the dream of return are in the paradoxical position of being both materially and psychologically displaced by humanitarian interventions and human rights discourses and practices that define them as victims who need to be returned to their original homeland for their protection, and for the restoration of national and international order and peace.[5] For the assumption of return is a fundamental premise of state, international and NGO policies vis-a-vis internally displaced people. The fact is that these policies might be contributing to prolong the conflict and being a cause of trauma for people who fled their home over five years ago. This is particularly true for women for whom restrictions on mobility are difficult. Many of these women who wish to settle in the place where they have found refuge are being kept dependent on relief handouts rather than being assisted to build new lives and livelihoods. Thus, ironically, relief might be prolonging the trauma of the very people it is supposed to assist.

Under these circumstances, an approach which conceptualises humanitarian work as part of a development continuum with gender sensitive post-conflict intervention, is especially necessary in instances where armed conflicts have lasted for several years with communities experiencing cycles of war and peace and displacement. While for some women the conflict has provided windows of opportunity for greater personal and group autonomy, and experiments with identity and leadership, for others there has only been trauma. Certainly this has been the case for many displaced Tamil women who have lost their husbands and sons in the conflict.[6] It is hence important that relief aid should be conceptualised to sustain women's empowerment and leadership roles that initially arose as an effect of conflict within an altered family structure.

Clearly the process of a woman becoming the head of a household is not transparent, un-ambivalent or free of guilt, and this is evident in many young widows' uncertainty about whether they should return home if and when the conflict ended. For them displacement clearly constituted the space of ambivalence: a place of regeneration with the hope for a future unfettered by the past, by loss and trauma. They were also concerned that returning home would mean a return to the pre-war caste and gender staus quo. Of course, anxiety about return is also related to qualms about personal security and trauma. Anxiety about return is clearest among young women who are heads of households at Siddambarapuram, who have integrated with the local economy and among those who had previously been landless.

Languages of Empowerment: Recasting Widowhood and the Return to Matri-focal Families

A generation of young Tamil war widows who have been displaced to and in the border areas for many years seem to be increasingly challenging conventional Hindu constructions of widowhood as a negative and polluting condition which bars their participation from many aspects of community life. Several young widows working in Vavunia town but resident in the camp displayed their sense of independence by wearing the red *pottu*, the auspicious mark reserved for the married Hindu women, despite being widows or women whose husbands had abandoned them. Likewise in Batticaloa, several women who had lost husbands to death, displacement or family fragmentation in the course of armed conflict and flight from bombing and shelling, increasingly refuse to erase the signs of *sumankali* (particularly the auspicious red *pottu*) they wore when married, and refuse to be socially and culturally marginalised and ostracised because they lack husbands and children. Displacement along with fragmentation and reconstitution of families around women in a conflict where men frequently have had to flee to avoid being killed or forcibly inducted into armed groups appears to have provided a space to redefine traditional Hindu Tamil perceptions of widows and single women as inauspicious beings.

Of course the demographic fact of a large number of young widows who are unwilling to take on the role of the traditional Hindu widow, who may not participate in auspicious social rituals such as wedding ceremonies and who are generally socially ostracised, facilitates the transformation of negative cultural patterns. Yet these young women's response to their changed circumstances marks the space for redefinition of what it means to be an unmarried or widowed woman in the orthodox Hindu tradition. Consciously and unconsciously, they appear to be redefining conceptions of the 'good woman' as one who lives within the traditional confines of caste, kin group and village. As they struggle with new gender roles and identities, many of these young widows also struggle to find a language and cultural idiom to articulate their changed roles. They refuse to wear the prescribed garb of widowhood and appear to break with the ideology of Kanaki (Paththini), the exemplarily faithful wife and widow of Tamil mythology and ideology. Rather, they seem to evoke the sign of the devadasi—Kanaki's alter ego—who transcends conventional gender roles, the professional woman married to immortality for her talent and skill, most familiar to South Asian audiences in the name of the famed dancer and courtesan Madhavi from the first century Tamil Hindu-Buddhist epic *Sillapaddikaram*.

Yet, with the exception of the young Tamil widows, many women who have found more freedom in the conflict still seem to lack a language to articulate this process of transformation and regeneration, and clearly feel guilty about expressing their new found confidence. But one woman directly told me, 'It is a relief now that he (her husband) is not with me. He used to drink and beat me up'. While she worries for her personal safety and that of her children in the absence of her husband, particularly at night, she said that she anyway had to support the children mainly on her own even when her husband was with her.

The victim ideology that pervades relief and rehabilitation as well as social health and trauma interventions for women in conflict situations needs to be problematised, especially as it may be internalised by some women with damaging consequences. Non-combatant women who have found spaces of empowerment in the conflict need sustained assistance to maintain their new found mobility and independence in the face of sometimes virulently nationalist assertions of patriarchal cultural tradition and practices during the conflict and in the period of post-war reconstruction. The return to peace should not mean a return to the pre-war gender status quo. It follows that humanitarian and development interventions must creatively support and sustain positive changes in the status of civilian women living in situations of conflict.

In the north and east of Sri Lanka, the reality of war for women has been the loss of their men folk, loss of physical safety, psychological insecurity and a struggle for survival and sustaining the family. In short, a double burden of keeping themselves and their families fed and sheltered while often assuming the sole responsibility for the vulnerable, the weak, the children, the elderly and the disabled. As a result, women have crossed the private/public barriers to contend with the military, to compete in the market, to survive economically. As they have done so many women who have been forced to take on various new roles within their families and communities during the years of armed conflict have also gained greater self-confidence and decision-making power in the process. Over time women have gone through a process of transformation despite, and because of, the difficulty of taking on the added burden of traditionally male roles (head of household/principal income generator), due to the loss of their men folk and displacement. A backlash against women's changing roles and patterns of mobility is arguably one of the reasons for increased levels of violence against women.

Historically, women who took on various non-traditional gender roles in situations of social stress, conflict, war and revolution have been 'pushed back into the kitchen after the revolution' as part of a return to everyday life (Enloe 1983; Jayawardena 1986). Arguably, one of the primary reasons why the return to peace often meant a return to the gender status quo was the lack of social recognition and a culturally appropriate idiom to articulate, legitimate and support women's transformed roles and empowerment in the midst of conflict, trauma and social disruption. The paper then has attempted to distinguish between the kinds of transformations that have occurred by exploring their long-term impact. For social transformation to be sustained there needs to be cultural transformation, an acceptance of the legitimacy of women performing their new roles. And it is hence arguable that the greater threat and the greater challenge to the gender status quo comes less from the women in fatigues who might be asked to do desk jobs after the conflict, and more from the women who refuse to erase the read *pottu*, the unsung civilian women who wage a daily struggle to sustain their families and themselves.

Unlike in Afghanistan where the situation of women had unambiguously deteriorated due to conflict and the rule of the Taliban, in Sri Lanka, the evidence suggests that despite women's experience of traumatic violence and displacement, some changes to the gender status quo wrought by armed conflict might have empowered women whose freedom and mobility were restricted by patriarchal cultural mores, morality and convention in peace time. Several women who have faced the traumatic loss and scattering of family members due to displacement, conflict and the breakdown of family structures have also assumed new roles which were thrust upon them as a result of the disruption of peace time community organisation, social structures and patriarchal values. Yet I do not wish to suggest that this is a general story that might be told of women living in conflict and displacement. Rather this paper has attempted to focus on some women's agency at moments when they seem most victimised, to excavate some hidden moments and routes of women's agency in situations of conflict.

It is hence that this paper has sought to develop an alternative framework for analysing women's agency and ambiguous empowerment in conflict situations while analysing changing gender relations. This has meant exploring gender relations outside the scripted frames of nationalist women's mobilisation as well as gender analyses of women in politics. For it seems to me that the arena of politics proper in South Asia is a violent space and process, where women politicians are stripped and humiliated, as has repeatedly occurred at election time in Sri Lankan politics in the past decade (1990s). In Sri Lanka, which celebrated 50 year of democracy and was considered a mature democracy with free fair and non-violent elections until recently, the crisis is acute.

I have argued elsewhere that nationalist women and women combatants in nationalist struggles waged by groups like the LTTE, or the nationalist women fighters in Ireland or Palestine are imbricated in ultra-conservative 'nationalist constructions of women' and tend to subordinate their gender identities to the nationalist cause (Rajasingham 1995). Suicide bombing is but the extreme version of this phenomenon, which might, in Durkheimian terms, be glossed over as altruistic suicide, when individual autonomy and personal agency is completely subsumed in the national cause. The question might well be raised as to whether women would be more given than men to altruistic suicide, given their socialisation in patriarchal Asian cultures where girl children and women are more often than not taught to put themselves second, and their male kin, family and community honour first. Clearly, non-combatant women are differently imbricated in nationalist discourses, and the return to peace (which entails the reassertion of the gender status quo) is as problematic for them as it is for combatant women, but for different reasons.

A multi-ethnic women's politics that crosses ethnic lines might be the best and last bulwark against growing ethnic chauvinism that is being built up by democratic politicians intent on shoring up vote banks and personal power at the cost of national peace. Moreover, liberal left feminist positions that seek to transcend ethno-religious differences seem less likely to succeed in advancing women's rights than nationalist politics. Given that ethnic identity politics is increasingly coterminous with politics proper, it is arguable that women will have to forge new spaces for activism—outside the sphere of politics proper, and by exploiting the social and cultural spaces that have thrust women into new roles. Violent deaths and armed conflict open up ambiguous spaces of agency and empowerment for women, within their families and communities, who have not been directly engaged in violence.

The Gender Status Quo in War and Peace

To end then at the beginning: women political leaders seem to have had little success in bringing about significant improvements in the lives and positions of women in the South Asian region, and in building bridges across ethno-religious lines. Both the Indian and the Sri Lankan record clearly show that women in leadership positions without fundamental cultural and structural changes in society and polity rarely result in the advancement of the position of women. It is hence that South Asian women activists now advocate an at least 33 per cent reservation for women in parliament in order to begin to change gender imbalances in politics and society. At the same time the case of Hindu women activists of the BJP in India and women in the LTTE in Sri Lanka might indicate that for too long pro-peace secular feminist analysis has denied nationalist women their agency and their place in the sun. For, ironically, it is arguable that the recent South Asian picture of women entering new public spaces in peacetime as well as due to war indicates that women's agency and rights might be more effectively advanced within a nationalist framework due to the dominance of cultural nationalism in the region. In India and Sri Lanka it would appear that women's rights have been most systematically advanced within an ethnonationalist framework. Of course the Hindu nationalist BJP women are calling for a uniform civil code to enhance the rights of Muslim women vis-à-vis Muslim men, in a clearly ideologically biased manner, while Tamil women who dissent with the LTTE project have paid heavily and in some cases with their lives.[7]

In this context, the argument that two decades of war and uncertain peace may result in the unintended empowerment of women (sometimes at the expense of their men folk) in Sri Lanka is dangerous and disturbing for those of us who believe in and advocate the peaceful resolution of conflicts arising from social injustice. Peace we still conceptualise as a return to things the way they used to be, and this also includes, in the case of Tamil women, caste structures that buttresses the (gender) status quo. For, after all, gender hierarchy is one of the old established institutions of society, and as Partha Chatterjee noted of women in the colonial period, they are frequently constructed as the central purveyors of a community's 'culture' and 'tradition', ironically precisely at a time that their lives and social roles might be undergoing great transformations. Chatterjee's argument pertained to the colonial and Indian nationalist construction of women. Moreover, as numerous feminist analyses have pointed out, in periods of violent nationalist conflict women are often constructed as the bearers of a threatened national culture, tradition and values. Hence often a return to peace is indexed in the return to the traditional gender status quo—and even women revolutionaries are pushed back into the kitchen.

Hence the notion that wars disrupt social, political and gender hierarchies in unexpected ways and may benefit marginal groups and individuals, while being obvious is yet inadequately explored. This lacuna in the understanding of conflict and the new wars and their effects have much to do with how we conceptualise peace—as a return to the (gender) status quo. Peace we still think constitutes a return to things the way they used to be: the certain certainties of familiar, older ways of being and doing. But to conceptualise peace thus is another kind of epistemic violence. For women, wives and mothers who have lost the head of household or seen him 'disappear' in the violence, there is no return to the old certainties of the nuclear family headed by the father, the patriarch. For the war's widows, for those who have lived intimately with war, the changes wrought by almost two decades of armed conflict and uncertain peace in Sri Lanka are deep, complex, structural and fundamental. They forcibly challenge our certainties about war and peace. In this context, peace is necessarily a third place divorced from the past, a utopia perhaps, somewhere arguably between the old and the existing, the past and the present.

There is a need to study the structures of the new wars. Social scientists, developmental workers and activists have hesitated to address the issue of how social structural transformations wrought by long term armed conflicts might have also brought about desirable changes in entrenched social hierarchies and inequalities such as caste and gender, among people exposed to it. We are weary of analysing the unintended transformations brought by war, of seeing positives in violence. Yet for many women who have lost family members peace can never be a simple return to the past. Rather, peace necessarily constitutes a creative remaking of cultural meanings and agency—a third space between a familiar, often romanticised past and the traumatic present.

Failure to conceptualise and assist the dynamic of social transformation in conflict and peace building might also impede recovery from traumatic experiences, particularly since women (and men), who have to take on new non-traditional roles due to the conflict might suffer secondary victimisation arising from the new roles that they perform. This is particularly the case with a growing number of young Tamil women who have been widowed in the course of the armed conflict, and are challenging conventional Hindu constructions of the 'good woman' as one who is married and auspicious, or *samangali*. Increasingly, many young widows who have to go out to work to sustain young families are redefining the perception of widows (and to a lesser extent unmarried women) as inauspicious beings (*amangali*) by refusing to be socially and culturally marginalised and ostracised because they have lost their husbands. Yet very few of these women seem to have found a culturally appropriate language to articulate the transformations that they have experienced, and many feel ashamed, guilty and/or traumatised by their changed circumstances and gender roles arising from conflict.

This paper has also attempted to trace languages and patterns of empowerment in the generally tragic story of displaced Tamil women's lives towards recognising and promoting positive changes wrought by conflict. The new spaces of cultural or ideological struggle opened by the social structural transformations engendered by long term armed conflict also enable the agents and ideologues of violence, and recently invented nationalist 'tradition', which are often oppressive to women. Sometimes for strategic reasons those who advocate peace have tended to exaggerate the violence, and seen it as an all-encompassing phenomenon. Analysis has been the victim of such an approach to the study of violence, gendered violence in war and peace. This paper has, thus, tried to rethink some of the gender dynamics of a return to peace by analysing women's new roles and the cultural frameworks that enable or disable them. For unless the cultural frameworks that denigrate (widowed) women are challenged and transformed, women and men who are coping and trying to recover from the wounds of war will carry a double burden—rather than be empowered by the new roles thrust upon them. This paper, then, has charted the shifting terrain of women's ambivalent agency in armed conflict and peace building, the new spaces opened and the old spaces closed, and the changing structure of gender relations, in the war scarred north-east of Sri Lanka.

Notes

1 Recently this picture has changed as the role of girls and women combatants has been recognised and women are being pressed to take on roles in the peace process and post-conflict reconstruction.

2 The social role of women: of holding the family together, of caring for children, the sick and the elderly, makes women the worst sufferers during conflict.

3 Reports of the UN Special Rapporteur on Violence Against Women.

4   Colonial evolutionary classifications of (primitive) societies presumed that fewer restrictions on women's freedom indicated a more primitive stage of civilisational advance.

5   For those in the conflict regions, the right to set up residence in an area of one's choice and the right to movement is seriously restricted by the LTTE's and the GoSL's security regimes. While the government restricts the movement of Tamils displaced southward, the LTTE will not permit Sinhalese to move or settle in the north. In fact, both the LTTE and the government have used displaced persons as security shields or buffers during military campaigns. The government's restrictions on the mobility of persons and their confinement to camps have other implications for the youth and children. Militant groups who infiltrate camps have very little difficulty in recruiting new cadres from the deeply frustrated and resentful youth, men and women, girls and boys.

6   Among internally displaced Muslim women, however, the pattern is slightly different. Depending on the location of camps and the resources that families had, some women feel they have gained autonomy in their new situations, while others complain of greater segregation.

7   In Sri Lanka the debate over secular and personal law as it applies to women is somewhat different and it is arguable that customary law in the case of Tamil Thesavalame and Kandyan Sinhala Law is more favourable to women than is secular law on many matters. However this is not entirely the case regarding Muslim personal law in Sri Lanka.

References

Adele, Ann. 1993. *Women Fighters of Liberation*. LTTE Publication Section. Jaffna: Thasan Printers.

Agarwal, Bina. 1996. *A Field of One's Own: Gender and Land Rights in South Asia*. Cambridge: Cambridge University Press.

Butalia, Urvashi. 1998. *The Other Side of Silence: Voices from the Partition of India*. New Delhi: Viking Penguin.

Chatterjee, Partha. 1989. 'The Nationalist Resolution of the Women's Question', in Kumkum Sangari and Sudesh Vaid (eds), *Recasting Women: Essays in Colonial History*, pp. 235–53. New Delhi: Kali for Women.

Enloe, Cynthia. 1983. *Does Khaki Become You? The Militarisation of Women's Lives*. London: South End Press.

Fuglerud, Oivind. 1999. *Life on the Outside: The Tamil Diaspora and Long Distance Nationalism*. London: Pluto Press.

Jayawardena, Kumari. 1986. *Feminism and Nationalism in the Third World*. London: Zed Books.

Jeffery, Patricia. 1999. 'Agency, Activism and Agendas', in Patricia Jeffery and Amrita Basu (eds), *Resisting the Sacred and the Secular: Women's Activism and Political Religion in South Asia*, pp. 221–44. New Delhi: Kali for Women.

Kaldor, Mary. 1999. *New and Old Wars: Organised Violence in a Global Era*. Stanford: Stanford University Press.

Menon, Ritu and Kamala Bhasin. 1998. *Borders and Boundaries: Women in India's Partition*. New Delhi: Kali for Women.

Rajasingham, Darini. 1995. 'On Mediating Multiple Identities: The Shifting Field of Women's Sexuality in the Community, State and Nation', in Margaret Schuler (ed.), *From Basic Needs to Basic Rights: Women's Claim to Human Rights*, pp. 233–48. Washington D.C.: Women, Law and Development International.

———.1999. 'The Dangers of Devolution: The Hidden Economies of Armed Conflict', in Robert Rotberg (ed.), *Creating Peace in Sri Lanka: Civil War and Reconciliation*, pp. 57–70. Washington D.C.: Brookings Institution Press.

Sachithanandam, Sathananthan. 1995. *The Elusive Dove: An Assessment of Conflict Resolution Initiatives in Sri Lanka, 1957-1996*. Colombo: Mandru, Institute for Alternative Development and Regional Cooperation.

Samuel, Kumudhini. 1998. 'Women's Activism and Peace Initiatives in Sri Lanka', paper presented at the 'Women in Conflict Zones' seminar, Colombo, December.

Schalk, Perter. 1990. 'Birds of Independence: On the Participation of Tamil Women in Armed Struggle', *Lanka*, December.

Thangarajah, C.Y. 2003. 'Veiled Constructions: Conflict, Migration and Modernity in Eastern Sri Lanka', in K. Gardner and F. Osella (eds), *Contributions to Indian Sociology: Special Issue: Migration, Modernity and Social Transformation in South Asia*, 37(1&2): 141–62.

Thiruchandan, Selvy. 1997. *Ideology, Caste, Class and Gender*. Delhi: Vikas Publishing House.

Wadley, Susan (ed.). 1991. *The Powers of Tamil Women*. New Delhi: Manohar.

Yalman, Nur. 1967. *Under the Bo Tree*. Berkeley: University of California Press.

8

CONTESTING 'INFANTALISATION' OF FORCED MIGRANT WOMEN

Rita Manchanda*

Innocence, in the sense of complete lack of responsibility was the mark of their rightlessness as it was the seal of their loss of political status.

—'Stateless Persons', *The Portable Hannah Arendt*

Gender and Migration: Conceptual Concerns

The contemporary image of the forcibly displaced—the refugee and the internally displaced, fleeing life and livelihood threatening situations—is usually of a woman, with maybe her children clinging to her. Be it the Rohingya refugees in Bangladesh, the Tamil refugees in India or internally displaced persons (IDPs) in Sri Lanka, the Chakma and Chin forced migrants in India, Afghan refugees in Pakistan and the Lhotsampas (people of Nepali origin from Bhutan) in Nepal, the image is of helpless and unwanted women and children, dislocated, destitute and uprooted.

Those forcibly uprooted from their social and political community—refugees, stateless persons, IDPs, escapees from violence, and natural as well as man made disasters—are configured by the international state system as the alien, the marginalised and the 'right less'. In the state

*An earlier version of this paper, titled 'Gender, Conflict and Displacement: Contesting "Infantalisation" of Forced Migrant Women', was published in the *Economic and Political Weekly*, XXXLX(37), September 2004: 4179–86 and is being reprinted with permission.

system, rights, or the right to have rights, flow from being recognised as a citizen. The woman IDP/refugee represents the epitome of the marginalisation and disenfranchisement of the dislocated. Her identity and her individuality are collapsed into the homogeneous category of 'victim' and of her community. She is constructed as being devoid of agency, unable and incapable of representing herself, powerless and superfluous. The fact that women and their children make up nearly 80 per cent of the forcibly displaced makes their abject rightlessness more easily naturalised—because women in our patriarchal acculturated state system are largely seen as non-subjects, enjoying at best secondary citizenship. Indeed, the dyad of women and children in the dominant statistical discourse of forcibly displaced persons of the United Nations High Commission for Refugees (UNHCR) and the humanitarian agencies reinforces the configuration of women IDPs/refugees as victims and deems them devoid of the possibility of agency.

In South Asia, women make up between 42 to 52 per cent of refugees, stateless persons and IDPs. Moreover, recent gender sensitive analysis of international labour migration reveals an emerging 'feminisation' in some labour exporting countries (Siddiqui 2000: 82). For example, in 1999, 90 per cent of Sri Lanka's international labour force was female. Indeed, the emerging focus on women in the knowledge/policy frameworks on migrants from Bangladesh or Myanmar (Rohingya and Chin) raises critical questions for the distinction between migrant and refugee and the ensuing international care and protection regimes. Ranabir Samaddar, a trenchant critic of the rational choice 'pull-push' framework of voluntary versus forced migration, argues, 'If refugees are escapees from violence, what of migrants like women sex workers from Bangladesh or the women workers engaged in various forms of sweat labour who have to leave Bangladesh for fear of endemic violence by husbands and other males, from unorganised garment industry, the village and society as a whole' (Samaddar 1997: 104).

The complex web of factors that often underlie migration, especially in South Asia, make determination of voluntarism and coercion not a particularly useful approach, for example, in understanding the labour migration of Sri Lankan women refugees. The practice of agents scouring the refugee camps in southern India recruiting 'maids' for the Gulf countries was part of a process that goes back to the conflict in the north and east of Sri Lanka. There is the demographic imbalance resulting from the violence, flight and refuge, the withering of the host state's political and humanitarian concern and the suspicious gaze that fell on women refugees in the wake of the media spotlight on Tamil female suicide bombers.[1] The vulnerability of women separated from their social community, the increasingly oppressive conditions in the camps, the willful indifference of the 'protecting' government and the lures of the recruiting agents, all created the situation of exit.

In this paper I propose to use a gender sensitive perspective to problematise the distinction made between refugees and migrants in the context of South Asia, which is characterised by mixed population flows and forced migration, by focusing on the question—why do women leave/flee? The answer has major consequences for humanitarian politics and existing international gender indifferent regimes of exclusion. It then discusses its reverse phenomenon of the internally stuck, where again the majority are women, children, the aged and the disabled. What conflict conditions produce the 'internally stuck'? The paper examines the continuing inadequacy of national and international gender insensitive regimes of care and protection. It challenges the construction of the refugee woman as a non-subject, that is, only as a victim and belonging to the community. It seeks to recover the heterogeneity of women IDPs/ refugees. Next, it interrogates the possibility of women's agency and the cultural particularities that enable or constrain it, and the implications for reworking gender relations. A gendered analysis prompts an exploration of the implications of the social construction of masculinities and femininities, and domestic violence resulting from 'angry men' disabled from performing their 'provider' roles and women pushed to take up 'non-feminine' roles. Arguably, an analysis of the way woman as a refugee subject is configured as a non-person will help us gain fresh insights on the 'infantilisation' and 'dematuration' of the refugee experience which is a fundamentally disenfranchising process. Also, it should prompt us to question the secondary status of women as citizens in our polities.

Forcibly displaced people are not a homogeneous group and are divided by class, caste, ethnicity, religion and gender. The use of gender as a category of analysis is premised on the assumption that women experience dislocation and displacement or becoming refugees in a particularly gendered way, and that protection, care, resettlement and migration regimes need to become more sensitive to women's experience of dislocation and population movements. The emphasis on using a gendered lens runs the risk of over-determining gender as a category of analysis and clearly, gender is intersected by other competing identities. Nonetheless, the fact that nearly half of those forcibly displaced are women predicates taking seriously the category of gender to analyse why women flee; how women are treated as refugee subjects in refugee management.

Gender based persecution is not recognised as a ground for asylum determination in the international refugee regime determined by the 1951 Convention. As the paper will show, women are vulnerable to gender based violence as an inducement to flight, during flight and in the place of refuge and return. Also, the substantive increase in conflict-related growth of female headed households among the forcibly displaced further emphasises the need of a gendered lens.

Why Women Flee?

In South Asia, population movements are marked by a pattern of mixed flows of forced migration that challenge any neat distinction between refugees/IDPs and migrants, i.e., between political and economic reasons. The minority Chakmas (Buddhists) of the Chittagong Hill tracts in Bangladesh were displaced by the construction of the Kaptai dam in 1964 and became 'environmental refugees'—they went across the border to India and eventually settled in Arunachal Pradesh. Another exodus in 1979 was the result of conflict induced displacement (Choudhury 2003: 249–80). The overlapping linkages are evident. It is the indigenous peoples and the ethnic minorities that are politically discriminated and persecuted in the state's homogenising nation-building project; it is their lands that are appropriated for resettlement of the dominant community and that become the sites of development projects that impoverish and uproot them.

Arguably, the protection determining criteria of 'well-founded fear of persecution' has been expanded to accommodate the phenomenon of masses in flight—of escapees from a fear of generalised violence. But how valid is the distinction between life-threatening and livelihood-threatening situations for the victims of structural violence? They both blur into one another in South Asia and violence cannot effectively distinguish a refugee from a migrant, as evident in interviews of Bangladeshi women 'migrants' to India (Samaddar 1997: 114).

In South Asia, the two discourses of migrants and refugees/IDPs are linked. For example in Nepal, national and international humanitarian agencies have tended to grossly under-report the phenomenon of an estimated 150,000 to 200,000 people displaced by the Maoist insurgency, categorising it as a spurt in seasonal migration. Officially, the government recognises only 7,343 persons/families, the criteria being 'a person who has been displaced due to murder of a family member by the terrorists' (Norwegian Refugee Council/Global IDP Project 2004; Kernot 2003). Since one out of three persons in Nepal depends upon seasonal migration for family survival, there is a need to interrogate the usefulness of definitions of 'voluntary migration' in a situation of structural violence. When infrastructure, and educational and health facilities in the rural areas are degraded by the conflict, and agricultural production and local markets disrupted, and economic blockades strain a fragile subsistence economy, the strategy of the International Committee of the Red Cross (ICRC) to view displacement as a mere increase in normal migration rates raises questions for humanitarian politics.

The UN Guiding Principles normatively defines IDPs as persons who have 'been forced or obliged to flee or to leave their home or place of habitual residence, *in particular* as a result of or in order to avoid the effects of armed conflict, situations of generalised violence, violations of human rights or natural or human-made disasters, and who have not crossed an internationally recognised state border'. The phrase 'in particular' widens their application, but only somewhat, as we see in the case of Nepal where national and international agencies have used the continuum between migration and conflict-induced displacement in Nepal as grounds for not giving priority to the plight of IDPs in Nepal.

Let us fragment the homogeneous category of the 'forcibly dislocated' and turn our focus to the subjectivity of why women flee. Rohingya, Chin, Bhutanese (Lhotsampas) and Bangladeshi forced migrants are viewed as economic migrants and illegal immigrants. A Rohingya woman refugee in Karachi explains, 'We have come all the way here, not just because we were trying to escape poverty and find a way to earn a better living like the Bangladeshis, but because it was our only option to save our lives' (Brunette 1999). The Rohingya Muslims from Myanmar's eastern state of Arakan fled discrimination and persecution from the majoritarian Burman (Buddhist) state and co-ethnic Rakhine (Buddhist) thugs. Made stateless by a discriminatory citizenship law, repeatedly enrolled for forced porterage by the military junta and beaten and starved, their lands confiscated as they were made 'alien' and the women systematically raped, some 200,000 of them fled to Bangladesh in 1978, and another 250,877 in 1991 (51.3 per cent of whom were women).

Chris Brunette in a study of Rohingya women refugees cites a UNHCR source in a camp in Bangladesh in claiming that the mass rape of adolescent girls in Myanmar triggered the 1991 exodus. 'Voluntary repatriation' aided by the UNHCR was halted in 1994 because of continuing gross abuse. The outflow continues. Deemed 'illegal aliens' in Bangladesh, the Rohingyas are unwanted in their first site of 'refuge'. Starvation rations, intimidation by police and the fear of being pushed back makes them 'voluntarily opt' to being trafficked as illegal migrants to Karachi in Pakistan.

Traffickers eagerly seek vulnerable adolescent girls or young widows whose husbands have been killed by repeated forced porterage and food deprivation. Destitute and often with dependent children, for them flight often begins with gang rape, and the sexual violence continues throughout their flight as they are likely to be raped by the Bangladesh Rangers, in the refugee camps or slum settlements and then by the Indian and Pakistani border police. Brunette's interviews with Rohingya migrants in Karachi shows how notional the idea of voluntarism in terms of rational choice theory is. Farida was raped and abandoned by her husband, who also kept the children. 'I chose to leave, alone'. Rahima came with two small children to Pakistan in 1998. She said, 'The army took away my husband as a porter and for two weeks he got no food. He died of beatings and starvation. I had a house with three acres of paddy land. The government took it away and gave it to the Maghs (Rakhine Buddhists). You are not our people, they said. I had relatives in Pakistan. I decided to join them' (Khandekar 2000).

Phenomenon of the 'Internally Stuck'

Internationally, discourses on displacement accept that the majority of the conflict-induced displaced are women and children. In modern conflicts there is no segregated battlefield. The home front is the war front. Today's armed conflicts—particularly internal wars and insurgencies/counter-insurgencies—produce conditions of generalised violence and terror that target women and children to undermine support bases for the struggle; ethnic conflicts target women—the purveyors of group identity. While protection and care regimes are focused on the displaced, there is the twin phenomenon of the 'internally stuck', often the most vulnerable. Those who cannot flee are women, children, the elderly and the disabled.

In 1998 this author visited the mid-western hill district of Rolpa in Nepal where the Maoist insurgency was particularly severe, and found villages with few able-bodied men around. They had gone *farar* (underground) to escape being caught by the police or the Maoists, some had joined the rebels, and others had migrated to cities or across the border to India in search of work and still others had melted into the jungle. Mirule was one such village with only a few men, where women were taking on new roles such as getting into local government and constituting all women wards, using the plough (earlier taboo for women) and trading sexual favours for male labour to thatch their homes (Gautam et al. 2000).

Subsequently, as the conflict expanded into a civil war in 2001, and the cadres of the Communist Party of Nepal (Maoist) spread their control over the villages and the security forces fortified district headquarters and bazaars, the numbers of the displaced swelled. Generalised violence, forced recruitment, the use of food as an instrument of war, and the disruption of agricultural production, food-for-work programmes and education and health services made thousands leave and thousands not to return from seasonal migration. But, as Esperanza Martinez in the first structured study of Nepal IDPs observed, it also produced the phenomenon of the internally stuck. 'The most vulnerable groups such as women, children, and the elderly have been left behind in their villages' (Martinez 2002). They are left there to face increasing deprivation and violence.

Arguably, the ideological nature of a conflict, protracted conflict, internal conflict, and particularly armed conflict structured around identity politics in which rape is a weapon of war, will impact differentially on the forced displacement of masses of families in flight. The general pattern points to the forced migration of first the men and young boys with the women left behind to take care of the children, the elderly, the lands and houses. This observation is consolidated by the field research of Judith Pettigrew and Sara Shneiderman who argue that the Maoists do not recruit young married women who are required to provide food and shelter (Pettigrew and Shneiderman 2003: 19–29). Policy frameworks for protection and care need to factor in the implications of gendered stages of the 'internally stuck' and the forced migration of families in protracted conflict situations.

In the case of ethnic cleansing in Bhutan, persecuted Lothsampa (ethnic Nepalese) men fled the country, leaving behind families who were labelled anti-national. Female heads of household, disabled women and girls were particularly abused. One refugee told Human Rights Watch, 'The officer raped me. I was thirteen years old at the time. They raped me three or four times a day for seven days. I was taken from my house along with two other girls, my aunt's daughter and daughter-in-law. After that, we didn't feel like staying there' (Human Rights Watch 2003).

Feminist social scientist Rada Ivekovic raises questions about the gendered implications of the social pattern of men at high risk fleeing, and women and children 'internally stuck', left to face the wrath of armed attackers who show equal violence towards men and women. Drawing upon the Guatemalan conflict experience, Ivekovic asks, 'Is it by chance that when soldiers approach, the men flee towards the mountains, if they haven't already gone away with guerrillas. And women are left behind. Men explain that they think the soldiers will not harm women (although the opposite is true). Women are left behind with children to drag to safety; the result is the army catches them. Rape and assassination follow' (Ivekovic 2002: 2–3). With regard to resettlement too, a gendered pattern can be picked up in the case of Sri Lankan refugees. There are reports of women who were sent back first to test whether it was safe to return or not.[2]

Women as Refugee Subject:
Infantilised and Disenfranchised

Narratives of the forcibly displaced and dislocated reveal how the 'refugee'/IDP experience is a fundamentally disenfranchising process. The refugee is denied the right to represent herself/himself. I argue that the construction of the woman refugee as a non person dramatically highlights the 'infantilisation' and 'dematuration' of the refugee experience. With women and children constituting the majority of those forcibly displaced, their rightlessness in national and international humanitarian discourses is considered normal, their presumed passivity in practice, is naturalised. The disenfranchising process of the refugee experience, especially for women, is a stark throwback to the secondary status of women as citizens in our polities.

State and Women

In South Asia, where women are hemmed in by oppressive and gender discriminatory social regimes, the patriarchal states, while affirming equality of citizenship, have in law and practice provided for gross inequalities and denial of rights to women as citizens. The work of Menon and Bhasin (1998) and Butalia (1998) in uncovering 'her-story' of the state project to recover women abducted during the partition of India and Pakistan in 1947, irrespective of what the abducted/resettled women wanted, exposed the denial of their right to represent themselves and the rejection of their claims to their children. It revealed the state's paternalistic bias and its configuration of women as citizens without rights. Between 1947 and 1955, the governments of India and Pakistan sought to recover 20,758 abducted women. The patriarchal state *infantilised* the abducted and raped women, denied them the possibility of representing themselves and in the process effectively disenfranchised them.

The same story was repeated in the wake of the violent separation of East Pakistan from West Pakistan in 1971, and the subsequent emergence of Bangladesh. Thousands of women who had been dislocated in Dhaka and other urban centres were corralled in camps and made available to Pakistani soldiers. Geoffrey Davis, then an Australian medical graduate specialising in advanced pregnancy termination procedures, recalled that the medical teams dealt with about a 100 MTPs (medically terminated pregnancies) a day in Dhaka alone. The *birangonas* (rape survivors) were diseased, malnourished and traumatised. When Davis arrived in 1972, the camps were being disbanded and the women were being sent home, often to be killed by their husbands because they had been dishonoured. He worked for six months in Bangladesh performing MTPs. Thousands of babies were given away for adoption to International Social Services, USA. Did the women consent? Was there a process for finding out what they wanted? He did not know (SACW 2002). President Mujibur Rahman, the first ruler of 'Bangladesh', had publicly denounced the children born of the rape of Bangladeshi women-citizens as aliens who had to be sent outside.

Institutional Regimes of Care, and Women

Institutional regimes of protection and care have only in the last few decades come under pressure to recognise gender based violence.

Feminist activism has resulted in the International Criminal Court of Justice recognising rape as an instrument of war. Gendered discourses have exposed the use of rape as an instrument of ethnic cleansing.

The 1951 Refugee Convention does not provide for a separate category for women who suffer gender specific persecution or human rights abuse in the private sphere of the home, or for women who suffer violence for gender based cultural transgressions. Since 1985, the UNHCR has tried to develop more gender sensitive frameworks as evident in the 1991 Executive Committee Guidelines for Protection of Women (IASC 1999). But as Mekondjo Kaapanda and Sherene Fenn elucidate, while it recognises that there may be a specific nature of an abuse suffered by a 'social group', and encourages women to be covered as a 'social group', it is left to individual states to follow it (IASC 1999; Kaapanda and Fenn 2000: 26–29).

In the case of South Asia, none of the states are signatories to the 1951 Convention or the 1967 Protocol. (However, they are signatories to Convention on the Elimination of All Forms of Discrimination Against Women, or CEDAW). UNHCR's protection mandate is subject to bilateral agreements. Thus refugee determination, protection and care become ad hoc and vulnerable to competing strategic and economic compulsions, as in the case of the Chin (Burmese) refugees in Mizoram, India. Following a review of India's hostile attitude to the military junta in Myanmar and with the security establishment keen to improve relations, from 1994 onwards the Chin refugees have been subject to expulsion. It coincided with a local 'sons of the soil' upsurge against 'aliens' (Mizos and Chins are co-ethnic but divided by post-colonial state borders). The Chin refugee camps in Mizoram were peremptorily closed down and a policy of push back threatened 40,000 persons—deemed by bureaucratic fiat to be 'economic migrants' (Manchanda 1997). The Chin refugees appealed, largely unsuccessfully, to the UNHCR in Delhi for protection and against refoulement, which for most meant arrest, rape and/or execution at the hands of the Myanmar army.

In the case of the Chin women, who constituted half of those dislocated, it is argued that the failure of UNHCR and the Indian authorities to recognise gender based violence as grounds for asylum has trivialised rape and placed women at great risk. A recent case of a Chin women asylum seeker exposes the crass lack of gender sensitivity in the interview process of the UNHCR office in Delhi. Nineteen-year-old Agnes (name changed) fled from her village on the Myanmar border and reached Mizoram on 24 March 2000 and from there Delhi on 6 May 2000. Her brother had been active in student politics and had escaped from the military junta to a third country. The army came after the family and Agnes claimed that she had been raped by an army captain. In her first interview on 23 September 2000 with a UNHCR protection officer called Bimla (name changed), she was asked to describe the structure of the room in which she was raped and physically detail what had happened there. Agnes was unable to be coherent. Her asylum request was rejected by the UNHCR. She appealed, and in her second interview on 13 March 2003 a legal officer called Cecilia (name changed) asked her, 'How did the captain rape you? Show how you were raped? Show all the actions of how the captain raped you and what you did?' Her appeal was rejected again. On the second appeal 'Agnes' was finally accorded recognition by the UNHCR in December 2003.[3]

The consequences of the UNHCR's gender insensitive attitude was painfully exposed in the case of Mary (name changed), the daughter of a Christian pastor who had sought refuge in Mizoram in 1993 after she was beaten and raped by an army officer for criticising the military junta. She was teaching in Mizoram till 2000, when she was pushed back into Myanmar. As she was marked for being politically active, the military went after her and raped and tortured her. She then fled to Guam. There she tested positive for tuberculosis during a skin test. Being pregnant, she could not have an X-ray done. She was kept in isolation for several months until she was rescued by a visiting reverend of the University Baptist Church (Banerjee 2002).

'Mary's' story reveals not only the trivialisation of rape as a grounds for protection and asylum, but also the prejudices and superficiality of the framework for understanding women's 'fear of violence' and consequently protection and care regimes. Also, her story as well as the stories of the Rohingya, Bangladeshi and Sri Lankan dislocated women emphasises the limits of trying to distinguish between 'economic' and 'political' migrants, and forced and voluntary dislocation. Above all, these stories reveal the abject rightlessness of woman as a refugee subject and its throwback on woman as a citizen in South Asia.

In South Asia, despite the 1991 Executive Committee Guidelines for the Protection of Refugee Women, the systems of protection and care in UNHCR aided camps remain largely gender insensitive, partly due to the lack of a national or regional refugee law and partly because national laws reinforce gender discrimination. In the case of the Bhutanese refugees (Lhotsampas) in Nepal and the Afghan refugees in Pakistan, respectively, bilateral agreements define the protection agency's mandate in Nepal and Pakistan.

Bhutanese Women Refugees

Discriminatory citizenship laws, persecution, violence, rape and forced 'voluntary migration' resulted in the flight of masses of ethnic Nepalese from Bhutan to India and then to Nepal. By 1990s there were 100,000 refugees in seven camps in Nepal, managed jointly by the Government of Nepal and the UNHCR, and aided by the World Food Programme and several international NGOs. More than 10 years later, the camps still exist and are regarded as models. Females comprise around 49 per cent of the camps' population. In 2003, Human Rights Watch on the basis of a survey in the camps indicted the UNHCR and the Government of Nepal for failing to protect refugee women's rights adequately. A key source of this failure is the continued use of a registration and ration distribution system based on household cards listed under the name of the male household head. The Government of Nepal would issue a separate ration card to a woman only if she obtained a legal divorce. But under Nepalese law, divorce endangers women's custody of children and their property rights on return to Bhutan. Consequently, Bhutanese refugee women who face domestic violence are either forced to stay in abusive and polygamous situations, or make ad hoc arrangements with the refugee camp management to collect their food rations separately, thus relying on the mercy of the management rather than a system fair to women. They are unable to obtain separate housing and have to find refuge with other family members in already overcrowded huts.

Also, the protection regime in the camps trivialise gender based violence as the reason for flight and domestic violence in the camps. The mechanisms for grievance redressal and the camp decision-making structures are both gender insensitive and tend to infantalise women. According to Geeta M. (name changed), a Bhutanese refugee, 'Sometimes I was beaten so badly I bled. My husband took a second wife. I didn't agree. He said, "If you don't allow me to take a second wife, then the ration card is in my name, and I'll take everything". I have asked my husband for the health card and ration card and he doesn't give it to me. I have not got approval to get a separate ration card'.

Refugee women are not entitled to register their children as refugees if they are not born of a Bhutanese (refugee) father. Camp administrators base registration procedures on Nepalese law, which discriminates against women by denying them the ability to transfer citizenship to their children. This discriminatory policy denies unregistered children access to food rations, clothes, education and health, and makes them ineligible for repatriation to Bhutan. Refugee men can register children born of non-refugee women. A Bhutanese refugee woman who marries a Nepalese citizen and separates (divorce means losing custody of children) and returns to the camps can have her rations reinstated, but her children will not be registered. Saver's sample survey of unregistered asylum seekers (SAFHR 2003) found that 41 per cent were children like three-year-old Samjhana born in Beldangi II camp. Samjhana's mother Rupa had been expelled from Bhutan in 1991, and she found refuge in the camp with her parents. She married a Nepalese man, but while she was pregnant her husband deserted her. She returned to the camp and her rations were reinstated. But Samjhana remains an unregistered child refugee.

The inability of refugee women to register their children not only deprives them of aid packages but also prevents them from participating in the verification and categorisation process that would allow them to be repatriated to Bhutan. Moreover, the verification process places women at a disadvantage to have their claims fairly considered. The Joint Verification Team conducting interviews at Khudanabari camp in 2003, for instance, had no women members. Women were unable to have independent interviews even if they were separated from their husbands. Furthermore, women and children who had found safety by living separately from abusive heads of households remained linked to and dependent on them for purposes of verification and repatriation. Kala G. (name changed) from the Khudanabari camp says, 'They asked my husband about why he left Bhutan. But I was not given a chance to tell my story, and I was tortured more than he was (in Bhutan)'. The Bhutanese refugee camps have been hailed as model arrangements. At the other end of the spectrum are the UNHCR aided Rohingya refugee camps in Bangladesh, where the fate of 21,000 refugees (and more unregistered 'new arrivals') remains undecided. Subsequent to the bilateral agreement negotiated with the UNHCR on protection and care in the camps nine months after the exodus began in 1990–91, the UNHCR chose not to make changes in camp arrangements which threatened women's physical security, i.e., location of latrines, water sources and dim lighting. Khandekar and Haider's account of the protection of Rohingya refugee women reveals that 'young and adolescent girls have become hostages in the hands of their own community. Refugee leaders are said to command a force of 200 men who have taken the camp population under their control ignoring directives of the government and UNHCR' (Khandekar 2000: 64).

'Return' and resettlement policies are rarely formulated to incorporate a gendered perspective. For dislocated women with small children, the camp provides a semblance of community. In a visit to a IDPs' camp in the Kokrajhar area of Assam, Roshmi Goswami of the North East Network observed that while others were talking of the need for resettlement, 22-year-old Phulmoni, a mother of three, looked lost and blank. Her husband had been hacked to death while they were fleeing. The relief camp was congested and uncomfortable, but she felt secure (Goswami 2000).

'Going through Men'—Aid Programmes Reproducing Local Patriarchies

Moreover, the cultural specificity approach of 'going through the men', for example as in the Afghan refugee camps in Peshawar, tend to reinforce oppressive local patriarchies. Sharon Krummel, an advisor on aid programmes for Afghan women refugees, observes that aid personnel tend to construct all women as 'vulnerable' and as 'victims'. Pakistani feminist Rubina Saigol argues that aid agencies prop up local patriarchies and justify the claimed necessity of male protection of women (Saigol 2000).

Humanitarian protection and aid discourses, especially service delivery strategies, emphasise 'cultural specificity'. International advisors on accessing displaced Afghan women have stressed the need to be sensitive to the culture and tradition of the Afghan tribes. However Saigol, who has been working with the Afghan refugees in Pakistan, argues that these advisors do not problematise 'culture and tradition'.[4] Culture and tradition are not permanently fixed; they are being reformed, especially in the changing social conditions created by conflict. The questions that need asking are: Who is making that culture? Who is invoking that tradition? Arguably, uprooting and dislocation, the loss of the male identity as breadwinner and the exigencies of the mixing of tribal ethnicities in a refugee situation produces and reforms 'tradition' and 'culture' as evinced in the reconstruction of the majority Pashtoonwali identity. In a refugee situation, the group's need to preserve community and culture intensifies. The *jihad* comes to be aggressively centred on women's bodies by making them invisible. A fatwa issued by the United Ulema of Afghanistan detailing restrictions on women reveals the hysterical paranoia of a conflict-destabilised society (Khattak 1995: 52–64). The more insecure the men the stricter the seclusion of women, the more extra-domestic activities are denounced and the more aggressiveness and domestic violence mark male identities.

Saigol argues that 'when women are helped in ways that reinforce an oppressive status quo the only people helped are the powerful males of the group'. Feminist analysts like Cynthia Haq, Nancy Dupree and Hanne Christensen have advised forums set up for the protection of Afghan refugee women and children to 'go through the men', that is, to first ensure the support of male leaders (Saigol 2000). This approach however tends to reinforce oppressive local patriarchies. Saigol warns that it will further marginalise alternative voices like that of the Afghan Women's Network (AWN) and the Revolutionary Afghan Women's Association (RAWA). Arguably, the reach of these urban educated women is limited and controversial, but Saigol emphasises the need to probe these gender sensitive approaches as practical alternatives. In particular, Saigol denounces strategies that seek to win space for women's education and income generating schemes by projecting them as enhancing *jihad*. Interviews with women refugees reveal that women do not perceive the violence as *jihad*—and this could be a potential resource for promoting peace.

Interviews of refugee women in camps in Peshawar and Islamabad reveal that they are not helpless and passive non-subjects. Some like Masooma assert, 'We think that women can do so many things. Afghan women are strong and have the ability to work. They can take steps on the way to peace provided conditions are made conducive for them to work and facilities are provided to them'. The AWN has been appealing to all international missions to involve women in peace-building work, as they unlike the men do not have a stake in the war and have seen from close quarters the suffering and deprivation caused by it. The hypocritical attitude of UN bodies on taking women seriously was exposed when Angela King's UN Gender Mission visited Peshawar and Islamabad and some women asked her to mobilise educated Afghan women in the peace-making process. King reportedly asked them to apply for UN jobs (Banerjee 2002). It is a reflection of the 'going through the men' approach that justified the surrender of the camps by the Pakistan government and international aid agencies to Taliban control.

Ambivalent Agency:
Reworking Gender Relations

In the iconography of conflict and displacement, women are the helpless victims in need of protection and care. Clearly, as we have seen, dislocated women suffer loss, deprivation and violence. Moreover, in South Asia conflict has produced 'nationalisms' and 'fundamentalisms' that have been particularly detrimental to women's autonomy and life fulfilment chances. However feminist research in recovering what women do in wartime has revealed that conflict has directly and indirectly opened up spaces for women to develop agency, effecting structural social transformations and producing new social, economic and political realities that redefine gender and caste hierarchies. The survival needs of the family have pushed women to take on new roles; women have been mobilised in support of conflict, but they have also been in the forefront of an (informal) politics of mitigating the impact of violence and peacebuilding. Women dislocated by conflict in South Asia, internally or across borders, have demonstrated what Darini Rajasingham, analysing the situation of IDPs in Vavuniya, Sri Lanka in this volume, describes as 'ambivalent empowerment', as it is born out of loss and devastation (Rajasingham 2000).

The 'gains' from conflict discourse are highly controversial and contested, especially when articulated by 'non victims' (Manchanda et al. 2001). But the need to validate the possibility of conflict producing spaces for ambivalent empowerment is crucial for reshaping humanitarian policy responses, peace-building and post-conflict resettlement policy frameworks, and shoring up women's rights. It involves the recovery of women's experience of conflict induced displacement as a resource, and value and policy frameworks that recognise that women are not just passive victims structured in the humanitarian discourse as 'dependent' on aid handouts. Instead, it asks for refugee/IDP situations to be viewed as an opportunity for seeding education, health, income generation and political awareness capacity. It also calls for factoring in women's agency in post-conflict resettlement policy frameworks and safeguarding these unintended 'gains' for reworking gender relations. Finally, it urges recognition of women's activism in peace-building and reconciliation as well as support for strengthening it.

Arguably the claim that conflict and displacement can create conditions that open up spaces for women begs the question: Is it meaningful to talk of agency or the ambivalent agency of women IDPs/refugees as a homogenous grouping when confronted with the reality of the situation of Afghan women IDPs/refugees? Researchers like Khattak and Saigol assert that their plight exposes the 'myth' of conflict producing spaces for developing agency (Saigol 2000; Khattak 1995). The Afghan refugee woman symbolises abject destitution, passivity and submission to increasingly restrictive, violent and oppressive regimes of seclusion and denial. Abducted, raped and tortured by all sides, the Afghan women— the embodiment of the honour of their nation—face continuing and often greater violence in the refugee camps. Frustrated and insecure men whose masculinity as the 'provider' has been undermined take it out on the women. Moreover, the need to provide sons for the *jihad* results in their reproductive capacity being appropriated by the ethnic group. The resurgence of fundamentalist attitudes towards women in the refugee population places them in totally dependent situations. The result, observes Nancy Dupree in 'The Afghan refugee family abroad', is greater confinement, depression, illness, and violence (cited in Saigol 2000). 'Our future is clear, there is nothing for us,' said a refugee woman (Mehdi 2000: 33).

Visits to the Afghan refugee camps show the men sitting idle while the women are busy and active. Several of the interviews done by the Sustainable Development Policy Institute (SDPI) with Afghan women refugees reveal a sense of self-worth and identity reminiscent of the interviews with internally displaced women in camps in eastern Sri Lanka. Selvy Thiruchandran, analysing the responses of the displaced Tamil and Sinhala female heads of household writes, 'These women did not feel powerless when we talked to them and they showed an individual capacity for political discourse' (Thiruchandran 1999). Indeed, the quotes of the refugee women cited by Saigol reinforce this assessment. Somia asserts, 'None of the leaders have worked for their people but for their own interests and hunger for power'. Fahima states, 'The majority of Afghans don't want to be involved in war. People have hatred towards those who fight (sic). The common man is fed up with this meaningless war'. Masooma understands that, 'Foreign hands work among Afghans. Every country seeks its interest in the destruction of our country. For example all our neighbours want a government friendly to their interests'.

Mosarrat Qadeem's study (2003) of Afghan IDPs reveals the complex adjustments that dislocated women have made to rebuild community for the survival of female-headed (and male disabled) displaced families in Kabul city. According to UNICEF, about 300,000–400,000 families were displaced by the conflict in 2000. Qadeem describes the complex forms of kin-related women households that emerged. 'So many men died in the conflict that it was not uncommon to find compounds run by charismatic matriarchs responsible for 8–10 married, widowed daughters and daughter-in-laws. Sometimes nuclear households without full time males would cluster around a respected female elder of the community.' Protection-less (without men) women with small children would gather informally in groups or cooperatives where food and other resources were shared and labour was divided.

However, in conditions of forcible displacement and exile, the initial 'decomposition' of social structures that provides space for loosening patriarchal reins and reworking gender, caste and community relations sometimes gives way to 'recomposition' of patriarchy. In the Afghan situation it has meant greater veiling and mobility restrictions for refugee women. Khattak and Saigol point out women were dislocated and forced to come out of their homes to sustain their families. This may seem like liberation and increased mobility, but closer examination shows that 'patriarchy had found another way to maintain its tenuous hold in the form of increased domestic violence'. The male ideal among Afghan refugees came to be centred on manifesting domestic aggression. Several women complained of greater violence by their maimed husbands.

In the midst of such shrinking space, however, it is important to recognise that women continue to demonstrate degrees of resistance. As Saigol points out, many women were beaten and tortured by their in-laws for not submitting to remarriage. They dared to challenge an interpretation of Pashtoon culture that sanctioned such remarriages. As Rahima asserted, 'Pakhtuns have no tradition that obliges a woman to leave her children and marry another one'. Their rejection was a practical one. 'He (brother-in-law) used to beat my children. He asked me to marry him. I told him I already have five children. I don't want to ruin my life … I don't want another husband to own me (Saigol 2000)'.

In Sri Lanka, the civil war for cultural and political rights of the Tamil people had transformed the north and east of the island into war-ravaged zones under shifting control of the government and the LTTE. It is estimated that about 55,000 women were widowed, more than 760,000 IDPs created, some 1,000,000 people made refugees and nearly a third of the affected households were headed by females. Selvy Thiruchandran (1999) exploring the structural implications of this phenomenon argues that they demonstrate that the 'domestic need not be fixedly gendered. Empirical studies of female-headed house-holds, particularly in a refugee-like situation, show a reworking of gender and familial relations'.

Feminist research about the experiences of women in the Sri Lankan conflict has sought to critically analyse how the difficulty of assuming the double burden of nurturing and being primary decision-maker and income earner in women-headed households has set off unintended processes of desirable structural transformation. This is not to minimise the psychosocial traumas that displacement entails, nonetheless, it is argued that long-term displacement has provided women the oppor-tunity for greater personal and group autonomy and experiments with identity. Circumstances are worse for displaced women who are forced to live in refugee camps, where privacy is non-existent and levels of generalised violence, alcoholism and domestic violence are high, but displacement has also produced a liberating displacement of caste and gender hierarchies.

Significantly, there is a stark contrast in the experience of dislocated Tamil women refugees in comparison to their Muslim counterparts. It underlines the need to fragment 'displaced women' and factor in particular cultural considerations. Some 75,000 Muslims were dis-placed to camps in Puttalam in 1990. There is the familiar pattern of an insecure community in exile reinforcing its cultural identity by exercis-ing greater control over its women, as evident in the new emphasis on *purdah*. Zackariya and Ismail's empirical study of the experience of women IDPs in 1992–97 reveals high rates of school dropouts, early marriage and a cycle of dependence perpetuated and sustained by vio-lence and legitimised by recourse to religious tradition. The official policy of a cash assistance of Rs 25,000 in lieu of dowry to a displaced couple marrying has been a further inducement to early marriage. In the Puttalam area where employment opportunities are limited, dis-placed men are largely unemployed. This has encouraged the phenom-enon of women migrating as housemaids to the Middle East (Zackariya and Ismail 1998: 25–51). This trend of feminisation of international labour movements in Sri Lanka raises questions for gender relations that are beyond the scope of this paper to examine.

The picture is clearly a mixed one, one that entails conflict opening up spaces for development of women's agency. Moreover, as in the case of the young Tamil widows, it is an ambivalent empowerment, for the women carry a burden of guilt about the empowering spaces that their loss has opened up. Rajasingham argues that the failure to develop cultural frameworks that legitimise these new empowering structural transformations add to the burden of guilt of these women. Moreover, it raises questions about the sustainability of these changes in the aftermath of conflict. In the current phase of Sri Lanka's ceasefire peace process, there is need to recognise the capacity of female heads of households as full agents. The workings of the 'Women's Committee' comprising nominees of the LTTE and the government are being closely watched all over South Asia as a possible model for the mainstreaming of gender in resettlement and peace processes.

For safeguarding the 'ambivalent gains' from conflict, solidarity networks need to be built at the local, national and international levels to make sure the spaces opened up do not close even before there is a realisation that they existed. Humanitarian and development discourses need to recognise and shore up these empowering changes during the resettlement process. Culturally enabling frameworks which legitimise new empowering roles and new realities need to be consciously strengthened, especially as the ideological frameworks of nationalist and ethnic struggles tend to configure women as purveyors of tradition and community identity. In the aftermath, the process of return to 'peace' should not mean a push back to the gendered status quo and secondary citizenship status of women. A gendered analysis of the forcibly displaced, by focusing on the way the experience of dislocation infantalises and disempowers women in particular, can provide critical insights on how to shore up women's rights in conflict and post-conflict situations.

Notes

1 The female suicide bombers Dhanu, Shanthi and Lakshmi, wives of co-conspirators in the Rajiv Gandhi assassination case, drew suspicion to the women in the refugee camps. Subsequently, women and children were kept in high-risk special camps (Hans 2003).
2 In the Sri Lankan resettlement process the women were sent first. In 1992 women made up 52 per cent of the refugee population, and by 1997 it was down to 21,606 females to 23,927 males (Hans 2003).

3 Personal communication with Anuradha Sai Baba of 'The Other Media', New Delhi, who is providing assistance to the Burmese refugees.

4 Saigol refers to Cynthia Lawrence Haq's 'Report to Women's Commission for Refugee Women and Children' (Haq 1989), Hanne Christenson's 'The Reconstruction of Afghanistan: A Chance for Rural Afghan Women' (Christenson 1999), Nicola Johnston's 'Afghan Refugee Women: What Room for Manoeuvre?' (Johnston 1999) and Nancy Hatch Dupree's 'The Afghan Refugee Family Abroad' (Dupree 1999).

References

Banerjee, Paula. 2002. 'Dislocating Women and Making the Nation', *Refugee Watch*, December.

Brunette, Chris. 1999. 'Trafficked from Hell to Hades', *Images Asia*, Report, November.

Butalia, Urvashi. 1998. *The Other Side of Silence: Voices from the Partition of India*. New Delhi: Viking Penguin.

Choudhury, Sabyasachi Basu Ray. 2003. 'Chittagong Hill Tracts: Uprooted Twice', in Ranabir Samaddar (ed.), *Refugees and the State: Practices of Asylum and Care in India*, pp. 249–80. New Delhi: Sage Publications.

Christenson, Hanne. 1999. 'The Reconstruction of Afghanistan: A Chance for Rural Afghan Women', *Afghanistan Studies Journal*, 7.

Dupree, Nancy Hatch. 1999. 'The Afghan Refugee Family Abroad', *Afghanistan Studies Journal*, 7.

Gautam, Shobha, Amrita Banskota, and Rita Manchanda. 2000. 'Where there are no Men: Women in the Maoist Insurgency in Nepal', in Rita Manchanda (ed.), *Women, War and Peace in South Asia*, pp. 214–51. New Delhi: Sage Publications.

Goswami, Roshmi. 2000. 'Women and Armed Conflict—North East India', paper presented at a WISCOMP conference on 'Women and Security', New Delhi.

Hans, Asha. 2003. 'Refugee Women and Children: Need for Protection and Care', in Ranabir Samaddar (ed.), *Refugees and the State: Practices of Asylum and Care in India*, pp. 355–95. New Delhi: Sage Publications.

Haq, Cynthia Lawrence. 1989. Report to Women's Commission for Refugee Women and Children, Internal Rescue Committee (IRC), New York, March.

Human Rights Watch. 2003. September. *http://www.hrw/org/reports/2003/nepal*.

IASC (Inter Agency Standing Committee). 1999. 'Mainstreaming Gender in the Humanitarian Response to Emergencies'. April 1999.

Ivekovic, Rada. 2002. 'Between Myth and Reality', *Refugee Watch*, June: 2–3.

Johnston, Nicola. 1999. 'Afghan Refugee Women: What Room for Manoeuvre?', *Afghanistan Studies Journal*, 7.

Kaapanda, Mekondjo and Sherene Fenn. 2000. 'The Story of Refugee Women', *Refugee Watch*, June: 26–29.

Kernot, Sarah. 2003. *Insurgency and Displacement: Perspectives on Nepal*, Paper No. 14, June. Kathmandu: SAFHR.

Khandekar, Zulfiqar and Ali Haider. 2000. 'Protection to Refugees: Case of Rohingya Women', in Abrar Chaudhury (ed.), *On the Margins*. Dhaka: Refugee and Migratory Movements Research Unit (RMMRU), Dhaka University.

Khattak, Saba Gul. 1995. 'Militarisation, Masculinity and Identity in Pakistan: Effects on Women', in Nighat Khan and Afia Shehrbano Zia (eds), *Unveiling the Issues*, pp. 52–64. Lahore: ASR Publications.

Martinez, Esperanz. 2002. 'Conflict Related Displacement', 31 July. Kathmandu: USAID.

Manchanda, Rita. 1997. 'Nowhere Peoples: Burmese Refugees in India', in Tapan Bose and Rita Manchanda (eds), *States, Citizens and Outsiders*, pp. 203–18. Kathmandu: SAFHR.

Manchanda, Rita, Bandita Sijapati and Rebecca Gang. 2001. *Women Making Peace: Report of the Kathmandu Workshop*. SAFHR. June.

Mehdi, Syed Sikander. 2000. 'Chronicles of Suffering—Refugee Women of South Asia', *Refugee Watch*, June: 33–35.

Menon, Ritu and Kamla Bhasin. 1998. *Borders and Boundaries: Women in India's Partition*. New Delhi: Kali for Women.

Norwegian Refugee Council/Global IDP Project. 2004. *Profile of Internal Displacement in Nepal*. Geneva.

Pettigrew, Jill and Sara Shneiderman. 2003. 'Women and the Maobadi', *Himal*, January: 19–29.

Qadeem, Mosarrat. 2003. 'IDP's in Afghanistan', *Refugee Watch*, August.

Rajasingham, Darini. 2000. 'Ambivalent Empowerment: The Tragedy of Tamil Women', in Rita Manchanda (ed.), *Women, War and Peace in South Asia: Beyond Victimhood to Agency*, pp. 102–30. New Delhi: Sage Publications.

Saigol, Rubina. 2000. 'At Home or in the Grave: Afghan Women and the Reproduction of Patriarchy', paper presented at a WISCOMP Conference on 'Women and Security'. New Delhi.

Siddiqui, Tasneem. 2000. 'State Policy and the Nature of Female Migration', in Abrar Chaudhury (ed.), *On the Margins*, Dhaka: RMMRU, Dhaka University.

Samaddar, Ranabir. 1997. 'Still They Come—Migrants in Post Partition Bengal', in Ranabir Samaddar (ed.), *Reflections on Partition in the East*, pp. 104–14. New Delhi: Vikas Publishing House.

South Asia Citizens Web (SACW). 2002. '(Dis) Appearing Women in Nationalist Narratives', interview with Dr Geoffrey Davis by Bina D'Costa, 1 June, The Australian National University. *www.sacw.net*.

SAFHR (South Asia Forum for Human Rights). 2003. 'Unregistered Bhutanese Asylum Seekers: A Pilot Survey'. Kathmandu: SAFHR.

Thiruchandran, Selvy. 1999. *The Other Victims of War: Emergence of Female Headed Households in Eastern Sri Lanka*, vol. II. New Delhi: Vikas Publishing House.

UNHCR. 2003. 'Sexual and Gender Based Violence Against Refugees, Returnees and Internally Displaced Persons: Guidelines for Prevention and Response', Geneva.

Zackariya, Faizun and Ismail. 1998. 'Early Marriage', in *Confronting Complexities: Gender Perceptions and Values*, Colombo: CENWOR.

9

Gender, Borders and Transversality: The Emerging Women's Movement in the Burma–Thailand Borderlands

Mary O'Kane*

Introduction

A dynamic women's movement is emerging—from within the exiled Burmese opposition movement—in Burma's borderlands with Thailand, China, India and Bangladesh. As this women's movement initially emerged from the Burma–Thailand borderlands, this study focused on the stories of women from Burma who were politically active in those locations.[1] Particularly significant about this women's movement is how its activists, displaced from Burma and marginalised at multiple intersecting levels—of gender, ethnicity and effective statelessness—have transformed dimensions of this extreme marginalisation into relative advantage. What miniscule yet vital portals have these women passed through to access new worlds of possibility while, paradoxically, remaining trapped in the liminal spaces of the Burma–Thailand borderlands?

Through the stories of politically active women exiled from Burma, and drawing on post-modern feminist and international relations (IR) theories of borders, transversality and identity, this paper discusses some significant factors leading to the emergence of this borderlands women's

*Mary O'Kane is very grateful to the women who participated in this research study for their support and generosity, and to Susan Blackburn for her ongoing support and advice. She would like to thank Navnita Chadha Behera, Richard Devetak and David Mathieson for their valued feedback and encouragement.

movement. It suggests processes through which these women's individual and collective identities undergo transformations in relation to the 'others' they encounter in the liminal spaces they inhabit and how, in turn, they have created a gendered political space for the emergence of a distinct dissident women's movement of Burma. As such, this paper focuses on historical-material processes concerning the interaction between women activists' identity, agency and social landscapes. It asks as to what are the processes by which these women are able to connect across legal, political, figural, material and symbolic borders to then transgress those borders and form a new collective female-dissident identity?

These women activists' stories reveal much about the inadequacies of dominant IR narratives about states, borders and movement. The dominant IR representation of interstate borders as fixed, natural and ahistorical works to ignore the paradoxes inherent in the construction of borders. States' continual (re)founding of their monopoly over the political through bordering practices points to the arbitrary nature of interstate borders, while the processes of border-isation simultaneously produce spaces in-between which are beyond resolution and state hegemony. Thus, inherent to the contradictory structure of borderland space is the *potential* for agents to access transversal space for political action. Transgressing borders is the *act* by which new, transversal space is created for encountering others and making new connections in ways filled with the potential for change and transformation. In this case, the potential that the Burma–Thailand borderlands holds for women activists is the possibility to access space beyond the total control of the state in which to purse their political struggle. Transversal space is made *actual* by women activists' capacity to avoid or negotiate states' attempts to control their movements in order to connect with, for example, global women's and human rights networks.

Through their capacity to cross borders in transformative ways, these women activists can be understood as agents of transversality. In claiming this, I draw on Nevzat Soguk and Geoffrey Whitehall's theory of transversality. Their approach rejects static, fixed and essentialist notions of territory and time to prioritise the transformative nature of all human beings. For Soguk and Whitehall, transversality defines the ontological condition of perpetual transformation through the interaction of movement, relation and identity. Transversality is informed by constant movement across and beyond borders, relations of domination and resistance and shared de-territorialisations (1999: 675). As a condition ontologically prior to the modern nation-state system, transversality 'exists prior to the conventional sovereign boundaries that enable political inclusions, exclusions and cultural separation across peoples and places' (ibid.: 676). Soguk and Whitehall see sovereign boundaries as temporary moments exemplary of the 'wandering grounds' of a transversal condition (ibid.). The modern state, because its own existence is sustained by continual attempts to instil its form over political life, is in constant tension with the driving human condition of transversality. As a result of the tensions generated by states' practices of imposing territorial borders over dynamic pre-existing social landscapes (Grundy-Warr 2002; Sturgeon 2004; Winichakul 1994), I argue that interstate boundaries are sites of heightened transversality.

As a consequence of the breakdown of the modern citizen-state relationship, accessing transversal non-state spaces can become vital for displaced people: not only for their physical survival, but also for their right to be self-determining political agents, and in preparation for political transformation in their home country. For the women activists I interviewed, the 'grey-areas' of the Burma–Thailand borderlands are the portals that make possible their struggle for human rights, women's empowerment and democracy in Burma.

As these paradoxical spaces and processes play central roles in the narratives of these women activists, their narratives regularly disrupt the dominant IR story and destabilise the sense of coherence or consistency it affects (Devetak 2001: 188). Consequently, states become intensely sensitive, not just to their presence in the borderlands, but particularly their movements around and beyond the borderlands. Both the Thai and Burmese states deploy varied and frequently contradictory strategies, differing over time and place, which work to exclude, entrap and depoliticise women activists and their displaced communities. Focusing on women activists' movements in the borderlands highlights the gendered character of these states' practices to exclude people from political membership, and therefore any guarantee of basic human rights.

The emergence of the women's movement of Burma in the Burma–Thailand borderlands is explained in three sections. First, woman activists' relationship with the state is briefly discussed to understand ways in which they are situated outside the modern nation-state system to become effectively stateless. In this theoretical context, women activists' stories are reflected on to gain insight into the characteristics of inter-state borderlands as sites of heightened transversality. Second, transformations in women activists' understanding of gender are discussed in relation to their displacement to refugee camps and un-documented migrant and political dissident communities (mostly) on the Thai side of the border. Transformations in gender consciousness are understood by women activists as foundational to the building of women's organisations in the Burma–Thailand borderlands. Third, the 'take-off' stage of the women's movement is explored, focusing on processes of de-territorialisation and women activists' negotiation of borders of ethnic identity to form Burma's first inter-ethnic political women's organisation, the Women's League of Burma (WLB). This enables women's agency to develop new and spatially complex strategies for acting politically specific to their circumstances.

Three arguments are presented in this paper. First, that the transversal character of interstate borders, and borders of gender, ethnicity and citizen/refugee, are fundamentally constitutive of processes leading to the emergence of this women's movement. Second, the abstract trans-versal spaces of the Burma–Thailand borderlands provide opportunities for these women's collective action not possible elsewhere—neither within Burma nor Thailand, nor in third countries where politically active woman from Burma may be dispersed. Third, the women's movement is both a modern political struggle for national democracy and gender equality, and objectively structured as a post-modern form of political dissent because of its globalised, multi-spatial, hybrid and diasporic characteristics.

Twenty-seven qualitative interviews with 24 politically active women (three women were interviewed twice) from Burma based in the Burma–Thailand borderlands provide the substantive data for this paper. The interviews covered a range of issues concerning their lives as activists in the Burmese opposition movement.[2] These activists, aged between 20 and 55 years, identified themselves as belonging to one of the nine ethnic nationalities from Burma: Karen, Karenni, Shan, Mon, Pa-O, Padaung, Burman, Kachin and Tavoy, as well as identifying them-selves as Burmese.[3] These women have lived on the borders for varying lengths of time experiencing a variety of circumstances.[4] Their education levels vary markedly, including university graduates, professionals and women who did not have the opportunity to complete primary school. Eight of the women were mothers and primary carers of young children.

All the interviews conducted for this research were in English, except for two that were translated into English.[5] Cross-cultural/cross-linguistic exchanges of this kind are laden with biases inherent in unequal power relations of researcher/subject, Western/Asian, race, class, native language/ non-native language, and so on. The nexus of language, culture and personal experience plays a crucial role informing both the expression and interpretation of experience, ideas and opinion. An indication of the impact of language in interpreting and analysing interviews is illustrated by Hallah Ghorashi in her study of Iranian political activists in exile in the Netherlands, of whom she is also one. An important process of achieving insight into Iranian women activists' narratives came through Ghorashi's psychological responses to the language and terminology interviewees used to discuss their identity. Hearing again a language/words used at a particular historical time and place during their political struggle in Iran triggered dreams and other psychological reactions relating to those experiences. This prompted Ghorashi to revisit the interview transcripts in ways that revealed insights unavailable to people outside their particular political experiences (Ghorashi 1997: 286).

While conducting and interpreting the interviews for this research study, I was cognisant of the absence of a shared native language, and cultural and historical experiences between myself and the women I interviewed. As a cultural, linguistic and racial outsider they had taken into their midst, I drew consciously and unconsciously from my experiences of living and working directly with them as a volunteer between May 1999 and February 2001 to interpret data for this research.[6] Through the friendship, trust and commitment that developed between my colleagues and myself over time, my 'outsider' status become blurred. This enabled me to observe and participate as women activists 'juggled' various issues, crises and processes in their overlapping working and personal lives. In this way, I was present to decision-making and prioritising processes in a wide variety of settings and could observe how past experiences of conflict and political struggle played significant roles in designing and implementing their present work.

Without Burmese or other ethnic language skills, I relied heavily on observation and my own culturally informed notions of non-verbal forms of communication, including body language, and emotional and psychological 'fallout' reactions/consequences. As they also responded to my reactions of what was going on at any particular time, we were constantly challenged to clarify and articulate our meanings and intentions in a way that reflexively adjusted our understandings of events and relationships. This raised my awareness of their sensitivity to terms and concepts such as 'Burmese', 'refugee' and 'feminism' which pose serious dilemmas for women activists.[7] For example, within communities from Burma the English word 'feminist' and its Burmese and ethnic language equivalents are strongly associated with notions of Western cultural imperialism, sexual orientation and negative social disruption. While most women activists agree with many feminist principles such as gender equality and empowerment, to publicly call themselves 'feminist' is to invite widespread criticism and further political marginal-isation, amongst other complex responses. As a Westerner writing about these women's experiences, an awareness of this 'politics of language' within the Burmese state, the opposition movement and beyond is necessary to help avoid unconstructive debate.

Nevertheless, there are aspects of these women's lives and work that remain hidden from me and are beyond my appreciation, such as political meanings communicated through culturally/linguistically spe-cific humour or the complications of bridging traditional and modern forms of relations. Additionally, whilst their political struggles continue, much information remains too sensitive to make public and too difficult to relate. Significant gaps and discrepancies will always exist between my interpretative lenses and the women with whom I talked. Therefore, this narrative represents one limited perspective of these women's ex-periences and the emergence of the women's movement of Burma in the Burma–Thailand border. These considerations inform the sig-nificant methodological and epistemological limitations of this paper.

At the request of the women interviewed for this research, for reasons relating to their security, names, locations of interviews and any inform-ation relating to their identities have not been included. Pseudonyms have been substituted for the interviewees' real names. To prevent pseudo-nyms from reflecting Burmese ethnic heritage, Western pseudonyms have been used.

Statelessness and Transversality: Inter-state Borders as Places of Possibility

The modern nation-state emerged as the form of political organisation mandated to protect the rights of its citizen-members. Thus, the pro-tection of individual human rights became inalienably linked with membership to a sovereign nation-state (Arendt 1958: 295). Accord-ingly, what is considered political occurs only *inside* the ordered bounds of the state and that which occurs *outside* the state is regarded as mere relations in a state of anarchy (Walker 1993).

The failure of the Burmese military state to protect its citizens' rights, including a failure to ensure political stability and economic growth, have resulted in ongoing human rights violations by both state and non-state actors.[8] This has caused widespread displacement throughout Burma, particularly from 1970 onwards, forcing millions to seek asylum across international borders. In fleeing to Burma's borderlands, women activists' relationship as citizens with the state of Burma has been severed,[9] and this has had profound consequences for them. In a global system of nation-states where all territory is carved up and claimed by a nation-state, their displacement from Burma and lack of acceptance into any other state means they are not recognised as belonging to any political community. In the absence of an alternative authority to guarantee their rights, the denial of membership to a political community, as Hannah Arendt identified, is equivalent to the denial of the 'right to have rights' (Arendt 1958: 296). Therefore, the right to belong to a political community is the most fundamental right lost to women activists displaced from Burma. Women activists and 'others' discursively located 'outside' political communities are not recognised as possessing political agency, and are thus denied a political voice. Their exclusion from membership of a state forcibly situates women activists, to varying degrees, in a liminal space outside the paradigm of the nation-state. This is a situation of effectively statelessness.

Through their persistent efforts to pursue their political goals from this position of statelessness in the Burma–Thailand borderlands, women activists are challenging this conventional political discourse. Ironically, in order to pursue political agendas with states' representatives and through UN agencies—whether it is politics of protection, democratisation in Burma, ethnic minority, women's, children's and environmental rights—they must escape the incapacitating incarceration of refugee camps and other intergovernmental refugee regimes to act independently.[10] This is achieved by women activists negotiating with and around states' border authorities to find spaces to live and pursue their political goals.

Women activists' stories of negotiating state boundaries in the course of survival and pursuing their political goals reveal several characteristics of the Burma–Thailand borderlands as sites of heightened transversality. First, borders may exist for the movements of people and things, but they also exist as routines in the spaces of transit (Soguk and Whitehall 1999: 677). In the Burma–Thailand borderlands, in places where the interstate border is actually enforced and represented, it is done so by the presence of state authorities at border checkpoints, customs offices, army patrols and police identity checkpoints in border towns and along arterial roads. In the ill-defined borderlands, Burmese and Thai state officials are stationed in proximity, policing the same people but often for different political reasons. One woman activist, 'Christine', expressed it thus:

> Every time we moved, there was change in the authorities—and not just one or two types of authorities. Then when we moved to another place again, there were other authorities again. This is how it is; some are soldiers, some are police or immigration, some are intelligence. But most of the intelligence stays in the town. Mostly on the border it is soldiers and immigration.

Understanding the different motives underlying Burmese and Thai border authorities' attempts to control their movements, and appreciating this in the broader cultural, social and economic context of cross-border, trade, labour and the general flow of people, allow political activists from Burma opportunities to create strategies to avoid capture. Both the porous character of the inter-state border and the ability of border-crossers to negotiate (to varying degrees) their passage and presence with border-keepers constitute borderlands as sites of possibility as well as danger.

Second, as occupants of transit zones, women activists make the uninhabitable habitable. They remake the spaces according to their needs (Hyndman 2000: 150; Malkki 1995). However, as Soguk and Whitehall emphasise, 'they do not make it under the circumstances chosen by them, but under the circumstances directly encountered, given and transmitted from the past' (1999: 677). Third, transversal space can be defined by a lack of structure, a foundationlessness where there is a collapse of space and time in the meaning of activities that constitute daily life (ibid.: 680). In the process of finding ways to negotiate state border authorities, women activists learn from and become changed by their experiences. Having escaped or negotiated the control of state authorities, they seek global connections in a slow process of personal and organisational development. In doing so, women participate in '"shared de-territorialisations", zones of proximity, non-localisable spaces of Relation, that brings the under ground and the above ground, movement and home, inside and outside, into proximity with one another to constitute complex spatial performances' (ibid.: 680).

Fourth, powerful memories of violent political struggle in Burma and those 'lost to the cause' are fundamental driving forces in women activists' search for transversal space. The memories of political resistance and survival become the cultural baggage that women activists carry with them as they travel. These memories represent the cosmological connection between women's roots in Burma and routes since displacement where their past, present and future collapse into the same space. Through constant reflection on their roots, a sense of presence-in-absence generates the utopic desire and courage that drives women to continue their work in their daily lives in the face of despair and grief. 'Catherine', a woman activist who witnessed the massacre in Rangoon's streets when the military opened fire on unarmed civilian demonstrators in 1988, explained it thus:

> It is something that I cannot forget in my life. That is why I am back here on the border. You know this is the conscience that I have to live. If people die on the street—the young kids, right on the street— the cause of death must be something reasonable. If they can die, we have to contribute something to the cause.[11]

Last, being located in the Burma–Thailand borderlands holds the potential for women activists to build bridges across political borders. This capacity is reflected by some women activists' deliberate *choice* to remain in the Burma–Thailand borderlands rather than seek resettlement through the UNHCR in third countries. They say that the borderlands provided the most suitable environment to continue their political resistance. In exercising their choice to stay, women highlight the contradictory and ambiguous character of borders as important sites of dis/connection with inside Burma, a relationship that is subjectively lived in a way that complicates dominant conceptions of exile. As one activist, 'Helen', relates:

> I don't like the word 'exile'. We are not running away from our own country for our own liberation. At the same time, we'll be going in and out of our country as part of the movement and struggle wherever we are. If you ask me, 'Are you in exile?' I will say 'No'.

Women activists' strong ambivalence towards the condition of exile in the Burma–Thailand borderlands points to how their appreciation of these sites for political struggle merge with feelings of loss generated through violence and displacement. Despite inherent dangers, the opportunities possible in the borderlands also constitute these spaces as the best places to engage in political resistance and gender empowerment.

Transformation in Gender Identity in the Burma–Thailand Borderlands

In the foundationless, fluid and morphing transversal spaces, distinctions between public/private, politics/survival, mother/activist, freedom fighter/illegal alien collapse and become inseparable experiences, what Soguk and Whitehall call the condition of 'dwelling in movement which is also movement in dwelling' (Soguk and Whitehall 1999: 678). The collapse and significant restructuring of how these binary categories of relations are lived in the Burma–Thailand borderlands has caused tensions between many women and members of their communities, resulting in shifts and transformations in many women's identities. Examples of how these shifts occurred and their meaning for the emergence of a distinct women's movement are explored in the contexts of women activists in camp-based communities, migrant communities and political dissident groups. It is important to note continuing differences in socio-political processes informing identity occurring in camp, town and city based settings (Malkki 1995) as they have important ramifications for how these women activists define themselves and relate to each other.

Refugee Camps

In relatively stable but intensely crowded refugee camps, women are increasingly mobilised in various, and at times seemingly contradictory, ways. Ethnic political structures governing camps' organisation and administration have encouraged the (re)formation of women's organisations where wives and relatives of ethnic political leaders took leading roles in ways that mirrored the structure of state-sponsored women's organisations inside Burma. The establishment or reinvigoration of women's organisations of this kind can be interpreted as examples of attempts by ethnic nationalist groups to develop recognisable state-like structures that harness the communities' human resources to support its political cause.[12] In refugee camps it is often (but not exclusively) the national women's organisation that provides the structure through which women can become mobilised politically in response to the extremely desperate needs of their communities.

Women's gender identities in camp-based organisations are mostly reinforced in line with traditional ethnic roles for women. However, their work to locate funds and resources to provide even the most basic survival needs for newly-arrived refugees and individuals in immediate crises raised some women's consciousness of the gendered dimensions of refugee displacement. Amongst these concerns, women activists cite male control of political and military decision-making and weaponry, women's susceptibility to rape and other forms of sexual abuse, increased domestic violence and increased vulnerability to maternal and infant mortality and morbidity. 'Elizabeth', leader of an ethnic women's organisation, made this point when discussing the reasons for her activism:

> Because the priority for the women's issue you can see in everyday life. I can see the needs and I have the feeling how to help. And I have many ideas; how we can do it, what is important to address.... These needs, regardless if you want to see them or not, are very clear. So you know this is what you have to do—for the women, the development of the women, the better living standard ... the health and the education.

The welfare-based responses of women in refugee camps raised serious questions for some women activists about the role of gender in perpetuating the conflict and its impact on all members of society. Paradoxically, through performing welfare duties in line with their traditional gender roles under the intensely pressured conditions of displacement and refugee camps, some women came to question, then challenge, some aspects of traditional gender norms through pursuing non-traditional roles in the community and education. The driving need to find solutions to immediate and long-term crises is leading women to self-advocacy, including demands for meaningful political participation in relevant decision-making processes. At the same time, their work is bringing them into contact with international organisations that provide new resources and ideas, such as new ways of understanding the phenomenon of domestic violence.

Undocumented Migrant Communities

The vast majority of women from undocumented migrant communities were not politically active before leaving Burma. The two women leaders interviewed who were politically engaged inside Burma pursued forms of activism different to the strategies they pursue currently.[13] This reflects a continuity of their political activism but a discontinuity in the forms of activism available to them related to their changed relationships with states. Unable to pursue peaceful or military political activities in direct opposition to the Burmese state from inside Burma, they are continuing their dissent from the borderlands by, amongst other strategies, lobbying members of the international community to support their cause.

Like many women based in refugee camps, they emphasised their activism in the borderlands as a response to the desperate needs of their displaced communities. There are an estimated 600,000 to 1.2 million migrant workers from Burma in Thailand (Human Rights Watch 2004). The challenges for survival faced by migrants significantly differ from those faced in camps because of the lack of access to humanitarian aid, geographical dispersal and black market employment. Nevertheless, the experiences of displacement of some migrant women leaders have similarly led to the raising of a gender consciousness.

Dispersed throughout the Thai population, migrants from Burma attempt to stay connected through loose social networks as they move, and are moved, through the extremely fluid and risky internationalised, gendered, racialised and illegal migrant labour markets. However, maintaining these networks and connections, which act as protection and support, is difficult because of their lack of access to legal protection. Many women and girls' vulnerability to exploitation and abuse is heightened by their physical isolation from their communities when working as domestic workers in private houses and in the sex industry, making the establishment of safety networks difficult and often dangerous (Aung Myo Min and Burmese Women's Union 2000).

It was predominantly loose coalitions of migrant women rather than the male dominated political organisations in the opposition movement that first began to respond to the needs of undocumented migrant communities.[14] In particular, women who had attained legal status (through resettlement in a third country or marriage) and who were multi-lingual[15] were called upon in emergencies to hospitals, police stations, courts and human rights fact-finding missions to assist with proceedings. Commonly, these problems involved women and girls caught in sexually, physically and psychologically abusive situations, often about to be deported back to Burma. Frequently, HIV-AIDS and other health conditions play a significant role. Women migrants with these skills and experiences were the first to become politically mobilised due to their growing awareness of the gendered nature of the problems they were repeatedly called on to assist. One woman activist, 'Sara', made the following comments about her colleague who was one of the first activists to campaign for the rights of trafficked women in Thailand in the early 1990s:

She became a translator for the courts and most of the girls that she translated for were trafficked persons. From there she really saw what is going on with this trafficking situation. Before that she just heard about the girls. And then she was a translator with Human Rights Watch. When she was translating, she heard these stories again and again. This is how she really saw the problem, and the need that we have to respond. And then, talking with some friends—it all clicked in her mind—that she really needs to do something.

The sense of injustice about the gendered nature of abuse suffered by exploited women belonging to their communities escalated among some women leaders. Their debriefing discussions triggered the realisation of the need to take coordinated action on behalf of women migrants and their families. This contributed to the establishment of women's organisations such as the Shan Woman's Action Network in 1998 and the Pa-O Women's Union in 2000.[16]

Student Activists

Women activists from dissident student backgrounds discussed the emergence of their strongly gendered consciousness in terms of their changing relationships with male student counterparts after reaching the borderlands. Having relocated to the border areas to pursue armed struggle alongside ethnic insurgent groups, women quickly realised the meaning of moving from a militarised society to a military zone. Implicit notions of equality that informed (rhetorically more than practically) female and male students' relations no longer applied. Traditional gender roles were suddenly enforced under conditions of danger, unfamiliarity, chaos and displacement, with an imperative to organise an army: the All Burma Students Democratic Front (ABSDF).[17] Several female students recalled with humour how they were presented with two choices by their organisation: they could become either teachers or medics.

Many female students, particularly those who had taken leading roles in organising demonstrations during the 1988 uprising inside Burma, felt marginalised and discriminated against on the basis of gender. The 'student' component of their identities was suddenly given lesser respect as they were forced to perform traditional female roles in the organisation of the student resistance. Feeling unjustly constrained by conventional gender roles imposed on them, women began questioning previously assumed meanings of politics and gender in ways that caused a shift in gender consciousness. The following narrative of 'Susan' illustrates how women's roles as activists, wives and financial 'housekeepers' become compressed into the same social space, creating tensions when women resisted traditional forms of control:

Some men wanted to control the shop[18] and tell us [women] what to do…. I told them, 'you shouldn't tell us how to run the shop, I know how to do it!' So we fought. I didn't like what they were trying to do. 'I came here because the (Burmese military regime) behave like that, so you also shouldn't do like that!' My resistance to them put my husband in a very difficult position. If they couldn't tell me what to do, then they told my husband. They accused him, 'You are very afraid of your wife. You cannot tell her what to do. Your wife is very crazy. You should control her. If you don't control her, then you are afraid of your wife.' … Sometimes he also would say, 'Please take care, you shouldn't speak to them like that.' 'No, you shouldn't tell me! I know my job, you do your job.' That time was very difficult. Such a *small* job, running the shop, but they could not give us any decision-making responsibility. They don't want us to be independent.... At that time I didn't know about women's rights or human rights.... I only knew that my feeling was, 'I can do it! Why do they want to control me? They shouldn't control me.'

The raising of gender consciousness amongst female student dissidents led, in 1995, to the formation of the first women's organisation in the borderlands founded on the principles of gender equality and increased women's participation in the politics of the Burmese opposition movement. A group of seven women in a remote jungle army camp on the Burmese side of the border, without access to funding, communication technologies, information or the benefit of formal bodies of feminist knowledge, organised the Burmese Women's Union (BWU) and quickly established a branch on the China–Burma border. Although the establishment of the BWU was (and continues to be) fraught with inter-ethnic tension and controversy, it filled a vacuum for women's solidarity amongst female students. As 'Susan' continues:

After that, the BWU started and they held the first Congress. When I came here, I learned about women's rights, and I knew that in every place women are suffering like that. Also I worry that maybe even if we gain democracy, women will not be able to participate in decision-making roles if we don't become more active. So we decided we should work for women's rights and democracy at the same time.

These narratives of women activists from refugee camps, migrant and political dissident communities reflect how, through travel and relocation, women moved back and forth through their memories to assess and reassess their past in relation to the present and their visions for the future. In the process, they formulated new understandings, developed new ideas and meanings, and asked new questions concerning gender roles. Women began to challenge established norms of gender relations in response to new and different situations faced in the Burma–Thailand borderlands. Transformations in these women's gender consciousness, in turn, led to either a transformation of the frameworks in which established women's organisations worked, or to the formation of new women's organisations. These developments within various women's organisations frequently occurred in parallel, and with limited communication between, them in these early days of the mid- to late 1990s.

Globalisation and the 'Take-off' of Women's Organisations in the Borderlands

Several challenges confronted women activists as they embraced their new directives working for women's rights and empowerment. Self-education was a top priority and required moving between various locations to organise and attend training sessions and participate in political meetings. The dialectic processes between negotiating Thailand's border enforcement practices and pursuing their new agendas transformed women's political agency and dimensions of local political spaces. Gradually they began to create and expand nascent gendered political spaces in which to pursue their varied agendas. These dynamic and empowering processes slowly enabled women to divert their energy and resources from addressing immediate security issues towards women's political activism and social welfare work. By doing so, women were able to adjust aspects of their uneven relations with the state; no longer were they running from the state for their survival, but their movement were now also driven by their own imperatives. As a woman activist 'Alice' explains:

> Before I had to move because we were forced by the Thai authorities or the SPDC (State Peace and Development Council) fighting.... But now I am working at (my organisation), we move because of our duties, not because we are forced by the authorities, it is different.

Gradual processes of self-empowerment and capacity building through this period enabled some women's groups to transform the meaning of movement and agency to new levels that exposed them to new horizons. These developments were foundational to the 'take-off' period of the women's movement on the Burma–Thailand border.

The 'take-off' stage of the women's movement was infused with new dynamic energy by women activists' engagement in two interlinking processes. First, globalised dimensions of the inter-state borderlands became a major focus of women activists. It was a place to connect and engage reflexively with people and processes operating at the global level to further their dissident and women's rights agendas. Second, as a result of women approaching their ethnic and political organisations with new gender-related ideas and agendas, they faced renewed opposition from male political leaders on the grounds of gender. This highlighted to women activists for the first time the need to develop a unified women's solidarity that overcame their ethnic divisions in order for their voices to be heard in the Burmese opposition movement.

The Globalised Borderlands and Women's Political Agency

Processes of globalisation can be characterised as flows of information, people, ideas, information, money and so forth, that interact and intersect as they cut across nation-state boundaries (Devetak 2001: 198). They are useful in explaining the emergence of the women's movement as they highlight processes 'through which interdependencies among geographical distant localities, places and territories are at once extended, deepened and intensified' (Brenner 1998: 42). Intersections between globalisation processes and women's activism occur in border locations as engagement between women activists and international NGOs, technologies and resources attracted to the borderlands for economic, political, military and humanitarian reasons. Women activists' capacity to tap into, connect with and participate in these globalising flows is strengthened over time by the movement of information, ideas and women themselves between borderland localities and other globalised sites.

The urgent need to communicate and seek funding to set up their own women's organisations slowly drew women activists out of the jungles, camps and villages to places where they could access communication infrastructure and technologies. Women activists' new direction in political resistance required overcoming spatial and temporal constraints by relocating to town-based offices. For women registered in refugee camps, this meant compromising what small degree of legal protection they held by leaving camp confines and increasing their dependence on cooperative relations with Thai security officials. The intersection of processes of relocation, de-territorialisation and negotiating security from the borderlands is clearly explained by this woman activist, 'Amanda':

Four to five years ago, when we stayed in the jungle, we couldn't build up and improve our activities. We couldn't show our activities at the international level, so we could not attract interest from the media. And then we tried to build up our individual groups so we slowly, slowly moved inside Thailand, because we had no technology; we had no telephone, we could not send a fax. If we wanted to send one letter, ohhh! It took such a long time (laughs). The whole world can send e-mails but we tried for a long time to send just one letter. We knew that if we stayed inside Thailand, we could work a lot for our activities. Therefore, we had to make good relationships with Thai authorities. It is really important for our movement. And now the border area is not just the border, no? It is the place to connect to the world!

International space presented a range of opportunities for women activists at a great many levels; not only encounters at the local levels through the internet, e-mail, NGO workers and other sources, but also with women activists travelling internationally. Women discussed at length the importance of their experiences of attending UN and other international and regional conferences and preparatory meetings on a range of issues including human rights, women's rights, Burma, the media, youth and racism. Opportunities to network around international issues such as trafficking provided paths leading to global networks. 'Caitlin', a woman activist, discussed the multiple benefits that women gained from participating at the UN level over time:

> I went to the Beijing Women's Conference in 1995. Only the NGO meetings—I didn't go to the government meetings. I went to the trafficking workshop and gave information on the experience I have here in Thailand. And on Burma. There were a lot of people. It was important for us to get into the network of these women's groups internationally working on all these issues because we had just come out and were trying to listen and learn. So that gave us a lot of support and resources that are translating into workshops in Thailand and other places. We learn by attending those workshops, we learn. That includes all the issues connected to UN conventions and meetings like the Beijing Plus Five (June 2000) and the CEDAW (January 2000).

Globalised spaces not only serve as important sites for political lobbying for democratic change in Burma. They are also sites where people from Burma seek vital education opportunities, not only for their intellectual development, but also for their social development. 'Caitlin' further says:

> There are younger people who went abroad to study. That is international space. I mean, our schools [in Burma] are closed! And then out here there are people like us talking about the future Burma! And also we want to have a better life, better society. So things are not matching at this moment. So we have to find a space…. To develop our society—so that that is the space that we are finding internationally. That is the international space.

Connecting with other women's organisations internationally and drawing on their real-life experiences of conflict in other parts of the world, women activists from Burma are bringing new strategies to play on the borderlands to reinvest new meaning in agendas of peace and reconciliation. As a woman activist, 'Sarina', says:

> I think the women have to start and talk about peace education and peace building…. Men try but it does not work out. I was at a refugee conference in Switzerland; it was very educating for me. Especially the Eastern European women—the Serbs and Bosnians. They started the women's group that started to teach peace education to their own people…. So the women started to talk. They brought their children to talk. That is how they started to build the peace.

As various women's organisations expanded their capacity for providing services and educational opportunities to women in their communities, a dialectic process of growth in individual and organisational capacity, membership and activism began to emerge. As they began to develop networks of support, funding opportunities and new ideas, women's organisations also began to actively recruit new members from diasporic locations. Young girls from refugee camps joined women's organisations to access rare opportunities to further their education, broaden their life experiences and work towards their political aspirations. Consolidation of the opposition movement's organisational infrastructure in Thailand also attracted women from around Burma's borderlands with China, India and Bangladesh. Individuals with leadership potential and other useful skills were recruited from inside Burma to work in the borderlands. Further, women who had studied and been granted citizenship or travelling documents returned to work in the border areas. They have assisted the emergence of the women's movement because of their capacity to travel more easily (locally, nationally and internationally) and by bringing important technical skills—including computer skills, English language skills, academic skills, translation skills—as well as their legal status and international connections. Their return to the border areas has enabled these women to do things that they could not do earlier.

Through accessing the transversal spaces of the borderlands, women were able to move and develop their organisations by connecting multiple spatial dimensions. In the process, they also gradually became transformed into agents of the transversal. They exemplify the processes of transversality where '(e)ither one is moving one's body through space in relation with others, or space—with its polymorphic forces, subjects, objects and identities—is moving through one's body without necessarily physically displacing one' (Soguk and Whitehall 1999: 691). The intensifying globalising processes that intersect through people and technologies located and moving through the ambiguous borderland spaces have made it possible for women to connect with international women's and human rights networks. However, this process of connection, engagement and transmission occurs unevenly both within and between women's organisations. The high mobility of some members of the movement juxtaposes sharply with the immobility of other women activists as well as their communities trapped within the bounds of displacement.

Encountering *one-an-other*: Building Women's Solidarity

For most women activists, the Burma–Thailand borderlands provided their first opportunities to engage with each other across barriers of ethnic difference. Women activists understood that to increase their capacities in the face of structural gender discrimination within the broader male-dominated Burmese opposition movement, they needed to unify on the basis of gender. To do this, they needed to form alliances across ethnic boundaries to put forward a unified voice, not only on 'women's issues', but on political processes in general. Intricately related to this, women's vision for political transition in Burma demands the participation of women at all levels of political dialogue, which also demands reconciliation across ethnic boundaries.

As women began to engage with each other, the differences between women's situations became apparent. These differences were not only based on ethnic cultural differences, but also related to differences in life experience and opportunity that strongly informed their capacity for political activism. Uneven social, political and economic status, as well as different experiences of conflict and displacement, characterised the relations between women as they embarked on this challenge for unification. Initial encounters between women activists revealed much to themselves about the extent to which militarised society inside Burma had generated a 'divide and rule' culture amongst politico-ethnic communities, and how the social structures of displacement in the border-lands operated to perpetuate these divisions in the absence of a collective women's rights consciousness. 'Amanda' recollected with humour the surprise women felt at their first Women's Congress in 1998, held somewhere on the Burma–Thailand border, when they realised the extent of the differences they needed to overcome:

> There were many, many funny things in our meeting. Because in the meeting, the Chin women's group, they didn't know who the Karenni women were. 'What is Karenni? What is this separate country?' they asked. Inside Burma we call the Karenni 'Kayah'. However after we left Burma we learned that the Karenni don't like being called 'Kayah'. There were many women's groups from western Burma and the India side, as well as from the Thai–Burma border. And they have different aims and objectives. Some women's groups chose [to work on] social activities, like safe houses for women who have trouble in Thailand and are returning to Burma. And a really funny thing was that some representatives from Mae Tao clinic,[19] they knew only about medical issues. Some other women knew only about education issues (laughs), some knew only social issues and some women knew only ethnic issues. So we couldn't talk with each other (laughs)! It was really funny, but it was really good because we could meet for the first time. And we decided that we needed another congress like that the next year.

Another important consequence of the 1998 Women's Congress was the spread of the idea for women to organise and engage in political processes at the ethnic-national level. Incentives for women to organise were often related to normative pressures of inter-ethnic rivalry and fears of continued Burman domination within the opposition movement. The 1998 Congress is considered by many women activists as an important watershed in instigating higher levels of gender organisation in the borderlands.

From then on, women's organisations began to organise forums at various locations around the inter-state borderlands to bring representatives of women's organisations together. In the beginning, engaging violently forged and deeply rooted feelings of ethnic suspicion was a slow, pit-holed journey occurring at the leadership level. Many women leaders organised training forums around women's rights and empowerment issues to create opportunities for women leaders to meet in politically safe environments where positive encounters at personal, political and social levels were possible. Women's Exchange, or 'WE', for example, are monthly meetings coordinated in various borderland localities by and for women of various ethnicities (including women not from Burma) to discuss issues concerning women. These meetings are a strategy developed by the women to create a space for ethnic reconciliation processes at community levels outside formal organisational structures. Training around women's issues facilitated transversal spaces in which women could 'play' and explore, with minimal risk of conflict, how to establish paths of contact between themselves. Accepting ethnic differences in the context of prioritising their common identity as women provided the foundational relationships for the emerging coalition of women's organisations. These relationships will always be characterised by differences that need constant negotiation and incorporation into common ground (Friedman 1998: 72). Importantly, the new connections made during this period opened the way for the next round of formal meetings at the organisational level.

At the third official meeting of women's organisations in December 2000, 12 organisations formed the WLB, an event considered the most significant development in gender politics in the borderlands. The WLB is not understood by the women's organisations as a new organisation, but as a facilitating body to channel resources more effectively from the global to the local level, to strengthen constituent women's organisations, to act as a unified voice of women, and to challenge the gendered boundaries of oppositional politics from which women have been effectively excluded. Combined, the variety of reasons that women's organisations give for forming the WLB reflect not only how each organisation's needs are constituted differently, but also illustrate the reflexive nature of globalised borderlands and women's attempts to harness that energy towards their own goals. Returning to 'Amanda', she further explains:

> Some women's organisations know that the international level can give a lot of support to the women's movement. And that some individual groups are better able to keep in touch with the international society. Other organisations know that if they cannot keep in touch with the international society, they have no support. I think most women's groups worry about this. And then, a few women's organisation leaders—they know it is time to improve the women's role in the political opposition movement and politics generally, that we need to show our unity and capacity through organising strong activities.... But some new organisations, they didn't have this idea yet, but they have difficulties to get funding. They don't want to stay individually, they want to join the umbrella group. So there are many ideas and ways of thinking. But they all accept the need to form the Women's League of Burma.

The WLB represents the most significant women's voice in the exiled opposition movement as it increasingly demands representation in exiled opposition political processes and meetings. While a primary function of the umbrella organisation was to channel information, resources and funding from the international level to the local organisations, it currently faces challenges in convincing international funding agencies not to deal with the WLB exclusively, but to continue to directly support constituent member organisations.

New Dimensions of Women's Political Activism

As the impact of the WLB on gender politics in the borderlands is becoming apparent, it is possible to see the spatial complexity with which women are working and how their positioning in the transversal borderlands has enabled them to develop strategies unique to their circumstances. The foundationless character of the transversal borderland spaces has enabled women activists to link political processes operating at diverse spatial levels. In doing so, these processes have become mutually constitutive of their strategies of political struggle in ways that have not previously been employed. Women activists are positioned as a medium for the conduct of ideas between the borderlands and various other globalised locations. Through constant movement from place to place in the course of their work, they are gradually transforming political space in the borderlands. This extract from a WLB report illustrates this point:

> On 27 August 2001, a petition signed by 51,487 internally displaced persons, refugees and migrants on the Burma–Thailand and Burma–India borders was submitted by representatives of the WLB to the Rapporteur of the Commission on Internally Displaced Persons, Refugees and Migrants, and the NGO declaration drafting committee at the World Conference against Racism (WCAR) in Durban, South Africa. At the international level, the petition was used as a lobbying tool for the inclusion of Burma as country specific issue in the WCAR NGO Declaration and to urge the WCAR delegates to address the consequences of racial and gender discrimination and related human rights violations committed by the current ruling authorities of Burma. At the local level, the signature campaign enabled the WLB to raise awareness on racism, racial discrimination, xenophobia and related intolerance in local communities. In the process, they built a greater sense of solidarity amongst people of Burma who participated and received support and suggestions from the people for the WLB's activities at WCAR (Lintner 2001: 31).

Conclusion

Activists in the women's movement of Burma trapped in the borderlands outside the nation-state system strive for survival, justice and a future envisaged as the return to the protective state/citizen relationship constituted through democratic process. These ethical imperatives shape their political, physical and ideological movement. Perceived as 'errant' movers by states, their movements are a focus of state control. Thus, women activists' imperative for continuing their movement positions them in tension with the state, forcing them to negotiate states' attempts to 'still' them.

Their negotiation of states' bordering practices is simultaneously the act of creating opportunities for new agency in the borderlands. Trapped in the temporal and spatial limits of the interstate borderlands, the 'interstitial spaces of indeterminacy' (Kaplan 1996: 144), these women activists' condition as ontologically transversal beings is intensified. Through converging lives and cultures in new roots, women act as transversal agents 'that now extend in all directions through networks and branches' (Soguk and Whitehall 1999: 682). The Burma–Thailand borderlands are thus vital sites of transversality for these women activists.

In this sense, the experiences of women activists from Burma support Soguk and Whitehall's proposition that 'transversality is both defined for migrants and movements and a place defined by migrants and movements' (ibid.: 676). Movements back and forth in time mark their narratives; recalling unresolved events of the past in ways that generate determination and courage to continue their activism today. There is a subtle but powerful paradox in the activism of these women. While on the ground woman activists are constantly on the move, and the women's movement is growing fast, they are at the same time suspended in a limbo, waiting for the time to return to Burma and implement the skills and knowledge they are developing in the Burma-Thailand borderlands and beyond. Many activists echoed 'Susan's' reflections:

This is a kind of transition period in which we are learning. We wish we could be like normal in our own country. In the time to come, we are hoping this will happen. We are also working for change at the same time. We are learning from other people's experiences. We are learning about the things we would like to have in our own country.

Women activists' ability to transform violent spaces into an enabling environment is demonstrative of how space is a constitutive of social processes, rather than a static condition. Precisely because these women have been able to create or produce a political space for their purposes, they are the 'major architects of their new-found lands of the transversal' (Soguk and Whitehall 1999: 676). Importantly, the dialogic nature of encounter in the transversal spaces between local and global becomes the practical method towards the gradual development of a rooted, sustainable women's movement. This grounding in strong networks of gender and political solidarity is vital not only for the continuing growth of the women's movement in the borderlands, but to develop a strong foundation for the future if/when political transition starts, and the movement crosses another 'border' into Burma.

Notes

1   Amongst people from Burma, the term 'Burmese' is associated with the dominant ethnic group in Burma, the Burmans, who constitute an estimated two-thirds of the population. As ethno-political conflict is a root cause of displacement from Burma, many women politically active in the Burma–Thailand borderlands are of non-Burman ethnic heritage and identify primarily with their ethnic nationality; for example, Karen, Shan or Mon. As a strategy to overcome inter-ethnic tension and work together, women activists in the Burma–Thailand borderlands refer to themselves as 'women from Burma' rather than 'Burmese women'. This convention has been followed in this paper.

2   These interviews were conducted in November 2000 and June–July 2001. The interviews (taped and later transcribed) lasted for an average period of one to three hours.

3   Some women identified themselves as 'Burmese' because of their mixed ethnic heritage. Some women of ethnic minority background identified most strongly with their state identity as Burmese. It is important to note that in this ethno-political conflict situation, ethnic identity is defined extremely narrowly. Being identified by one's self or community as being of a particular ethnic identity is a process of community inclusion/exclusion. This has serious ramifications for an individual's acceptance into various political groups.

4   Some women had been in the borderlands for most of their lives, displaced by ethno-political conflict or life threatening poverty, arriving at refugee camps or border villages as young children. Others arrived in the aftermath of the 1988 pro-democracy civil uprising. Women have been continuously arriving, leaving and returning to the Burma–Thailand border for a variety of reasons.

5   English was either their second or third, and sometimes even fourth or fifth, language. Most women were self-taught with scant opportunities to practice speaking English. The author herself does not speak Burmese or other ethnic languages.

6   The author had worked as an English language teacher, and office and project management assistant. Additionally, she had lived in and visited this region of north-western Thailand regularly since 1990.

7   The author would like to thank Richard Devetak for clarifying this point.

8   Political oppression in Burma today can be linked to two connected root causes. First, the breakdown of trust in ethno-political relations shortly after independence from British colonisation in 1948 resulted in an on-going conflict between the central Burmese state and insurgent ethnic minorities. Second, the Burmese military, which took power in a coup in 1962 has, over the past five decades, redirected national resources away from developing the country towards building military capacity.

9   However, it can be argued that the state/citizen relationship never practically existed for many, particularly ethnic minority, people in Burma. However, this discussion is beyond the scope of this paper.

10 A few post-structuralist IR writers such as Nevzat Soguk (1999), Jennifer Hyndman (2000) and Peter Nyers (1999) have begun to critique the disempowering and marginalising affect of conventional refugee discourse on refugees and asylum seekers.

11 Reference is made here to the 1988 student-led civil uprising throughout Burma against the military dictatorship in which an unknown number of unarmed civilians were killed by the military (estimates range from 3,000 to 10,000), causing an estimated 10,000 students to flee to the border areas to join the armed resistance of the ethnic minority insurgency groups.

12 Most people's experiences of the state in Burma are limited to the Burmese military. As such, the political structures of the ethno-political groups often resemble the military regimes' patterns of political organisation. This is an important contributing factor to the military character of the ethno-political groups.

13 One woman was a member of a well-known political family. The other was a soldier.

14 Up to the late 1990s, issues of migrant workers from Burma were not considered by male political leaders to be important to the 'high politics' of regime change in Burma.

15 Important languages were Thai, Burmese, English, Shan, Karen, Karenni and Mon.

16 Other factors also contributed to taking the actual steps of forming some of these organisations, such as significant women's meetings and the rise in activity of other women's organisations at the time.

17 Helia Lopez Zaroza's experience as a Chilean woman suddenly finding herself in exile in England with her husband imprisoned in Chile by the military dictatorship highlights some interesting parallels (from quite different circumstances) of how displacement and exile can result in a sudden change in gender identity that can be oppressive as well as positive for women (Zaroza 1998: 191).

18 This shop, on the China–Burma border, was set up to earn basic living costs for the students. Students noted significant differences between the Chinese, Thai, Indian and Bangladeshi governments in response to their presence. While Chinese/ Yunnanese officials were tolerant of the Burmese students and displaced peoples' efforts to earn money to support themselves, they did not permit any form of political organising or activism. In Thailand the situation was the reverse.

19 The Mae Tao clinic was established by Dr Cynthia Maung in the Mae Sot area after the mass migration of student activists to the borderland areas in 1988.

References

Arendt, H. 1958. *The Origins of Totalitarianism*. London: Harcourt Brace and Co.

Aung Myo Min and Burmese Women's Union. 2000. *Cycle of Suffering: A Report on the Situation for Migrant Women Workers from Burma in Thailand and Violations of their Human Rights*. Bangkok: Human Rights Documentation Unit/Burmese Women's Union.

Brenner, N. 1998. 'Beyond State-Centrism? Space, Territoriality, and Geographical Scale in Globalisation Studies', *Theory and Society*, 28: 39–78.

Devetak, Richard. 2001. 'Postmodernism', in S. Burchill, R. Devetak, A. Linklater, M. Paterson, C. Reus-Smit and J. True, *Theories of International Relations*, pp. 181–208. New York: Palgrave.

Friedman, S.S. 1998. *Mappings: Feminism and the Cultural Geographies of Encounter*. Princeton: Princeton University Press.

Ghorashi, H. 1997. 'Shifting and Conflicting Identities: Iranian Women Political Activists in Exile', *European Journal of Women's Studies*, 4: 283–303.

Grundy-Warr, Carl. 2002. 'Forced Migration and Contested Sovereignty along the Thai–Burma/Myanmar Border', in C. Schofield, D. Newman, A. Drysdale and J.A. Brown (eds), *The Razor's Edge: International Boundaries and Political Geography*, pp. 337–83. London: Kluwer Law International.

Human Rights Watch. 2004. *Out of Sight, Out of Mind: Thai Policy Towards Burmese Refugees and Migrants*, 16(2) (C), February. http://hrw.org/reports/2004/thailand0204/, accessed 20 March 2004.

Hyndman, J. 2000. *Managing Displacement: Refugees and the Politics of Humanitarianism*. Minneapolis: University of Minnesota Press.

Kaplan, C. 1996. *Questions of Travel: Postmodern Discourses of Displacement*. Durham: Duke University Press.

Lintner, H.N. 2001. 'Signature Campaign for the World Conference Against Racism', *Dove*, 17: 31–33.

Malkki, L. 1995. *Purity and Exile: Violence, Memory and National Cosmology among Hutu Refugees in Tanzania*. Chicago: University of Chicago Press.

Nyers, P. 1999. 'Emergency or Emerging Identities? Refugees and Transformations in World Order', *Millennium*, 28(1): 1–26.

Soguk, N. 1999. *States and Strangers: Refugees and Displacements of Statecraft*. Minneapolis: University of Minnesota Press.

Soguk, N. and Whitehall, G. 1999. 'Wandering Grounds: Transversality, Identity, Territoriality, and Movement', *Millennium*, 28(3): 675–98.

Sturgeon, J. 2004. 'Border Practices, Boundaries and the Control of Resource Access: A Case from China, Thailand and Burma', *Development and Change*, 35(3): 463–84.

Walker, R.B.J. 1993. *Inside/Outside: International Relations as Political Theory*. Cambridge: Cambridge University Press.

Winichakul, T. 1994. *Siam Mapped*. Honolulu: University of Hawaii Press.

Zaroza, H.L. 1998. 'Refugee Voices, Internal Exile, and Return: A Gendered View', *Journal of Refugee Studies*, 11(2): 189–98.

10

CAN THE WOMEN FLEE?—GENDER-BASED PERSECUTION, FORCED MIGRATION AND ASYLUM LAW IN SOUTH ASIA

Oishik Sircar*

Introduction

The majority of the world's refugees are females,[1] who bear the brunt of the most extreme forms of human rights abuse. Yet the 1951 United Nations Convention Relating to the Status of Refugees (hereafter Refugees Convention) does not recognise 'gender' as a separate and independent ground for persecution. Not a single woman was present amongst the plenipotentiaries when the drafters of the Convention had met in Geneva. It was the dominant image of a political refugee—someone fleeing persecution resulting from direct involvement in political activity—which informed the minds of the drafters. This understanding does not often correspond with the reality of women's experiences, and the 'law has developed within a male paradigm which reflects the factual circumstances of male applicants, but which does not respond to the particular protection needs of women' (Romany 1994: 88).

*Work on this paper has been supported in part by the WISCOMP Women in Security, Conflict Management and Peace 'Scholar of Peace' Fellowship that the author was awarded in 2004. The author is grateful to the South Asia Human Rights Documentation Centre (SAHRDC) and the Centre for Feminist Legal Research (CFLR), New Delhi for library and computer support. Special thanks to Navnita Chadha Behera and Mary O'Kane for their comments and criticisms. Thanks are also due to Jyoti Sanghera, Yasmin Tambiah, Sharmila Rege, Ayesha Sen Choudhury, Bikram Jeet Batra, Gareth Sweeney, Christopher Rickerd, Paula Banerjee and Chirantan Chatterjee for their ideas, input and inspiration.

Even the existing bank of jurisprudence on the meaning of persecution is primarily based on experiences of male claimants where '[persecution] is [understood] by the criterion of what men fear will happen to them' (Charlesworth 1994: 71).

Female-specific experiences such as genital mutilation, bride-burning, forced marriages, domestic violence, forced abortion or compulsory sterilisation have not been widely understood to qualify as persecution. Rape has been the only exception (Macklin 1995: 225).

In South Asia, where violence against women is endemic, they are most defenceless in their ability to seek protection from violence through the implementation of international law. State adjudication practices, as well as the non-existence of a regional 'gender asylum law' regime, does not afford them an opportunity to seek surrogate protection[2] under International Refugee Law. The result is a growing number of internally displaced women who are at greater risk because the government that should have protected them often commits the abuses they seek to escape. Moreover, because they have not crossed any international border to seek refuge or asylum, displaced persons can claim only minimal protection from international law (Human Rights Watch 1995: 101). While the UNHCR is responsible for providing protection and assistance to refugees, no similar agency exists within the UN system for IDPs.[3]

The problem is compounded by the fact that none of the South Asian countries have signed the Refugees Convention, nor has a regional refugee policy been developed. There is very little legal input available in a gendered sense for the protection of women fleeing violence and governments have been insensitive in failing to recognise the special needs and requirements of women refugees (Hans 2003: 356). While some migrate to refugee camps in neighbouring countries, a small minority seeks protection either as asylum seekers or through refugee resettlement processes. Although few in number, the issues they confront are fundamental to the protection of women's human rights (Newland 2003: 1).

Looking at forced migration from a gender perspective is therefore important to understand the circumstances which give rise to women's fear of persecution that are unique to women. Refugee women face gender-specific violence and have gender-specific needs. During armed conflicts, international or internal, women are targeted for sexual violence, as their bodies become markers for the nation or community they represent. In flight, women and girls risk further violations of their human rights through rape and abduction. Often, their passage to safety is bought at the price of sexual favours, sometimes even within the relative security of a refugee camp. Frequently bearing additional social responsibilities as heads of households they face discrimination in food distribution, and access to health, welfare and education services—thus doubly disadvantaged as refugees and as women (Goodwin-Gill 1996: 225).[4]

This paper argues that South Asian women forced to migrate due to gender-based persecution can be best protected through the establishment of regional and national 'gender asylum law' regimes. It draws leads from the gender asylum jurisprudence that has been developed by the UNHCR and some industrialised countries which have advanced asylum to women from the global South who have been victims of gender based persecution perpetrated by both state and non-state actors.

It further seeks to place women and their experiences within the framework of international refugee law and explore the linkages between gender-based persecution/violence, forced migration and asylum law protection to suggest directions, spaces and sites for further investigation.

Gender-based Persecution in International Refugee Law

Article 1A(2) of the Refugees Convention, as amended by the 1967 Protocol relating to the Status of Refugees, defines a 'refugee' as:

> ... any person who ... owing to a fell-founded fear of being persecuted for reasons of *race, religion, nationality, membership of a particular social group or political opinion*, is outside the country of his/her nationality and is unable or, owing to such fear, is unwilling to avail himself/herself of the protection of that country; or who, not having a nationality and being outside the country of his/her formal residence, is unable or owing to such fear, is unwilling to return to it (author's emphasis).

There exists no comprehensive definition of the concepts of 'persecution' and 'well-founded fear of persecution' in international law. The drafters of the Refugees Convention framed an open-ended and flexible approach to the concept of persecution in the form of a universal framework. The UNHCR's 'Handbook on Procedures and Criteria for Determining Refugee Status' gives direction in this regard:

> ... it may be inferred that a threat to life or freedom on account of race, religion, nationality, political opinion or membership of a particular social group is always persecution. Other serious violations of human rights—for the same reasons—would also constitute persecution (UNHCR Handbook 1992: para 51).

The definition of persecution in refugee law contains two elements: first, persecution not only requires that a claimant be at risk of sustaining serious harm, and second, that the claimant cannot expect meaningful protection from that harm in her home country. Thus, recognising that gender-related harm which threatens basic human rights of women constitute serious harm alone is not sufficient to warrant the label of 'persecution'; the harm feared must be directly or indirectly attributable to the state, and it must also be that the individual cannot expect meaningful protection from these state authorities in the country of origin (Adjin-Tettey 1997: 54). In other words, the criterion that are particularly significant in cases dealing with gender persecution, and that differ from other asylum application, is which acts amount to persecution.

The term 'gender-based persecution' refers to asylum applications of women premised on issues pertaining specifically to their gender.[5] These claims can be separated into two general categories. The first focuses on persecution commonly faced by women, such as rape,[6] genital mutilation, domestic violence and bride burning, among others. The second category includes claims that constitute persecution because of the applicants' gender; that is, persecution for disobeying repressive gender-discriminatory laws or for not conforming with social mores that are offensive to women. This category also includes situations that discriminate against women and strictly prohibit them from engaging in certain activities (Bahl 1997: 34).

Although the definition of a refugee in the Refugees Convention appears to be gender neutral, behind it lies the narrow interpretation and assumption of conventional refugees that rarely fit the experiences of women. In practice, women have greater difficulty in satisfying the legal requirements for refugee status because of certain inherent male biases in the law. Women are less likely to meet the eligibility criteria for refugee status because of non-recognition of gender based persecution, as well as the social and political context in which their claims are adjudicated. According to Nancy Kelly, the problem is twofold: first, the Refugees Convention definition of 'refugee' does not specifically identify gender as a base for protection. Second, in applying the refugee definition, adjudicators have traditionally neglected to incorporate gender in their interpretation of the grounds of persecution enumerated in the Refugees Convention (Kelly 1993: 265). This is especially true of male adjudicators who tend to regard gender based persecution as a private and personal matter rather than as a socially significant phenomenon. Applications are continuously considered as falling outside the requirements of the Refugees Convention and rejected on the basis that the perpetrator is a private actor for whom the state cannot be made accountable. At times, fear of treading on state sovereignty has led advocates for cultural relativism to warn against interpreting traditional and historically sanctioned practices as persecution.

This is also due to the general failure of the international refugee and asylum law regime in not recognising systemic denial of social and economic rights while emphasising individual targeting and specific deprivation of civil and political rights. Besides, human rights law and discourse tend to privilege male dominated public activities over the activities of women, which take place largely in the private sphere (Crawley 2000: 17).[7] The key criteria for being a refugee are drawn from the public realm dominated by men. With regard to women's activities in the private sphere there is primarily silence, which assigns the critical quality 'political' to mostly public activities. Thus, state oppression of a political minority is likely to be considered political unlike gender oppression at home (Indra 1987: 3). Moreover, in rejecting gender as a legitimate ground for persecution, state authorities may easily dismiss people, especially women whose economic, cultural and social rights have been violated, as 'economic migrants' (Raj 2001: 170).

The barriers to seeking an asylum may also be logistical, informational or psychological. Since more women are illiterate, it becomes harder for them to get information about how and where to apply for asylum, or even to learn about their options. In some societies women are prohibited from interacting with strangers, including government authorities. This could become an obstacle not only for seeking asylum, but also in gaining legal assistance. Women may find it more difficult to reach a location to claim asylum, as they tend to be less mobile than men, and have less control over resources. Often being solely responsible for their children, the logistics of travelling with children become more complicated than travelling alone (Kelson 1997: 183). When they are travelling with male relatives, the men are often treated as the 'primary' asylum seekers, even if it is the women's experiences that might more clearly fit the requirements for granting asylum. They may not be asked about their own experiences, but those of their male relatives (Newland 2003: 4).

This omission of gender as a separate ground for persecution (the existing five grounds being *race, religion, nationality, membership of a particular social group* and *political opinion*) has had severe implications for many female asylum seekers across the world. As a consequence, debates have focused on whether women's experiences can and should be interpreted so that they may be included into the already existing grounds, or whether it is instead necessary to introduce gender as a sixth ground. The question is whether the addition of gender as a sixth ground can bring about a reconceptualisation that would reveal, instead of concealing, the persecution that has its origin in women's distinctive existential and material state of being? (Lyth 2001: 28). Heaven Crawley responds by stating, 'simply adding gender or sex to the enumerated grounds of persecution would not solve the problem. The bars to women's eligibility for refugee status lie not in the legal categories *per se*, but in the incomplete and gendered interpretation of refugee law, the failure of decision-makers to acknowledge and respond to the gendering of politics and of women's relationship to the state' (Crawley 2000: 17). Still how refugee law could be more effective in strengthening other forms of protection is that refugee law, in part, takes an integrative perspective on women's rights. 'By interpreting forms of violence against women within mainstream human rights norms and definitions of persecution, refugee law avoids some of the problems of marginalising women's rights in international law' (Anker 2002: 133). For almost two decades now there has been an increased recognition by the international community and the UNHCR of the need to interpret the notion of persecution in a gender sensitive fashion. In 1984, one of the first efforts to recognise gender based persecution claims occurred when the European Community admitted it under the category of membership in a particular social group (Goldberg 1995: 346). The European Parliament in 1985 called on states to grant refugee status 'to women who suffer cruel and inhuman treatment because they have violated the moral or ethical rules of their society'.[8] During the same year the Executive Committee (EXCOM) of the UNHCR issued a recommendation which acknowledged that states may recognise claims of gender-based persecution under the 'particular social group' category.[9]

Finally, in 1991, the Guidelines for the Protection of Refugee Women were adopted by the UNHCR. The guidelines acknowledge that women and girls 'have special needs that reflect their gender: they need, for example, protection against manipulation, sexual and physical abuse and exploitation, and protection against sexual discrimination in the delivery of goods and services'.[10] They cover most of the physical and legal problems that women refugees can face and recognise that women refugees should seek asylum if confronted with violence. At a later stage, the EXCOM issued a Conclusion on Violence against Women that called for the 'development by states of appropriate guidelines on women asylum seekers, in recognition of the fact that women refugees often experience persecution differently from refugee men' (UN Doc. A/AC.96/XLIV.CRP.3).

Pursuant to the UNHCR Guidelines, some countries developed a new 'gender asylum law' jurisprudence. In 1993, the Canadian government first implemented such guidelines on gender based persecution in the assessment of refugee claimants. The USA (1995), Australia (1996), Norway (1998) and Sweden (2001) followed. These guidelines are an important step, but they only apply to women who have made it to one of the above countries to claim refugee status. A body of case law has also evolved while examining women claimants' appeals, which have mostly afforded protection to women fleeing persecution on the Refugees Convention ground of belonging to a 'particular social group'. Although this option may have produced socially desirable results, it does not fully recognise the importance of persecution on account of gender. Gender as a social group might be an appropriate remedy if the persecution of women were isolated or temporary, but that approach does not afford women enough protection within the context of society's recognised, widespread and institutionalised persecution of women worldwide. Still, this increasing recognition of gender based persecution by courts is an indication of the developing sensitivity towards claims based on it in some jurisdictions.

However, there is a need for scholars, activists and policy-makers working on refugee rights to be cautious of the kind of repercussions that inclusion of 'gender' as a separate ground for persecution might entail. While this would be a significant development, it might homogenise the 'woman' category by assuming that women's experiences of persecution everywhere follow the same patterns and trends, irrespective of their cultural and geopolitical locations. To avoid essentialising both gender and culture, the framework for asylum determination needs to be transformed to accommodate the inclusion of women not as a special case, but one among many different categories where women's experiences are contextualised with regard to their gender as well as its linkages with their caste, colour, race, and national and political identities. This approach suggests that the problem is not so much the invisibility of women but rather how their experiences have been represented and analytically characterised (Crawley 2000: 19).

Right to International Protection, Gender-based Violence and State Responsibility

The UN Declaration on the Elimination of Violence Against Women defines violence against women as:

> … any act of gender-based violence that results in, or is likely to result in, physical, sexual or psychological harm or suffering to women, including threats of such acts, coercion or arbitrary deprivation of liberty, whether occurring in public or private life.

In 1990, the UNHCR EXCOM affirmed the linkage between a violation of the rights guaranteed under the CEDAW and persecution for the purposes of the Refugees Convention, stating that severe discrimination prohibited by CEDAW can form the basis for the granting of refugee status.[11]

In October 2003, the UNHCR EXCOM adopted a Conclusion on Protection from Sexual Abuse and Exploitation highlighting the need for measures to empower women in refugee situations, codes of conduct for humanitarian staff, prompt investigations of allegations of sexual abuse and exploitation, and the need for accountability mechanisms. The conclusion also recognises that states, the UNHCR and other implementing and operational partners all have the responsibility to take concrete measures to prevent and respond to sexual and gender based violence.

In spite of being parties to the CEDAW and holding membership of the UNHCR EXCOM, India, Pakistan and Bangladesh are still to recognise the importance of the rights of women refugees. This insecurity is compounded by the cultural and societal positions of women in South Asia, where they still occupy a subservient position to men. Effectively, their education, resources and recourse to justice for wrongs committed against them are limited (Peters 1996: 232).

Governments in South Asia have failed to fulfil their duty to secure legal redress for women victims of persecution. Gender based discrimination in this area includes the persistence of inadequate laws against abuses and institutional failings on the part of the criminal justice process, including the police and the judiciary. Often these failings mutually reinforce each other. Scholars have extensively documented the kinds of treatment South Asian women have to undergo at the hands of state and non-state actors.[12] As a result, these women become refugees, or are internally displaced, where they remain as victims of persecution without access to protection mechanisms—domestic or international.

Perhaps the most pervasive form of gender-based persecution in South Asia occurs in the context of domestic violence, where the state's omission to act to stop such violence results in its complicity in perpetuating it. Equally significant are the systematic violations of their rights during armed conflicts. During conflicts—internal or international—violence against women is often used as a weapon of war, in order to dehumanise the women themselves or persecute the community to which they belong. Women are likely to form the greatest proportion of adult civilian population killed in war and targeted for abuse. Women are also usually the majority of refugees and internally displaced persons forced to flee their homes because of armed conflict (Amnesty International 2004: 50).

While rape and sexual violence are the most commonly recognised forms of gender-specific persecution, there are other forms of persecution that also qualify as being gender specific. These include cultural and religious traditions inhibiting women's right to life, liberty and security, such as genital mutilation, honour killings, dowry deaths, *sati* (widow burning) and other traditional practices harmful to women/ girls. Similarly, women are often subject to inhumane and discriminatory treatment for transgressing customary and religious laws such as dress codes, taking up employment and ignoring educational restrictions or restrictions on women's freedom of movement (Binder 2001: 173–174). Women and girls are sometimes not even safe from sexual and other forms of exploitation by humanitarian aid workers—the very people who are charged with responsibility for the welfare of refugees and the displaced.

Many governments, eager to avoid their responsibility to provide protection to refugees, are applying an increasingly restrictive definition of who qualifies for refugee status. A number of countries deny refugee status to people persecuted by armed opposition groups and other private actors, and only a few countries grant asylum where the state has failed to protect against torture by private individuals.

This issue of the state's role in persecution suffered has been a vexed problem in asylum law. Traditionally in refugee law, persecution was understood as an act of the state or those acting in their capacity as state agents. This view only recognised persecution perpetrated by public authorities and failed to recognise the rights of women to be free from gender persecution perpetrated in the so-called 'private' sphere. Notwithstanding the fact that women throughout the world are most often subjected to gender-related abuse perpetrated in the 'private' sphere of intimate relationships, the unwillingness of states to intrude into that domain has allowed such violations of women's human rights to continue with impunity (Randall 2002: 305–06).

If eligibility for asylum is defined on the basis that the government in the country of origin must either refrain from committing violations or provide adequate protection from such violations, then it can be strongly argued that women who suffer gender based human rights abuses and/or flee because of well-founded fear of gender based persecution must be eligible for refugee protection.

In understanding the relation between the woman seeking protection and the state it is important to point out that women suffer due to lack of infrastructure that protects them, or due to non-enforcement of the existing laws providing them with effective redress (Bahl 1997: 41). In other words, the state is responsible to the extent that it fails to provide or utilise the apparatus that could prevent or redress the wrongs. The state has an affirmative obligation to protect and prevent violence. Its inability to do so amounts to persecution from nonfeasance, that is, liability is conferred on the state for commission of those persecutory acts. The state would definitely be in breach of its obligations under international law, which requires it to punish those individuals— government agents or private actors—who commit human rights violations. The breach of such obligations, and the inability or unwillingness to protect a woman's human rights, is tantamount to the state's connivance in the act of persecution.

Over the past decade, the jurisprudence of different states, the UNHCR and national gender guidelines have addressed various issues critical to the recognition of status and availability of protection for women asylum seekers. It is argued that the assessment within the refugee determination process to find out whether there has been a failure of state protection must be based on the state's international human rights obligations to protect against systematic abuse on the grounds of gender (Crawley 2000: 50). The UNHCR Handbook states that acts of violence in the private sphere may be considered persecutory if the authorities condone them, or if they refuse to or are unable to provide sufficient protection. It also states that where an applicant's country has denied her this assurance, such denial of protection may confirm or strengthen the applicant's fear of persecution and may indeed be an element of persecution.

Proposed Strategies for a National/Regional 'Gender Asylum Law' Regime in South Asia

Governments in South Asia have not yet realised the urgency for proposing a mechanism for protecting women who need to flee from gender-based persecution. Their unwillingness to submit their responses to asylum seekers and refugees on their territory to international scrutiny is reflected in the non-existence of any regional/national refugee regime as well as no accession to the Refugees Convention. The UNHCR is allowed access to camps and displaced populations in the region only with the permission and cooperation of the respective national governments, and such permission is not always granted. However, the general principle of non-refoulement[13] prohibiting forced repatriation is now acknowledged as customary international law that binds even non-signatories, including of course the South Asian countries. Non-refoulement applies where there is fear of torture or violation of refugees' right to life.

Despite the grave nature of the refugee problem in South Asia, countries in the region have not developed any formal structure to deal with the issue. Instead, refugees are frequently subjected to the same national laws as illegal aliens and/or are dealt with under ad hoc administrative arrangements, which by their very nature can be arbitrary and discriminatory affording few rights to refugees. The most important hindrance to developing a formal refugee regime in South Asia has been the adherence to the policy of working out political solutions through bilateral negotiations between the host country and the country of origin, with an emphasis on sovereign jurisdiction (Abrar 2001: 21). That is because they have yet to de-link refugee issues from their national security concerns. Especially post-9/11, many states are finding it difficult to reconcile the need to control their borders with their international obligations to assist and protect refugees. As Castro-Magluff notes:

> This is a modern manifestation of the classical dichotomy between states' claim to sovereignty and their participation in the international community. The international instruments providing for the protection of refugees are seen as restraining states' jurisdiction to control the admission of foreign nationals into their territory. The idea of policing one's borders to control the entry and residence of non-citizens plays an important role as the primary symbol of sovereignty, both in terms of the separation of independent states' exercise of jurisdiction, and in the general perception of independence and nationhood. For states immigration control is thus viewed as one of the last remaining symbols of national security (Magluff 2001: 63).

A leading South Asian scholar, B.S. Chimni, has argued that South Asian countries should refrain from acceding to the Refugees Convention as the instrument is being dismantled by those very states which had framed it. And, any talk of accession should also be linked to the withdrawal of measures that constitute the non-entrée and temporary protection regimes (Chimni 2003: 443). James Hathaway, on the other hand, argues for reinvigorating refugee law through a theory of 'solution-oriented' temporary protection and burden sharing through 'common but differentiated' responsibility (Hathaway 1997: xxiii, quoted in Ray 2001: 180). But how can one convince governments of temporary protection while still ensuring that the rights of refugees are protected and their futures are not permanently put on hold? The norm in international refugee protection has been that of permanent protection eventually leading to citizenship. The issue of temporary protection will continue to evoke security concerns for countries in South Asia as well as around the world, and also generate new concerns regarding refugees' basic rights. In this context, it is a challenge for South Asian states to either accede to the Refugees Convention and its

Protocol or develop a regional instrument and demonstrates to the Western world how the spirit and scope of refugee treaties can be implemented and respected (Gorlick 1998: 27).

Given the realities of South Asia, efforts should be geared towards developing comprehensive national laws that uphold the universal principles of international refugee protection while taking into account the distinctive traits of the region. This will be a more solution-oriented approach that will be far more pertinent and fair in light of current displacements within South Asia. Moreover, if such a national legislation were adopted by South Asian states without acceding to the Refugees Convention, it would be a rare example of national legislation superseding international obligations (Raj 2001: 181). The absence of national laws have meant that refugees are dependent on the benevolence of the state rather than on a regime of rights to reconstruct their lives in dignity. A consistent legal framework is vital to the prevention of political ad hocism, which often translates into forcible repatriation for refugees (Nair 2001: 20).

With specific reference to violence against women, the absence of regional or national laws have also meant that women facing persecution on grounds of gender can only apply for asylum to a developed country. This not only adds a practical constraint but is also culpable of creating the stereotypical image of the Third World woman-as-victim subject. An examination of case law in various developed countries makes it evident that most cases of gender-based persecution concern women from the (global) South who face culturally sanctioned forms of violence. Similar to the problems of addressing 'gender' as a special ground for persecution, the present politics of asylum jurisprudence considers the Third World 'native' woman to be tradition-bound, incarcerated in the home, illiterate and poor, and most importantly, in need of Western intervention for 'protecting' and 'saving' her from violence (Kapur 2002: 18). The need for a 'gender asylum regime' in South Asia is thus necessary for not only advancing asylum jurisprudence in the region, but also challenging and countering the existing constructs of the Eastern-native-disempowered woman, which at best victimises and at worst infantilises them.

The initial attempt at formulating a draft regional law for refugee protection was first formulated in 1966 when the African-Asian Legal Consultative Committee adopted the Bangkok Principles on the Status and Treatment of Refugees. These principles have since been in cold storage and only the text was finalised at a meeting in New Delhi in 2001. The Bangkok Principles recognise 'gender' as a separate ground for persecution.

In November 1997 the Eminent Persons Group (EPG) for South Asia set up by the UNHCR approved a model national law at their Dhaka Consultation.[14] This model law is the first step in the process of building a consensus on preventing, managing and solving the problems accompanying refugee flows within South Asia in a comprehensive and humane manner. The purpose of the law is to establish a procedure for granting refugee status to asylum seekers and those forced to migrate due to a well-founded fear of persecution, to guarantee them fair treatment and to establish the requisite machinery for its implementation. This model law incorporates 'ethnic identity' in its categorisation of people who would qualify to gain refugee status. It is commendable to note establishing membership of a 'particular social group' will also include gender-based persecution. The model law provides a comprehensive definition suiting the needs of the region (Abrar 2001: 22). Unfortunately, it has only remained a legal fiction with states showing no inclination towards incorporating it in their respective national legislations.

Since India is the largest receiving country in South Asia,[15] it should take the initiative for establishing a gender sensitive refugee law regime in the region by first making a national law on refuge protection. This would be an extension of India's obligations under various international human rights instruments that it has acceded to.[16] Such an initiative will also show that India takes its membership of the UNHCR EXCOM[17] seriously, and wants to strengthen its role there. To remain a member of the EXCOM without either acceding to the 1951 Convention or passing a national legislation shows an opportunistic attitude towards UN institutions that does the image of the country little good in the international community (Chimni 2003: 443).

Conclusion

While a reformulation of the refugee definition to include gender is desirable, political realities and trends in immigration policies inevitably lead to the conclusion that this approach can be effective only if efforts are also focused on improving national legal and judicial practices to supplement the existing conventional international refugee law framework. The issuance of gender guidelines by some Western countries and the undertakings by the UNHCR demonstrate important steps toward a more gender-sensitive refugee regime, and a very gradual increase in the willingness of states to recognise violence against women as an issue deserving the intervention of the protection that refugee law provides.

It is important that, along with national and regional legislation on refugee protection, South Asian governments expand the UNHCR gender guidelines in the interest of protecting women in South Asia who have very specific needs. This should ideally lead to developing a uniform 'gender asylum law' in the region. A regional refugee treaty would be the most effective way of making sure that states remain bound to their obligations. It is also recommended that a treaty monitoring body be established with powers similar to those of human rights treaty bodies. This body should have the authority to issue general recommendations, view state reports and receive individual complaints of women facing persecution.

The process of developing a 'gender asylum law' regime in South Asia must include governments, NGOs and protection agencies alike because it is important to take a holistic view of this phenomenon. Along with advocating and campaigning for the establishment of a national/regional 'gender asylum law' regime, civil society institutions must urge states that are not signatories to these other international human rights law instruments to accede to them, and also press those states that have acceded but have not made enabling legislation to do so.

Violence against women needs to be prioritised by South Asian governments and civil society organisations as especially grave and pervasive aspects of discrimination. To this end, the efficacy of 'gender asylum law' in providing 'real' protection to women facing persecution at the hands of state and private actors must be recognised. Governments must be more concerned about protection of women facing persecution, rather than thinking of how a refugee regime might open the floodgates to illegal immigrants. Rather, it is a substantive law that would facilitate states' efforts to identify illegal immigrants as opposed to refugees.

A step in this direction would not only be a landmark achievement in the development of asylum jurisprudence in the region, but would also be a major addition to intervention mechanisms for the protection of women facing violence globally.

Notes

1 UN Doc. HRC/IP/2/Rev (1986). Because UNHCR does not segregate refugee figures by gender, the precise number of women refugees is not known.

2 Refugee law provides surrogate national protection to individuals when their states have failed to fulfil fundamental obligations, and when that failure has a specified discriminatory impact. Under the Refugees Convention, the responsibility to provide international protection—a surrogate to the ruptured, national protection—is placed in states that are parties to the convention.

3 At present there is no internationally agreed upon definition for the internally displaced. The UN Guiding Principles on Internal Displacement normatively defines IDPs as: 'persons who have been forced to or obliged to flee or leave their homes or places of habitual residence, in particular as a result of or in order to avoid the effects of armed conflict, situations of generalised violence, violations of human rights or natural or human-made disasters, and who have not crossed an internationally recognised state border'.

4 Feminists have argued the need for recognising women's agency and not necessarily treating them as victims in situations like these. This argument is premised on studies that have shown how displaced women have actually been empowered because of being put in positions where they have control over resources and can take decisions. Goodwil-Gill's submission however does not challenge this understanding. His concern is not meant to be taken as 'protectionist', but asserting the need for special protection for refugee women.

5 Gender-based issues include:

> State-directed and state-approved violence against women; violence against women by private actors that is legally endorsed; violence against women that is illegal but is tolerated by the state through discriminatory enforcement of the law; ... discriminatory laws and practices, ... and abuses that are gender specific either in the form—such as forced pregnancy and forced virginity exams—or in that they target primarily women—such as rape and the forced trafficking of women for purposes of sexual servitude (see Human Rights Watch 1995: xiii–xxi).

6 Rape is also widely faced by men in conflict related situations, although not to the extent faced by women. Rape of men is yet to become an issue of public debate.

7 Feminists have argued that the public/private distinction is one of the major obstacles to the achievement of women's rights. (See, for example, Burrows, Noreen. 1986. 'International Law and Human Rights: The Case of Women's Rights', in Tom Campbell et al. (eds), *Human Rights: From Rhetoric to Reality*, Oxford: Blackwell, pp. 80, 86–96.

8 UNHCR. 1997. *The State of the World's Refugees: A Humanitarian Agenda*, Box 5.2: 'Gender-related persecution', Geneva.

9 UNHCR Executive Committee Conclusion No. 39.

10 Guidelines for the Protection of Refugee Women, 7 (1991).

11 UN Doc. EC/SCP/59, UNHCR Executive Committee, Note on Refugee Women and International Protection.

12 See generally, Human Rights Watch (1995), Amnesty International (2001, 2004).

13 'Non-refoulement' is an important principle of international refugee law which acts as a complete prohibition against the forcible return of people to a place where they will be subject to grave human rights violations or where their life or personal security will be seriously endangered. The principle applies equally to refugees at the border of a state and to those already admitted, and it remains in force until the adverse conditions which prompted people to flee in the first place are alleviated.

14 SAARC Law has also contributed substantially to developing a model national legislation for refugees. SAARC Law is a regional body recognised by SAARC, which brings together national associations of judges, legal administrators, academics and lawyers from the five SAARC countries. Its Delhi Seminar of May 1996 favoured framing national legislation before formulating a regional instrument.

15 India's multi-ethnic, multi-lingual and relatively stable society has often made it an attractive destination for a lot of asylum seekers. Refugees from Afghanistan, Iran, and even Sudan, Tamil refugees from Sri Lanka, Jumma people from Bangladesh and Chin, and other tribal refugees from Burma comprise the bulk of India's refugee population.

16 India has ratified the International Convention on Civil and Political Rights (ICCPR), the International Convention on Economic, Social and Cultural Rights (ICESCR) and the Convention on the Elimination of All Forms of Discrimination Against Women (CEDAW). It is also a signatory to the Convention Against Torture (CAT) and is bound by the Universal Declaration of Human Rights (UDHR). However, India declined from signing or ratifying the Rome Statute of the International Criminal Court (ICC).

17 Pakistan and Bangladesh are also members of the EXCOM and have not formalised their commitment to protecting and assisting refugees through adopting an international or national framework.

References

Abrar, C.R. 2001. 'Legal Protection of Refugees in South Asia', *Forced Migration Review*, 10: 21–23.

Adjin-Tettey, E. 1997. 'Failure of State Protection within the Context of the Convention Refugee Regime with Particular Reference to Gender-related Persecution', *Journal of International Legal Studies*, 3: 53–86.

Amnesty International. 2004. *It's in Our Hands: Stop Violence Against Women.* London: Amnesty International.

———. 2001. *Broken Bodies, Shattered Minds: Torture and Ill Treatment of Women.* London: Amnesty International.

Anker, D.E. 2002. 'Refugee Law, Gender, and the Human Rights Paradigm', *Harvard Human Rights Journal*, 15: 133–54.

Bahl, A. 1997. 'Home is Where the Brute Lives: Asylum Law and Gender-based Claims of Persecution', *Cardozo Women's Law Journal*, 4: 33–73.

Binder, A. 2001. 'Gender and "Membership in a Particular Social Group". Category of the 1951 Refugee Convention', *Columbia Journal of Gender and Law*, 10: 167–94.

Castro-Magluff, J.M. 2001. 'The Inadequacies of International Regime for the Protection of Refugees', in Sanjay K. Roy (ed.), *Refugees and Human Rights: Social and Political Dynamics of Refugee Problem in Eastern and North-Eastern India*, pp. 63–79. New Delhi: Rawat.

Charlesworth, H. 1994. 'What are Women's International Human Rights', in Rebecca J. Cook (ed.), *Human Rights of Women: National and International Perspectives*, pp. 58–84. Philadelphia: University of Pennsylvania Press.

Chimni, B.S. 2003. 'Status of Refugees in India: Strategic Ambiguity', in R. Samaddar (ed.), *Refugees and the State: Practices of Asylum and Care in India*, pp. 443–71. New Delhi: Sage Publications.

Crawley, H. 2000. 'Gender, Persecution and the Concept of Politics in the Asylum Determination Process', *Forced Migration Review*, 9: 17–20.

Goldberg, P. 1995. 'Where in the World is there Safety for Me?—Women Fleeing Gender-based Persecution', in J. Peters and A. Wolper (eds), *Women's Rights, Human Rights: International Feminist Perspectives*, pp. 345–58. London: Routledge.

Goodwin-Gill, Guy. 1996. *The Refugee in International Law*. Second edition. Oxford: Clarendon Press.

Gorlick, B. 1998. 'Refugees and Human Rights', *Seminar*, 463: 23–27.

Hans, A. 2003. 'Refugee Women and Children: Need for Protection and Care', in R. Samaddar (ed.), *Refugees and the State: Practices of Asylum and Care in India*, pp. 355–95. New Delhi: Sage Publications.

Human Rights Watch. 1995. *The Human Rights Watch Global Report on Women's Human Rights*. New Delhi: Oxford University Press.

Indra, D. 1987. 'Gender: A Key Dimension of the Refugee Experience', *Refuge*, 6: 3–4.

Kapur, R. 2002. 'The Tragedy of Victimisation Rhetoric: Resurrecting the "Native" Subject in International/Post-Colonial Feminist Legal Politics', *Harvard Human Rights Journal*, 15: 1–37.

Kelly, N. 1993. 'Gender-Related Persecution: Assessing the Asylum Claims of Women', *Cornell International Law Journal*, 26: 625–71.

Kelson, G.A. 1997. 'Gender-based Persecution and Political Asylum: The International Debate for Equality Begins', *Texas Journal of Women and Law*, 6: 181–213.

Lyth, A. 2001. 'Where are the Women?—A Gender Approach to Refugee Law', LL.M thesis, Lund University, Sweden.

Macklin, A. 1995. 'Refugee Women and the Imperative of Categories', *Human Rights Quarterly*, 17: 213–77.

Nair, R. 2001. *Refugee Protection in India*. New Delhi: South Asia Human Rights Documentation Centre (SAHRDC).

Newland, K. 2003. 'Seeking Protection: Women in Asylum and Refugee Resettlement Processes', Issue Paper for the UN Division for the Advancement of Women, Expert Consultation on Migration and Mobility and How this Movement Affects Women, Malmo, Sweden.

Peters, T.L. 1996. 'International Refugee Law and the Treatment of Gender-based Persecution: International Initiatives as a Model and Mandate for National Reform', *Transnational and Contemporary Problems*, 6: 225–50.

Raj, S. 2001. 'The Gender Element in International Refugee Law: Its Impact on Agency Programming and the North-South Debate', *Indian Society of International Law Yearbook on Humanitarian and Refugee Law*, 1: 164–82.

Randall, M. 2002. 'Refugee Law and State Accountability for Violence Against Women: A Comparative Analysis of Legal Approaches to Recognising Asylum Claims Based on Gender Persecution', *Harvard Women's Law Journal*, 25: 281–318.

Romany, C. 1994. 'State Responsibility Goes Private', in Rebecca J. Cook (ed.), *Human Rights of Women: National and International Perspectives*, pp. 65–115. Philadelphia: University of Pennsylvania Press.

UNHCR (United Nations High Commissioner for Refugees). 1992. 'Handbook on the Procedures and Criteria for Determining Refugee Status'. Geneva: UNHCR.

11

GENDER-BASED PERSECUTION: THE CASE OF SOUTH ASIAN ASYLUM APPLICANTS IN THE UK

Anthony Good*

To be accepted as refugees under the 1951 UN Convention, asylum applicants must demonstrate a 'well-founded fear of being persecuted for reasons of race, religion, nationality, membership of a particular social group or political opinion'. Gender based persecution was deliberately excluded from the Convention's scope, but over the past half century it has become increasingly common for asylum claims to be based upon matters such as sexual assault or domestic violence. Because the Convention itself provides no guidance, female asylum applicants face particular difficulties in demonstrating that their experiences, however horrific, can be brought within the scope of the Convention. For example, courts may fail to recognise gender related differences in how political opinions are expressed in conflictual situations. This chapter examines these issues with special reference to asylum applicants in the United Kingdom from Sri Lanka, Pakistan and India, and looks at the implications of key cases in the international jurisprudence, such as the 1999 British House of Lords decision in the case of Islam & Shah.

One of the first international agreements of the post-World War II order was the Universal Declaration of Human Rights in 1948. Article 14(1) of the Declaration stated: 'Everyone has the right to seek and to enjoy in other countries asylum from persecution' (UNHCHR 1998). This Article was greatly elaborated in the 1951 UN Convention Relating to the Status of Refugees, the key international instrument covering

*Research for this paper was supported by the Economic and Social Research Council's Research Grant No. R000223352.

asylum applicants. The Convention's preamble states that refugees should enjoy fundamental human rights, recognises that this requires international cooperation and charges the United Nations High Commissioner for Refugees (UNHCR) with coordinating measures by signatory states to deal with refugee problems. Article 1A(2) of this Convention, as modified by the 1967 Protocol, defines a 'refugee' as someone who:

... owing to well-founded fear of being persecuted *for reasons of race, religion, nationality, membership of a particular social group or political opinion*, is outside the country of his nationality and is unable or, owing to such fear, is unwilling to avail himself of the protection of that country (italics added).

One hundred and twenty-six countries signed both the 1951 Convention and the 1967 Protocol, while eight more signed one or the other.[1] Countries to have signed neither the Convention nor the Protocol include India, Pakistan, Sri Lanka, Nepal and Bangladesh—even though Pakistan was on the drafting committee. The decisions by India and Pakistan to remain non-signatories reflected definitional disagreement; both countries, faced with huge numbers of displaced persons in the aftermath of Partition, thought that 'refugees' should be defined so as to include such people. India stated that 'it was not convinced of the need for an international organisation whose sole responsibility would be to provide legal protection, when its own refugees were dying of starvation' (Goodwin-Gill 1996: 264).

UK Legislation

The Convention per se is not part of British law, but underlies domestic legislation in the sense that the UK has committed itself not to violate its Convention obligations. The basic legislation is the Immigration Act 1971, as amended by the Asylum and Immigration Appeals Act 1993, the Asylum and Immigration Act 1996, the Immigration and Asylum Act 1999, and the Nationality, Immigration and Asylum Act 2002. The Human Rights Act 1998, incorporating the European Convention on Human Rights (ECHR) into United Kingdom law, has also applied to asylum cases since October 2000. This frenzy of recent legislation, unparalleled in any other area of public policy, reflects the moral panic surrounding the issue of asylum in the UK and other European Union states in recent years.

The administrative and legal procedures to which asylum claims are subjected under this legislation have been summarised elsewhere (Good 2004: 115–17) and the focus here lies on the case law generated thereby. That case law is vitally important because the drafters of the Convention left virtually every term undefined, even the notion of 'persecution' which is arguably most central of all. Partly as a result, every phrase of Article 1A(2) has undergone extensive, and evolving, legal interpretation ever since (Symes and Jorro 2003). Because the Convention and Protocol arose directly out of human rights concerns associated with the founding of the UN, their interpretation must be firmly grounded on the principles of the UN Charter (von Sternberg 2002: 3), and even though asylum decisions are framed by national legislation and local administrative procedures, the jurisprudence necessarily has a strong international dimension. British courts regularly draw on legal precedents from other countries, especially those with shared common-law traditions such as Canada, Australia, New Zealand and the USA.

The Five 'Convention Reasons'

All elements of Article 1A(2) have been subject to conflicting legal interpretations, but this paper limits itself to the five 'Convention reasons'. To qualify as a refugee, a person must have a well-founded fear of persecution 'for reasons of race, religion, nationality, membership of a particular social group or political opinion'. This paper focuses on the last two of these, in relation to the fact that the Convention does not explicitly consider issues of gender.

Naturally enough, the Convention reflects rather outdated understandings of these concepts. Regarding *race*, for example, it was far less widely recognised in 1951 that the issue at stake was not biological differences per se, but culturally variable ideas about such differences. To some extent, the UNHCR's explanatory 'Handbook' (1992: para 68) updates earlier understandings by advocating a definition which includes 'all kinds of ethnic groups that are referred to as "races" in common usage'. Belonging to a particular 'racial' group is not in itself sufficient to claim refugee status, of course, but the existence of racial discrimination may be, if it affects 'human dignity'.

The Universal Declaration of Human Rights guarantees the right to freedom of *religion*, including freedom 'to manifest it in public or private, in teaching, practice, worship and observance'. The most common cases in which religion forms the basis of asylum claims in the UK at present concern Ahmadis in Pakistan, regarded as heretics by many other Muslims, and Falun Gong members claiming persecution by the Chinese government. Matters of definition do not generally arise, but while the courts have accepted without question that the Ahmadis, say, practice a distinctive religion, they have shown less certainty over the religious status of West African secret societies.

The inclusion of *nationality* among the Convention reasons may seem odd: why would a state persecute its own nationals simply for being its own nationals? As UNHCR's 'Handbook' (ibid.: para 74) explains, however, this term too may refer also to membership of ethnic or linguistic groups and may overlap with the term 'race'. Hathaway (1991: 144), one of the leading academic authorities, explains that it was meant to cover cases where inferior forms of citizenship exist, as in apartheid South Africa, or where ethnic minorities define their nationalities in ways other than those imposed upon them by the state, as in the former USSR.

Political opinion is only a ground for refugee status if it leads to a fear of persecution, which implies that the person's opinions are known to the authorities or are imputed by them to that person, for example, when someone belongs to a political family. Politics is, however, left undefined, so there is clearly scope for interpretation as to whether particular views are political or not. Moreover, the Convention's stress on opinions leaves it unclear as to how political *actions* by would-be refugees are to be assessed.

Finally, the most problematic category is *membership of a particular social group*. The problems arise largely from the fact that almost no discussion took place from which later legal decision-makes could deduce what the Convention's drafters had in mind. Remarkably, the sum total of debate at the founding conference consisted of an assertion by the Swedish delegate that 'certain refugees had been persecuted because they belonged to particular social groups. The draft convention made no provision for such cases, and one designed to cover them should accordingly be included' (UN Doc. A/CONF.2/SR.3, p. 14; see Grahl-Madsen 1966: 219). Asylum courts worldwide have dealt as best as they can with this lack of clarity over what the phrase was meant to cover (Haines 1998).[2] In particular, there has been much legal wrangling over the extent to which persons who have been persecuted for reasons related to gender can bring themselves within the scope of the Convention by claiming that the persecution resulted from their membership of a 'particular social group'.

Gender

After the briefest of discussions, the drafting conference for the 1951 Convention deciding against adding 'sex'[3] to the list of Convention reasons in Article 1A(2), because its members doubted that 'persecution on account of sex' would ever arise (UN Doc. A/CONF.2/SR.5)! The Convention was of course meant to apply to women and men equally, but it has increasingly been argued that this omission, coupled with the Convention's use of masculine pronouns throughout, led to distinctively female experiences being marginalised (Crawley 2001: 5).

For this reason among others, feminist critics tend to assume that women are discriminated against in asylum decision-making, and 'may not benefit equally from [Convention] protections' (Berkowitz and Jarvis 2000: 1). The reality seems more complex, however. It does not seem to be the case that women as a whole are less successful than men in their asylum claims; if anything, rather the reverse holds true (Spijkerboer 2000: 39). What is true, though, is that 'the asylum cases of men and women are always different' (ibid.: 5). In other words, the refugee identities of *both men and women* are gendered social constructs. What is more, the parties involved in processing their claims—the immigration officers or case workers who interview them on behalf of the state; their own legal representatives who record their statements; the administrative officials who make initial decisions on their claims; and the judges who determine their appeals—tend to construct these identities using such received gender stereotypes as masculine rationality, activity and autonomy, or feminine emotionality, passivity and dependence (ibid.: 7).

Another consequence of the Convention's 'gender neutrality' is that is generally unclear which 'Convention reason' is the most appropriate peg upon which to hang a claim of gender based persecution. Lawyers have generally chosen, however, to present such claims in terms of their client's membership of a 'particular social group'. This paper considers asylum claims involving rape and domestic violence, but similar arguments could be made for cases involving gendered discrimination based upon female genital mutilation, notions of family honour or violations of reproductive rights.

The International Case Law

Aleinikoff (2003) distinguishes two broad approaches in the international jurisprudence concerning particular social groups: (i) the 'protected characteristics' or 'immutability' approach exemplified by the US Board of Immigration Appeals' decision in Matter of Acosta, and the decision of the Canadian Supreme Court in Ward; and (ii) the 'social perception' stance of the Australian High Court in Applicant A. It is the former which has dominated, with consequences which seem unfortunate from an anthropological perspective, as we shall see.

Matter of Acosta is noteworthy for its influential use of the legal doctrine of 'ejusdem generis' (of the same kind), a form of argument by analogy which states that when statutes contain lists of items such as that in Article 1(A)2, any items whose meanings are problematic should be read in the same spirit as those whose meaning *is* clear.[4] Acosta had belonged to a taxi drivers' co-operative in El Salvador which was targeted by guerrillas for refusing to take part in anti-government strikes. He claimed that the co-operative constituted a 'particular social group' for Convention purposes, but the Board ruled against him. It argued that 'race', 'religion', 'nationality' and 'political opinion' were all immutable characteristics in the sense that either it was beyond the individual's power to change them, or that they were fundamental to that individual's individual identity or conscience. The occupation of 'taxi driver', on the other hand, was neither immutable nor fundamental to Acosta's personal identity.

An alternative version of the 'immutability' approach, stemming from the Canadian case of Ward, is to define the essence of the 'particular social group' itself. Ward had belonged to the paramilitary INLA (Irish National Liberation Army) in Northern Ireland, and was imprisoned by the British government for that reason. He sought asylum in Canada on his release, claiming to fear persecution because of his membership of a particular social group. The Canadian Supreme Court ultimately decided that the INLA was *not* a 'particular social group' in Convention terms, because although independence was a legitimate political aim, being required to give up violent means of achieving that aim would not constitute an abdication of his human dignity. Justice La Forest based his leading judgment upon the decision in *Matter of Acosta*, and the UNHCR 'Handbook's' statement that 'A "particular social group" normally comprises persons of similar background, habits or social status' (1992: para 77). These led him to propose a new three-part definition of his own:

1. Groups defined by an innate or unchangeable characteristic (on such bases as gender, linguistic background and sexual orientation);
2. Groups whose members voluntarily associate for reasons so fundamental to their human dignity that they should not be forced to forsake the association (for example, human rights activists); and,
3. Groups associated by a former voluntary status, unalterable due to its historical permanence (one's past is an immutable part of oneself).

This definition has been highly influential, not least in that courts have repeatedly adopted similarly polythetic definitions of 'social group'.[5] However, it has also been criticised on the ground that it is hard to see any coherent principle underlying the three categories (Aleinikoff 2003: 271).

Much less widely influential, but anthropologically more satisfactory, is the 'social perception' stance adopted by the Australian High Court in *Applicant A* (Aleinikoff 2003: 271–73). Faced with applicants fearing forced sterilisation because of opposition to China's 'one child policy', the court decided that the 'ordinary meaning' of the phrase 'social group' referred to 'a common attribute and a societal perception that they stand apart' (McHugh J.), or a 'characteristic or element which unites them and enables them to be set apart from society at large … making those who share it a cognisable group within their society' (Dawson J.). However, while this analysis is undoubtedly more sociologically nuanced, its impact is lessened by the failure of the judges to adopt a vocabulary more in tune with their arguments. As even these brief excerpts show, the court continued to use the term 'group' for what would in anthropology, at least since Scheffler (1966), be termed instead a social *category*.

Case Law in the UK

British jurisprudence on 'social group' starts from the 1995 case of
SSHD v. Savchenkov, concerning a security guard in a St Petersburg
hotel, 'SSHD' being the Secretary of State for the Home Department.
Savchenkov claimed persecution by the Russian mafia, who were trying
to coerce him into being an informer. The Secretary of State argued that
being a victim of violent crime did not qualify him for asylum, and the
adjudicator agreed that he was persecuted as a law-abiding person who
would not join the mafia, not as a member of a particular social group.
Consequently, there was no basis for any claim under the Convention.
At his second appeal, however, the Tribunal decided that (my italics):

> ... given the evidence of the existence and insidious power of the
> mafia, individuals which the mafia seeks to recruit and who refuse
> *do* form a social group. They are identified by the approach and
> refusal. [So] we see the group as identifying and identified by an
> important recognisable social attribute. Whether or not the group is
> liable to persecution is then a question of evidence.

But although it was argued in the Court of Appeal that Savchenkov
belonged to a particular social group of La Forest's second or third
type, Lord Justice McCowan could see no evidence that those refusing
to join the mafia associated with one another, or shared a former voluntary status. The only 'group' to which Savchenkov could with any plausi-
bility be said to belong, was the group of people threatened by the
mafia; but this group, if it could be so called, was identifiable only by
virtue of its members' shared fear of persecution by the mafia. In
MacCowan's subsequently influential view, the Convention could never
have been intended to cover groups whose existence stemmed solely
from fear of persecution. To allow 'membership' of 'groups' of this
kind to qualify applicants for refugee status would simply be tautological,
because anyone able to demonstrate that they would be persecuted
would thereby become a member of a social group comprising all those
at similar risk, and would automatically qualify for asylum. This, reasoned MacCowan, could not possibly be what was intended by the
Convention, as shown by the very fact that it explicitly limited its scope
to those suffering persecution for one of the five 'Convention reasons'.

The next important 'particular social group' case was ex parte Adan, in which the House of Lords had to decide whether the danger to the life of a man from Somalia, whose clan was engaged in civil war, could be regarded as persecution for a Convention reason. They decided that it could not, unless Mr Adan could show 'differential impact', i.e., that he was at greater risk of ill-treatment than other members of his clan. Clearly, one factor underlying this decision was the knowledge that, had they decided otherwise, virtually every Somali would qualify for asylum, given the chaotic situation there. One effect of their decision was, however, to establish the legal precedent that, at least in cases of clan-based civil war, persecution for reasons of clan membership *need not* constitute persecution for reasons of 'membership of a particular social group', a situation which is bound to strike all anthropologists weaned on Fortes and Evans-Pritchard (1940), and accustomed to thinking of African clans as the very epitome of corporate groups, as bizarre in the extreme.

The implications of this decision for asylum applicants are 'alarming' (Scannell 1999: 77), but there remain crucial matters of definition. What forms of disorder qualify as 'civil war'? For example, should Adan apply also to Sri Lanka, whose ethnic conflict, also commonly described as 'civil war', is plainly not a war of all against all in the same way as segmentary clan warfare in Somalia. One does not (or *should* not) become a combatant merely by being Tamil or Sinhalese; moreover, one of the warring parties is recognised internationally as the legitimate government of the country. A key tribunal decision (Rudralingam) argues that Adan is generally applicable 'to situations of civil war and armed conflict. Sri Lanka is obviously one such situation', but given the different contexts, this is in fact not at all obvious. In Juvenathan, where the Tribunal had cited Adan as one reason for dismissing the asylum appeal, counsel argued in the Court of Appeal that Sri Lanka was crucially different from Somalia because both sides had declared themselves to the UN as being bound by the rules of war. Otton LJ was 'not persuaded' that the tribunal had been wrong to consider Adan, but as he found their decision justifiable on other grounds, he did not come to a definite conclusion.

What if a person has a well-founded fear of persecution in parts of their home country, but there are arguably other parts where they would have no such fear? Seeking refuge elsewhere in the country has been termed the 'Internal Flight Alternative' (IFA), and the UNHCR 'Handbook' states that:

> The fear of being persecuted need not always extend to the whole territory of the refugee's country of nationality ... persecution of a specific ethnic or national group may occur in only one part of the country. In such situations, a person will not be excluded from refugee status merely because he could have sought refuge in another part of the same country, if under all the circumstances it would not have been reasonable to expect him to do so (1992: para 91).

This is phrased in inclusive rather than exclusive terms, and was rarely invoked in the 1980s as a ground for refusing asylum (ELENA 2000: 64). Its increasing use to exclude admittedly persecuted persons from Convention protection has coincided with the growth in applications. The UK Home Office usually claims, for example, that Tamils persecuted in Jaffna can live safely in Colombo, or that Sikhs with a well-founded fear in the Punjab will be safe in other parts of India.

The Court of Appeal decided in the Sri Lankan Tamil case of ex parte Robinson that two questions arise in this connection: (i) is there part of their own country where the asylum applicant would not have a well-founded fear of persecution, because the authorities are able and willing to provide sufficient protection there?; and (ii) would it be 'unduly harsh' to expect them to live there? Factors affecting 'harshness' include the accessibility of the safe region; the dangers and hardships involved in travelling to or staying there; and whether protection would meet human rights norms (IND 2002: para 3.4). For example, an IFA does not exist if one is required to undergo great physical danger or hardship, or hide in an isolated area (Goodwin-Gill 1996: 75), whereas separation from family and friends does not in itself constitute undue harshness (ex parte Gunes). There was some controversy at the Tribunal level over the standard of proof to which 'undue harshness' must be determined; was it the 'reasonable likelihood' standard generally employed in asylum decisions or the 'balance of probabilities' as in civil cases? The Court of Appeal decided in Karanakaran that there was no need to adhere strictly to any specific standard, because in deciding whether relocation would be 'unduly harsh', cumulative account should be taken of a whole range of disparate factors, however likely or unlikely each was deemed to be (Storey 1998; Symes 2001: 259).

It has increasingly been argued internationally that the IFA label is inappropriate, as the real issues are 'questions of protection, inability, unwillingness and the presence of a well-founded fear for one of the recognised Convention reasons' (Re S: New Zealand Refugee Appeal No. 11/91). The term 'Internal Protection Alternative' is now seen as preferable because 'it helps to reinforce the point ... that the issue is not one of flight or relocation, but of protection' (Refugee Appeal 71684/99; see also Michigan Guidelines 1999; Symes 2001: 247).

Sexual Violence

One consequence of the exclusion of 'sex' from the list of Convention reasons was that the words 'sex', 'gender' and 'rape' were never even mentioned in the founding texts—the Convention itself and UNHCR's 'Handbook' (1992)—though UNHCR did address such issues later (for example, UNHCR 2002). In the UK, the Home Office's Asylum Policy Instructions (APIs) follow Hathaway (1991: 112n) in stating explicitly that 'rape and other serious sexual violence' constitute persecution 'if they are committed for a Convention reason and the authorities are unable or unwilling to provide effective protection' (IND 2002: para 1.2.8.2).[6] But what precisely *are* the circumstances under which sexual assault constitutes 'persecution for a Convention reason'? In Sri Lankan appeals, for example, the Secretary of State almost always argues that sexual assaults were individual actions not condoned by the state, and hence did not amount to persecution—even when rape has been perpetrated against detainees by those very agents of the state who were holding them in custody.

Such arguments have even sometimes been accepted by the courts. Mr Justice Ognall, for example, hearing a judicial review application (ex parte Roomy) in the High Court from a Muslim man who had been raped by his captors while detained by the Sri Lankan Army, agreed with the adjudicator's conclusion, at the earlier appeal, that these had been criminal acts rather than instances of torture:

> ... the adjudicator was saying ... that undoubtedly this was violent conduct by two persons in positions of authority, that undoubtedly it was perpetrated upon the applicant for whatever reason while he was in their custody, but that no material had been placed before

him which served to demonstrate that that brutal conduct was the
product of persecution. [...] It is well known ,,, that persons in
positions of authority not infrequently abuse their position to violate,
in whatever way captives [sic]. That is regrettably a fact of life. It is
another to demonstrate that violation by soldiers is to be viewed
as the product of a policy of persecution to the captive in question.
[D]eplorable though that conduct was ... the soldiers ... were as-
saulting him in this way to gratify their own licentiousness, and ...
it was not the product of whatever reason had led the applicant to be
within their otherwise lawful custody.

As this illustrates, many decisions are grounded on the erroneous
view that rape—even in the context of generalised conflict—is primarily
an act of sexual gratification rather than of violence (Crawley 2001: 35).
Yet, as the Medical Foundation's report on sexual abuse of male detainees
in Sri Lanka has since pointed out, the most likely motive in such cases
is 'the demonstration of complete control over the victim' (Peel et al.
2000). The perpetrators, they point out, 'do not perceive themselves or
their acts as homosexual'. This medical evidence accords with cultural
views surrounding homosexuality, as explored in an interview with the
award-winning Canadian novelist Shyam Selvadurai, himself a gay
Tamil brought up in Sri Lanka. Use of the terms 'gay' and 'homosexual'
in the Tamil and Sinhalese cultural contexts is, he points out, problematic. For young men in Sri Lanka, pre-marital heterosexual sex is
generally unavailable. Many therefore engage in same-sex activity, but
it is the receptive partner who is perceived as homosexual, while the
insertive partner retains his masculinity, his heterosexual identity, and
his social status.[7] In other words, the intense social stigma associated
with homosexuality applies principally to the receptive participant,
which is of course precisely the situation of the detainee as a rape victim
of the soldiers holding him in custody.

The misperception of rape as being essentially sexual rather than
violent in character is, of course, even more likely when it is perpetrated
against women. Spijkerboer analyses the Dutch authorities' treatment
of the rape of 'Anne', a Tamil woman from Jaffna, as revealed by her
interview report and the decision stating reasons for refusing her asylum
application. He points out that:

The version of the facts presented in the decision lacks any reference
whatsoever to political issues. Even the fact that the son was suspected

of being an informer immediately prior to his execution ... is overlooked. What is not overlooked, however, is the fact that the LTTE men were drunk. The decision thus presents alcohol as the cause of Anne's first rape (2000: 52).

One can find similar examples in the British courts. In SSHD v 'D',[8] the Home Office successfully appealed against the granting of asylum to a Sri Lankan Tamil woman. The adjudicator (a woman, which may or may not have been significant) had not believed that the appellant faced persecution on political grounds, but granted her asylum because she had twice been raped by soldiers. The (all-male) Tribunal did not believe, however, that her rape constituted torture, or that it put her at risk of future persecution for a Convention reason:

> These were not systematic rapes to humiliate a prisoner in custody; but escapades by lecherous soldiers.... Clearly rapes by security forces do occur in the north and east of the island, as is unfortunately often the case where troops of any power are occupying an area with a population they see as different from themselves. It is not easy for the authorities to deter this sort of activity on the part of their more brutal and licentious soldiery; but there is evidence that those in Sri Lanka have taken firm action where they could, in one case resulting in death sentences against members of the security forces.[9] It cannot be said that there is a general risk of rape, with no effective protection against it, for Tamil girls in the north and east. [Her barrister] was equally unable to explain ... *why being raped twice in these circumstances should put this asylum-seeker at any greater risk of it on return.* [While] 'systematic rapes to humiliate a prisoner in custody' might well amount to torture, what is said to have happened in this case could not be so described, as a matter of ordinary English (italics added).

Compare the granting of asylum by this same chairman, when still an adjudicator, to 'N', an 'attractive young Tamil girl', with his comment in refusing the appeal of 'TM', a Tamil woman aged 50: 'Without wishing to appear unchivalrous, we have to say that there can be no significant risk of rape at her age'. While not the sole criterion in these two decisions, because the situation in Sri Lanka had changed in the interim, the sexual desirability of the victim was clearly seen as a dominant factor.

Such decisions are grounded upon several tacit and mutually re-inforcing cultural assumptions. First, men's involvement in public activities such as demonstrations and strikes is seen un-problematically as an expression of political opinion, whereas women's behaviour in veiling or refusing to veil, or their domestic activities such as preparing food for political activists, may not be, especially if the latter are her relatives (Akram 2000; Crawley 2001: 21–26; Spijkerboer 2000: 4–5). This exemplifies the ambiguities in defining 'politics', which were touched on earlier. In fact, alternative 'political' interpretations of their rapes were available for at least three of the Tamil women mentioned here. For example, the rape of 'Anne' was precipitated by her refusal to provide rice for the men who raped her, yet the Dutch authorities did not even consider the possibility of interpreting this as a political act of opposition to the LTTE (Spijkerboer 2000: 47, 51).[10] 'D' had been de-tained twice by the authorities, and her entire family was suspected of association with the LTTE. As for 'TM', her father had been shot dead by the security forces, her brother had joined the LTTE, and she herself had been questioned and later required to report regularly to the author-ities, under suspicion of providing medical care for wounded LTTE cadres. Yet the British courts downplayed these political contexts, just as Spijkerboer suggests, and assumed that sexual desire was the primary motive.

Second, the presumption is regularly made by decision-makers that sexual intercourse is an 'inherently private' activity (Crawley 2001: 95). This was vividly illustrated by the case of Campos-Guardado in the United States, where an El Salvadorean woman was raped after being forced to watch the torture and murder of her male relatives; the court recognised the men's deaths as politically motivated but concluded that her rape was not political but 'personal' (ibid.). Whilst one cannot find so stark a contrast within a single appeal involving Sri Lankan Tamils, the same point is made in a rather different way by the case of Roomy cited earlier. The victim here was a man, but because his suffering was interpreted as sexual in nature and hence as personal in motivation, its political character was denied. Consequently, like all the women whose appeals are discussed in this section, his acknowledged persecution was deemed not to fall within the ambit of the Refugee Convention.

Third, and underlying the previous two assumptions, there is the presumption that male sexuality is 'an innate, independent and quasi-biological drive which … can suddenly overwhelm a man' (ibid.: 96).

Its violent expression can then be dismissed as 'the aberrant act of an individual which is to be expected, rather than as behaviour condoned or encouraged by the government' (ibid.), so even when the rapist is a soldier, policeman or government official who is actually on duty, he is 'perceived as acting from personal motivation' (ibid.: 35).

There is evidence that such presumptions are ethnically determined. Thus, while rapes of Tamil women are usually considered by the British courts to be sexually-driven offences committed by delinquent individuals, rapes of Bosnian women tend to be seen as examples of politically motivated ethnic cleansing (Spijkerboer 2000: 101). That view works to the Bosnians' advantage, of course, but why this concern with motivation in the first place? Strikingly, the argument that violence by a state agent is a private act and not politically motivated seems largely restricted to cases involving sexual violence (ibid.: 113, 128).

Domestic Violence: Islam & Shah

The other major decision by the House of Lords on the 'particular social group' issue concerned the joint appeals of Shahana Sadiq Islam and Syeda Khatoon Shah. Both had been forced out of their marital homes in Pakistan by violent husbands, and both claimed to fear persecution in the form of false accusations of adultery if forced to return home, on the grounds that they belonged to a 'social group' of women persecuted in this way.[11] As in Adan mentioned earlier, the Lords reached conclusions which from an anthropological perspective were distinctly odd.

Sadiq Islam had married in Pakistan as long ago as 1971, but her husband had often been violent towards her. In 1990 she attempted to stop a fight between rival political factions in the school where she taught. One faction made allegations of infidelity to her husband, who was one of their supporters. He assaulted her and she was twice admitted to hospital. She left her husband and sought refuge with her brother, but had to leave after he received threats. She arrived in the UK with two children in 1991 and claimed asylum for reasons of membership of a particular social group, and political opinion. The Tribunal decided she had been persecuted but was not a member of a 'particular social group' because women in her situation had no 'innate or unchangeable characteristic' in common, nor were they 'a cohesive homogeneous group whose members are in close voluntary association'.

Her appeal against this decision was heard by the Court of Appeal along with an appeal by the Home Office concerning Khatoon Shah. She too had been thrown out of her marital home in Pakistan by a violent husband. She arrived in the UK in 1992, giving birth shortly afterwards. She claimed asylum, citing her fear that her husband might assault her, or deny that the child was his and accuse her of sexual immorality under Sharia law. The adjudicator found her fear of persecution to be well founded, but decided she did not belong to a 'particular social group', the only Convention reason which could conceivably apply. The Tribunal refused leave to appeal, but she sought judicial review of this decision, and Justice Sedley directed the Tribunal to hear her appeal. It was the Home Office appeal against that decision which came before the Court of Appeal.

At that time the Home Office's APIs (IND 1998: para 1.2.9.4), citing Savchenkov, defined 'particular social group' in a way which was also clearly influenced by the formulae in the earlier mentioned Matter of Acosta and Ward:

(a) The group is defined by some innate or unchangeable characteristic of its members analogous to race, religion, nationality or political opinion, for example, their sex, linguistic background, tribe, family or class; or

(b) The group is cohesive and homogeneous. Its members must be in close voluntary association for reasons fundamental to their rights (for example trade union activists). Former members of such a group are also included; or

(c) The particular social group was recognised as such by the public. Whatever the binding factor is, it must be independent of persecution.

Paragraph (a) clearly exemplifies the ejusdem generis approach, and paragraphs (a) and (b) together express what Aleinikoff (2003: 269) termed the 'immutability' approach to the question of 'particular social group'. By contrast, paragraph (c) seems to make a cursory nod in the direction of the Australian 'social perception' approach in Applicant A. To an anthropological eye, however, what is most striking about these paragraphs is their congruence with anthropological arguments over descent theory from the 1950s and 1960s. Thus, paragraphs (a) and (b) irresistibly recall those arguments premised upon the existence of behaviourally observable, corporate *descent groups*—an assumption shared, despite their differences over 'complementary filiation', by both Fortes (1970) and Leach (1961: 5)—in relation to which paragraph (c) can be seen as corresponding to Scheffler's (1966) contrasting portrayal of *descent categories* as forms of indigenous classification.

The Court of Appeal found that Sadiq Islam's claim under 'political opinion' failed on the facts, so the sole issue was whether either or both women were members of 'particular social groups'. All three judges agreed, along the lines set out in Savchenkov, that there was no common uniting attribute, independent of the feared persecution, which entitled either woman to claim membership of such a group. There were, however, divergent views regarding issues raised by paragraph (b) of the Home Office definition. Whereas Lord Justice Staughton accepted the Home Office argument that 'cohesion' was an essential feature of a 'particular social group', Lord Justice Henry held—with explicit reference to Applicant A—that a group might be said to exist if it was 'recognised as such by the public'.

At the subsequent House of Lords appeal the arguments took a rather different course, not least because of a substantial change in the Home Office's own position. Their barrister, David Pannick QC, announced that the Secretary of State no longer supported paragraph (a) of his own definition of 'particular social group'. The implications of that reached far beyond this particular case, because the Home Office was, in effect, dropping the main criterion on which its preceding asylum decisions regarding 'particular social group' had been based. The reason seems clear. If Sadiq Islam and Khatoon Shah were to win their appeals on this basis, many other abused women in Pakistan would also qualify for asylum. Lord Justice Staughton's view based on 'cohesion' was far more attractive to the Home Office because, if accepted by the House of Lords, it would allow eligibility to be restricted yet further.

The principal issue to be decided, therefore, was whether 'cohesiveness' was a necessary property of a 'particular social group'. Lord Steyn, in his leading speech, declared his preference for the approach in Matter of Acosta. He also pointed out that the only precedent in English law for the view that cohesiveness was an indispensable characteristic of a 'particular social group' was Lord Justice Staughton's argument in the lower court in this very case. Lord Steyn did not, therefore, accept that 'cohesiveness' was an essential feature of such groups. Lord Hoffmann agreed, and Mr Pannick ultimately had to concede this.

But could these two specific women be seen as members of a 'particular social group'? Nicholas Blake QC, their counsel, argued that a combination of 'gender, the suspicion of adultery, and their unprotected status in Pakistan' set the two applicants apart as members of a separate group. The Court of Appeal had rejected this view, on the Savchenkov principle that the group should exist independently of the persecution, but Lord Steyn argued that the lower court's reasoning had been invalid. 'The unifying characteristics of gender, suspicion of adultery, and lack of protection', he explained, 'do not involve an assertion of persecution.' In any case, Lord Steyn continued, the Savchenkov principle had to be qualified along the lines indicated in Applicant A, namely, that 'while persecutory conduct cannot define the social group, the actions of the persecutors may serve to identify or even cause [its] creation'. He concluded that on this ground too the appellants could be seen as belonging to 'a particular social group', a view supported also by Lord Hutton.

A majority of the Lords ended, however, by supporting an argument made by one of their own number, which was far broader in scope than that advanced by Mr Blake. Lord Hoffmann's passionately argued view focused on the existence, in Pakistan, of '[d]iscrimination against women in matters of fundamental human rights on the ground that they *are* women' (my italics). Consequently, he reasoned, 'women in Pakistan', without further restriction or qualification, do form a particular social group 'because they are discriminated against and as a group they are unprotected by the state'. Although, as Mr Pannick argued, many Pakistani women were able in practice to avoid the impact of persecution, that had also been true 'under even the most brutal and repressive regimes' such as Nazi Germany and Stalinist Russia. It would be totally contrary to the principles of the Convention to refuse asylum on such a basis. Lord Steyn agreed, describing Lord Hoffmann's stance as 'a logical application' of the reasoning in Matter of Acosta.

Only Lord Millett argued for dismissal, agreeing with the Appeal Court that the social group was defined by the persecution. Though women in Pakistan *were* legally discriminated against, he argued, these appellants had been persecuted 'because they refuse to conform, not because they are members of the social group'. Even Lord Millett agreed, however, that cohesiveness was not a necessary attribute of a social group, but merely one possible feature of such groups.

The Consequences of Islam & Shah

The Islam & Shah decision established, therefore, that under certain circumstances even very broad categories of women might indeed be regarded as members of 'particular social groups'. One inevitable outcome was that the Immigration and Nationality Directorate (IND) had to make substantial changes to the definition of 'particular social group' in its APIs, which were revised to read as follows:

(i) Members of a social group have to have in common an immutable characteristic which is either beyond the power of an individual to change, or is so fundamental to their identity and conscience that it ought not to be required to be changed.

(ii) Whilst a social group must exist independently of persecution, discrimination against the group could be taken into account in identifying it as a social group, i.e., discrimination against the group could be a factor contributing to the identity of a social group (IND 2002: para 1.2.9.4).

Another, and less direct, consequence of the Lords' decision was that, in the eyes of the Court of Appeal, its acceptance that there was gender based persecution in Pakistan added the clinching extra weight to the argument that the Home Secretary's inclusion of Pakistan among the so-called 'White List' of countries for which 'there is in general no serious risk of persecution', was unlawful (SSHD v. Asif Javed and others).

There was some discomfort among the Law Lords over the possibility that their decision in Islam and Shah would be read as a direct attack on the customs and legal system of Pakistan. Indeed, the Tribunal which had heard Sadiq Islam's appeal previously, had actually rejected evidence of discrimination against women in Pakistan, because it contained 'overt and implicit criticisms of Pakistani society and the position of women in that and other Islamic states'. 'We do not think,' it stated, 'that the purpose of the Convention is to award refugee status because of a disapproval of social mores or conventions in non-western societies'. For Lord Hoffmann, however, that was not the issue. There was no suggestion, he said:

... that a woman was entitled to refugee status merely because she lived in a society which, for religious or any other reason, discriminated against women. Although such discrimination is contrary not merely to western notions but to the constitution of Pakistan and a number of international human rights instruments, including the Convention on the Elimination of All Forms of Discrimination Against Women, which Pakistan ratified in 1996, it does not in itself found a claim under the Convention. The Convention is about persecution, a well founded fear of serious harm, which is a very different matter. The ... findings of fact as to discrimination have not been challenged. They cannot be ignored merely on the ground that this would imply criticism of the legal or social arrangements in another country. The whole purpose of the Convention is to give protection to certain classes of people who have fled from countries in which their human rights have not been respected. It does not by any means follow that there is similar persecution in other Islamic countries or even that it exists everywhere in Pakistan. Each case must depend upon the evidence.

Though the internal logic of this argument is questionable, the sentiments are clear, and the courts have subsequently been anxious to resist any notion that Sharia law, in itself, persecutes women. In rejecting an asylum claim based on domestic abuse in Yemen, one Tribunal (Dahsan) argued as follows:

The finding by the House of Lords ... that women in Pakistan constitute a particular social group was based upon a detailed analysis of the law and constitution in that country in relation to women. Mr Ahmed [the barrister] has simply made the general assertion to us that because Sharia law applies in Yemen, women must per se constitute a particular social group there, and presumably in any other countries which apply Sharia law. However he has conspicuously failed to provide any evidence or detailed argument to support this proposition.

In general, despite the Home Office's all-too-obvious fear, the floodgates did not open in the sense of a massive upsurge in similar asylum claims. There were in fact surprisingly few such cases, and among these the influence of Islam & Shah was, of course, particularly strong in cases involving other women from Pakistan or neighbouring South Asian countries.

In a Tribunal appeal (Begum) heard immediately after the Lords' decision in Islam & Shah, for example, the appellant was a 50-year-old single woman living in Pakistan with her young niece, and whose relatives were all overseas. She claimed to have suffered harassment from policemen following her in the street and ringing her doorbell. This was either for sexual motives, because she was wrongly perceived as a single mother, as her sister claimed in evidence; or because she was an active supporter of the Mohajir Quami Movement, as she herself implied. Her barrister argued that she belonged to the social group of 'single women with no male protection and perceived as single mothers'. The tribunal doubted the sister's credibility, but accepted that Begum did belong to a 'particular social group' and that 'she would be persecuted for a Convention reason namely her perceived political opinion and that she is a single woman without male protection, and that she falls within the social group of a woman [sic] in Pakistan, as defined in the judgment in Shah and Islam'. It reads as though the tribunal was so strongly influenced by Islam & Shah that it continued to use arguments from that case even though it was allowing the appeal on grounds of imputed political opinion!

A later example involved an Indian appellant. Balvir Kaur came to the UK as a visitor in 1991, then claimed asylum on the grounds that she had suffered harassment because of her husband's membership in the Babbar Khalsa. By the time her appeal came before an adjudicator she had given birth to a son following a brief affair with a Sikh man she had met in the UK, and she claimed that in addition to her initial fear of the police she now also feared ostracism and persecution from the Sikh community, and violence from her husband. The adjudicator accepted that she would face discrimination, but found that this would not amount to persecution and would not in any case arise from her membership of a 'particular social group' comprising what he called 'fallen women'. While noting the antiquarian ring to this phrase, the tribunal nonetheless felt that 'the expression has more potency when looked at in the light of the background evidence as to how the Appellant would be treated in India'. Clearly impressed by expert evidence from Dr Purna Sen of the London School of Economics, Professor Patricia Jeffery of the University of Edinburgh and Hannana Siddiqui from the Southall Black Sisters, it concluded that 'on balance we have come to the view that, looking at the Appellant's background in rural India in the light of the social, cultural and religious mores, women in the Appellant's circumstances are identifiable as a particular social group'.

It is strikingly in line with Spijkerboer's argument cited earlier, that in cases such as these two, women succeeded in making good their asylum claims on the basis of evidence of past and likely future persecution of a kind which would not even get to first base in a claim by a male appellant. Indeed, attempts to extend the Islam & Shah approach to men have so far been unsuccessful even where the groups argued for are closely akin to those which, according to Goodwin-Gill (1996: 46n), had been in the minds of the Convention's drafters. In SSHD v. Diallo (Sierra Leone), for example, the social group argued for was 'member of a wealthy, educated, mine-owning family', while in SSHD v. Montoya (Colombia), the claimed social group was 'private landowners'. Both appeals failed, however.

Even for women's claims, moreover, the broad scope of the Islam & Shah decision has not always been decisive. In the appeal of 'M', for example, the adjudicator accepted that rape by soldiers had taken place but ruled, citing Savchenkov, that this did not place the appellant in a particular social group within the meaning of the Convention, because such a group ('Tamil women raped by the security forces') would have no existence independent of the claimed persecution. Further, the rape was not considered to have been a means of state persecution: in the argument familiar to us from the earlier discussion of sexual violence, the adjudicator found that it 'occurred because of the individual actions of individual soldiers acting in a criminal manner, in abuse of their powers'. Finally, the Tribunal hearing her second appeal, reasoning in line with Adan, considered that her subsequent detention, strip-searching and threatened torture in Colombo were insufficient to subject her to the risk of any 'differential impact'. On all these points, the Court of Appeal agreed.

Here, then, the potentially broad scope of the Islam & Shah decision was almost explicitly limited by recourse to other precedents of comparable authority. Consequently, it has not so far been possible to extend the 'particular social group' approach taken in Islam & Shah from domestic violence cases to cover gender-based persecution in situations of armed conflict.

Conclusion

Notwithstanding the partial clarifications which have taken place as a result of the key decisions examined above, the meaning of 'particular social group' under the Refugee Convention continues to cause the British courts difficulty, especially in relation to gender based claims. Even so, the temptation for lawyers representing female asylum applicants—especially those who have experienced domestic violence but also, for want of any obvious alternative, victims of sexual assault—must be to couch their arguments in social group terms, citing Islam & Shah. It is worth reiterating, however, that 'political opinion' may sometimes be a more appropriate ground. The IAA's own gender guidelines note that 'an asylum seeker may be persecuted in a gender specific manner for reasons unrelated to gender (for example, being raped because of her membership in a political party)' (Berkowitz and Jarvis 2000: 3), and—perhaps influenced by those guidelines—the Home Office APIs now openly recognise the possible gender-specific character of political action and opinion: 'It should be remembered that political acts can also include less direct actions such as hiding people, passing messages or providing community services, food, clothing and medical care' (IND 2002: para 1.2.9.5).

A woman who opposes institutionalised discrimination against women or expresses views of independence from the social or cultural norms of society may sustain or fear harm because of her actual political opinion or a political opinion that has been imputed to her. She is perceived within the established political/social structure as expressing politically antagonistic views through her actions or failure to act. If a woman resists gender oppression, her resistance is political (2002: para 1.2.9.5).

One can draw similar conclusions for the USA, where some gender-related applications have succeeded on particular social group grounds, yet arguments based on political opinion have also been successful. With regard to female genital mutilation, one notable success for 'particular social group' arguments was Matter of Kasinga, but in Matter of MK a woman from Sierra Leone was granted asylum partly because of the political opinions which led her to reject this aspect of her society's cultural practice.[12] A close parallel to Islam & Shah, in the sense that it too concerned domestic violence, was furnished by Matter of RA, in which the court found that resistance to domestic abuse, on the part of a woman from Guatemala, caused her abusive husband to impute political opinions to her, leading to an escalation of his violence (Musalo and Knight 2001: 53–58). It would clearly be a strategic error on the part of female applicants' lawyers, then, to put all their eggs unreflectively into the 'particular social group' basket.

Finally, and despite its beneficial humanitarian implications, the reasoning leading up to the Lords' decision in Islam & Shah appears antiquated, to say the least, from a social science perspective. 'Women in Pakistan' cannot be described as a social *group* because they are not corporate. One can certainly say that they form a recognised social *class* or *category*, but the law has generally not recognised that distinction. In this sense, as we saw, disagreements over 'particular social group' in the UK asylum courts can be seen as replaying theoretical debates in anthropology during the decade following the drafting of the Refugee Convention. The ways in which the dominant 'immutability' approach to the issue developed in British jurisprudence—particularly the initial Home Office stress on 'cohesiveness'—expressed a kind of structural-functionalist understanding of 'social group', pre-dating Scheffler's (1966) crucial distinction between 'groups' and 'categories'. Yet although the less influential 'social perception' approach of the Australian High Court in Applicant A appears in that sense far more sociologically sophisticated, that decision was, as we saw, rendered less clear than it deserved to be by not being expressed in equally sophisticated terminology.

Both legal approaches, in other words, might gain something from greater awareness of cognate developments in the social sciences. And this is far from a mere academic quibble; decisions are routinely being made by the British courts on the basis of outdated criteria, which prevent them from recognising that women at risk of rape in situations of armed conflict may indeed have a 'well-founded fear of persecution' for reasons falling within the scope of the Refugee Convention.

Notes

1 As the Protocol involves acceptance of all key Convention clauses, it makes little practical difference if the Convention itself was not signed.
2 Goodwin-Gill (1996: 46n) explains the lack of debate by suggesting that, given the time and context in which the discussions took place, delegates must have had clearly in mind members of the former capitalist classes in Soviet Eastern Europe.
3 In 1951 it was not yet routine to distinguish 'gender' from 'sex' as social and biological constructs respectively.
4 For example, in the phrase 'cats, dogs and other animals', the final term should be interpreted as meaning 'other *domestic* animals'.

5   On polythetic definitions generally, see Needham (1975); for examples of their anthropological use to define 'marriage', 'religion', and 'kinship', respectively, see Leach (1961), Southwold (1978) and Barnard and Good (1984).

6   This is the work manual for IND caseworkers, instructing them on how to receive, assess and decide asylum claims.

7   *www.greatwest.ca/ffwd/Issues/1998/1015/book2.html*, accessed 17 February 2003.

8   Here and in several other cases below I have concealed the asylum applicant's name even though the case is in the public domain, in order to protect her from gratuitous further public exposure.

9   In fact the case referred to involved the rape *and murder* of a Tamil schoolgirl; no soldier was brought to court solely on rape charges during the entire ethnic conflict, still less found guilty.

10 Conflicted-related rapes in Sri Lanka are almost always committed by members of the security forces; 'Anne's' account of being raped by the LTTE is virtually unique in my experience.

11 Both women had been granted leave to remain in the UK on humanitarian grounds, but still sought full refugee status.

12 Female genital mutilation is practised by the Bohra Muslims in India and Pakistan (Crawley 2001: 176), but no asylum claims on this ground appear to have been made by such women, in the UK at least.

References

Akram, Susan Musarrat. 2000. 'Orientalism Revisited in Asylum and Refugee Claims', *International Journal of Refugee Law*, 12: 7–40.

Aleinikoff, T. Alexander. 2003. 'Protected Characteristics and Social Perceptions: An Analysis of the Meaning of "Membership in a Particular Social Group"', in Erika Feller, Volker Türk and Frances Nicholson (eds), *Refugee Protection in International Law*, pp. 263–311. Cambridge: Cambridge University Press.

Barnard, Alan J. and Anthony Good. 1984. *Research Practices in the Study of Kinship*. London: Academic Press.

Berkowitz, Nathalia and Catriona Jarvis. 2000. *Asylum Gender Guidelines*. London: Immigration Appellate Authority.

Crawley, Heaven. 2001. *Refugees and Gender: Law and Process*. Bristol: Jordans.

ELENA (European Legal Network on Asylum). 2000. *The Application of the Concept of Internal Protection Alternative*. London: ELENA. *http://www.ecre.org/research/ipa.doc*, accessed 10 January 2001.

Fortes, Meyer. 1970. *Time and Social Structure, and Other Essays*. London: Athlone Press.

Fortes, Meyer and Edward E. Evans-Pritchard. 1940. *African Political Systems*. Oxford: Oxford University Press.

Good, Anthony. 2004. '"Undoubtedly an Expert?" Country Experts in the UK Asylum Courts', *Journal of the Royal Anthropological Institute*, 10: 113–33.

Goodwin-Gill, Guy. 1996. *The Refugee in International Law*, second edition. Oxford: Clarendon.

Grahl-Madsen, Atle. 1966. *The Status of Refugees in International Law*. Leiden: A.W. Sijthoff.

Haines, Rodger. 1998. 'Membership of a Particular Social Group', Interim Reports of Inter-Conference Working Parties, International Association of Refugee Law Judges. *www.iarlj.nl/wp/wp2.htm*, accessed 23 December 2003.

Hathaway, James. 1991. *The Law of Refugee Status*. London: Butterworths.

IND (Immigration and Nationality Directorate). 1998. *Asylum Policy Instructions*. London: Home Office.

———. 2002. *Asylum Policy Instructions*. *www.ind.homeoffice.gov.uk/default.asp?PageId=711*, accessed 15 April 2002.

Leach, Edmund R. 1961. *Rethinking Anthropology*. London: Athlone Press.

Michigan Guidelines. 1999. *The Internal Protection Alternative*. University of Michigan Law School. *www.refugee.org.nz/Guidelines.htm*, accessed 11 January 2005.

Musalo, Karen and Stephen Knight. 2001. 'Steps Forward and Steps Back: Uneven Progress in the Law of Social Group and Gender-based Claims in the United States', *International Journal of Refugee Law*, 13: 51–70.

Needham, Rodney. 1975. 'Polythetic Classification: Convergence and Consequences', *Man*, 10: 349–69.

Peel, Michael, A. Mahtani, Gail Hinshelwood and Duncan Forrest. 2000. 'The Sexual Abuse of Men in Detention in Sri Lanka', *The Lancet*, 355 (9220): 2068–69.

Scannell, Rick. 1999. 'Asylum and People at Risk', in Nicholas Blake and Laurie Fransman (eds), *Immigration, Nationality and Asylum Under the Human Rights Act 1998*, pp. 73–91. London: Butterworths.

Scheffler, Harold W. 1966. 'Ancestor Worship in Anthropology: or, Observations on Descent and Descent Groups', *Current Anthropology*, 7: 541–51.

Southwold, Martin. 1978. 'Buddhism and the Definition of Religion', *Man*, 13: 362–79.

Spijkerboer, Thomas. 2000. *Gender and Refugee Status*. Aldershot: Ashgate.

Storey, Hugo. 1998. 'The 'Internal Flight Alternative' (IFA) Test and the Concept of Protection', in Frances Nicholson and Patrick Twomey (eds), *Current Issues of UK Asylum Law and Policy*, pp. 100–32. Aldershot: Ashgate.

Symes, Mark. 2001. *Case Law on the Refugee Convention*. London: Refugee Legal Centre.

Symes, Mark and Peter A. Jorro. 2003. *Asylum Law and Practice*. London: Lexis Nexis.

UNHCHR (United Nations High Commissioner for Human Rights). 1998. *Universal Declaration of Human Rights*. Geneva: UNHCHR.

UNHCR (United Nations High Commissioner for Refugees). 1992. 'Handbook on Procedures and Criteria for Determining Refugee Status'. Geneva: UNHCR.

———. 2002. *Gender-related Persecution*. (Guidelines on International Protection, 1), Doc. HCR/GIP/02/01. Geneva: UNHCR.

Von Sternberg, Mark R. 2002. *The Grounds of Refugee Protection in the Context of International Human Rights and Humanitarian Law: Canadian and United States Case Law Compared*. The Hague: Martinus Nijhoff.

About the Editor and Contributors

The Editor

Navnita Chadha Behera is Reader in international relations at the University of Delhi. She has previously been Assistant Research Professor at the Centre for Policy Research; Assistant Director, Women in Security, Conflict Management and Peace (WISCOMP), New Delhi (1999–2000); and Visiting Fellow at the Brookings Institution (2001–02). She has received the Asia Fellows Award (2005–06) for a research project on 'Engendering Security Analyses in South Asia: A Case Study of Bangladesh'.

Dr Behera has published widely in India and abroad on issues pertaining to international relations and violence. She has previously published *State, Identity and Violence: Jammu, Kashmir and Ladakh* (2000), *State, People and Security: The South Asian Context* (editor, 2001), *Perspectives on South Asia* (co-editor, 2000), *People-to-People Dialogues in South Asia* (co-author, 2000), and *Beyond Boundaries: A Report on the State of Non-Official Dialogues on Peace, Security and Co-operation in South Asia* (co-author, 1997). Her forthcoming publications include *Demystifying Kashmir, IR in South Asia: Search for an Alternative Paradigm?* (editor), and *Facing Global Environmental Change and Globalisation: Re-conceptualising Security in the 21st Century* (co-editor).

The Contributors

Anasua Basu Raychaudhury is an Indian Council of Social Science Research Fellow at the Centre for Studies of Developing Societies, New Delhi. She completed her Ph.D. in international relations from Jadavpur University, Kolkata. She was awarded the Kodikara Fellowship by Regional Centre for Strategic Studies, Colombo, to work on 'The Energy Crisis and Sub-regional Cooperation in South Asia', which was later published as *RCSS Policy Studies* 13 (2000). She has presented papers in various national and international conferences and has also contributed to several reputed journals in India and abroad. Her research interests include regional cooperation, energy politics, partition refugees and violence against women in South Asia.

Urvashi Butalia is a publisher and writer based in Delhi. She writes on issues related to gender, fundamentalism, communalism and questions of identity. Her best known work is the award winning *The Other Side of Silence: Voices from the Partition of India* (1998). Her other published works include *Women and the Hindu Right: A Collection of Essays* (co-edited, 1995) and *Speaking Peace: Women's Voices from Kashmir* (2002).

Anthony Good is Professor of Social Anthropology in Practice at the University of Edinburgh. His initial field research involved marriage practices and life-cycle ceremonies in South India and Sri Lanka. Later, he studied the economy of a medium-sized Hindu temple in Tamil Nadu. He has carried out extensive policy-related work on community development in rural Asia. His current research involves the legal process of claiming asylum in the UK. He is the author of *The Female Bridegroom* (1992) and *Worship and the Ceremonial Economy of a Royal South Indian Temple* (2004), and *Research Practices in the Study of Kinship* (co-author, 1984).

Furrukh A. Khan teaches at the Lahore University of Management Sciences. He also teaches English as a Foreign Language in the UK during the summer. He has been published extensively in various books and journals. He is also a recipient of the Social Science Research Council's South Asia Regional Fellowship as well as the Asian Scholarship Foundation's ASIA Fellows Award. His research interests include post-colonial literature, Shakespeare, modern literary theory, and South Asian and African literatures.

Saba Gul Khattak is Executive Director, Sustainable Development Policy Institute, Islamabad. She has also taught international relations and comparative politics at the Universities of Peshawar and Hawaii. She provides regular policy advice to the government on issues of women, refugees and governance.

Dr Khattak has been the recipient of several honours and awards for academic excellence and has served on a number of national and international committees in a voluntary capacity. Her research interests revolve around the political economy of development, feminist and political theory with special emphasis on state theory. She has contributed to various journals and books and has co-authored *Hazardous Home-based Work: A Story of Multi Tiered Exploitation* (2005).

Rita Manchanda is currently the Gender Expert at the Commonwealth Technical Fund in Sri Lanka. She has been Programme Executive, South Asia Forum for Human Rights and Director of its women, conflict and peace, and media and conflict programmes. She has written extensively on security and human rights and among her many publications is *Women War and Peace in South Asia: Beyond Victimhood to Agency* (edited, 2001).

Nayanika Mookherjee is Lecturer at the Department of Sociology, University of Lancaster, UK, and Fellow of the Society for South Asian Studies, British Academy. Her doctoral research from the University of London explores the public memories of sexual violence of the Bangladesh Liberation War and will soon be published as a book. She has been published in numerous books and journals and her current research examines the relationship between genetics and the nation through the prism of 'war-babies' in Bangladesh. Her other research interests include anthropology of politics, memory and human rights; violence and the body; political kinship, race and genetics; gender and feminist theories; medical anthropology; and diasporic communities and South Asia.

Mary O'Kane is a Ph.D. candidate with the Department of Politics, Monash University, Melbourne. Her research includes the political agency of people in refugee-related situations focussing, in particular, on the Burmese opposition movement-in-exile. She is especially interested in contemporary notions of the 'political' as experienced in Southeast Asia. She has worked in refugee advocacy in Australia and with women political activists from Burma on the Thai-Burma border. She has lived and worked in north-west Thailand from time to time since 1990.

Darini Rajasingham-Senanayake is an anthropologist and Senior Fellow at the Social Scientists' Association and the International Centre for Ethnic Studies, Colombo. She has written extensively on multiculturalism, identity politics and gender transformations in conflict situations and in South Asia. Her recent research is on developmentalism and the political economy of post-conflict reconstruction. She obtained her Ph.D. from Princeton University and has previously published *Ethnic Futures: The State and Identity Politics in Asia* (co-author, 1999) and *Building Local Capacities for Peace: Rethinking Conflict and Development in Sri Lanka* (co-edited, 2003).

Oishik Sircar is a human rights lawyer and an independent researcher who divides his time between Pune and Kolkata. He has studied at ILS Law College, Pune, and at the Women's Studies Centre, University of Pune. He has worked as a campaigner, researcher and trainer with Amnesty International, South Asia Human Rights Documentation Centre and the International Committee of the Red Cross. He was awarded the WISCOMP Scholar of Peace Fellowship by the Foundation for Universal Responsibility, New Delhi, in 2004. He presently teaches a course in gender and human rights at the Women's Studies Centre, University of Pune, and is consultant-coordinator of the Human Rights Education Initiative with the Centre for Communication and Development Studies, Pune. His research interests include issues of gender, sexuality, law, culture and migration.

Index

306 Gender, Conflict and Migration